Matt Dawson

Matt Dawson

nine lives

THE AUTOBIOGRAPHY

with ALEX SPINK

HarperSport

An Imprint of HarperCollins*Publishers*

First published in hardback in 2004 by
HarperSport
an imprint of HarperCollins*Publishers*
London

First published in paperback in 2004

3

A CIP catalogue record for this book is
available from the British Library

ISBN-13 978-0-00-716567-4
ISBN-10 0-00-716567-6

Set in Linotype Meridien by
Rowland Phototypesetting Ltd,
Bury St Edmunds, Suffolk

Printed and bound in Great Britain by
Clays Ltd, St Ives plc

The HarperCollins website address is
www.harpercollins.co.uk

All photographs supplied by Matt Dawson with
the exception of the following: **Action Images:**
/Peter Jay: p.12 (top), /Tony Henshaw: p.7 (top),
/Alex Morton: p.10 (top), /Tony O'Brien: p.10 (centre);
Getty Images: /Odd Andersen: p.16 (top),
/Robert Cianflone: p.13 (centre), /Phil Cole: p.12 (centre),
/Sean Garnsworth: p.13 (top), /Stuart Hannigan: p.14 (top),
/Ross Kinnaird: p.9 (bottom), /Alex Livesey: p.8 (bottom),
/Chris MacGrath: p.15 (centre left), Damian Myer: p.15 (bottom left),
Mark Nolan: p.14/15, /David Rogers: p.7 (bottom), p.8 (top),
p.9 (top and centre), p.10 (bottom), p.11 (top and bottom),
p.12 (bottom), p.13 (bottom), p.15 (bottom), p.16 (centre left),
p.16 (bottom), /Jim Watson: p.16 (centre right),
/Nick Wilson: p.11 (centre).

To my late Grandad Sam. I know you've been watching Grandad, and I hope I've made you as proud as the rest of the Dawson–Thompson clan. We never did find that eight iron!!!

Contents

Acknowledgements   ix

Prologue   xi

1 Growing Up   1

2 Losing Ground   23

3 Return of the Artful Dodger   37

4 Heaven and Hell

  (i) *Lion Cub to King of the Pride*   61

  (ii) *The Making of a Captain*   73

5 Misunderstood

  (i) *Hate Mail, Hated Male*   93

  (ii) *Striking Progress, Strike in Progress*   119

6 Foot in Mouth   133

7 Going Off the Rails   181

8 Headstrong to Humble

  (i) *Bashed by the Boks*   207

  (ii) *Grand Slam at Last*   219

9 Shooting for the Pot

  (i) *History Lesson Down Under*   247

  (ii) *The Greatest Day of All*   279

10 Celebration Time   347

11 A Step into the Unknown   353

Career Statistics   371

Index   386

Acknowledgements

I've looked back on my life and realised there have been hundreds of influential people that have paved the way to my ultimate goals, happiness and success. To my friends, thank you for the tireless support, constructive criticism, and unlimited laughs along the way. To my rugby colleagues, coaches and players, I am indebted for the commitment and abuse you have dished out most mornings and on even more nights out; without the honesty and straight-talking my career would have ceased years ago. Most of all I want to give my eternal love to Big R, Mum, Emma, Joanne and the rest of my beautiful family. *Carpe Diem*. Enough said.

Prologue

Kick it to the shit-house . . .

That was the last thing I remember saying before the whistle blew, before I dropped to my knees, before my life changed forever.

There was no time left on the clock inside the Olympic Stadium, my very own theatre of dreams. Extra time had come and was now gone. We just had to get the ball out of play. It came to me and I flung it to Mike Catt: the ball and that less than eloquent line.

Paul Grayson, my best pal, got to me first. We shouted and screamed at each other as the raw emotion of the moment took over. I looked up into the stand to where I knew Mum, Dad and my girlfriend Joanne were sharing our joy. For a moment I was overwhelmed. It had been a long journey to the summit and the realisation that I had finally arrived stole my breath away. Almost exactly a year ago to the day I had been told my career was over due to a neck injury. Yet here I was on top of the world.

If there really is a place called Heaven on earth then I was there. I floated over to the end of the stadium occupied by the thousands upon thousands of England fans. They were singing my song, *Wonderwall* by Oasis. Well, of course they were. I was in dreamland. I stood in front of the bank of white shirts conducting the singing and mouthing the words along with them. 'Sing my tune, baby,' I yelled, as though I was on stage at Knebworth. I could see nobody I knew but I was picking people out – watching them cry, watching them hug each other – and revelling in their joy.

'Suck it all in,' I told myself. 'Remember what you are seeing, remember what you are hearing. Lock away these images forever.' It was awesome, simply awesome. It also seemed too good to be true. Because for as long as I could recall, my rugby life hadn't been like this. For me, and those who care for me, there had been a lot of rough to go with the smooth.

I have won two World Cups and a host of titles with England but am still remembered for being captain of the side which 'snubbed the Princess Royal' when we didn't go up to collect the Six Nations Cup after we had lost at Murrayfield in 2000.

I have not only won a series with the British Lions but scored the try which some say was the defining moment of our triumph over South Africa in 1997. Yet it sometimes seems I am as well known for the Lions diary I wrote in the *Daily Telegraph* four years later in Australia.

I have spent 13 years with Northampton, helping them to four cup finals, yet was never offered the captaincy and was instead rewarded for my loyalty by being hauled in front of an internal disciplinary committee after a nothing incident in the 2002 Powergen Final, and then effectively forced out of the club in the summer of 2004.

Through it all I have never given anything but my best, and yet it feels my motives and I have often been misunderstood. I have been called arrogant and worse. I have been upset by it, I have come close to chucking it all in. But I have also learned from it and, I think, become a better person for it.

'Gradually,' my mother said recently, 'people are realising that Matthew is not the arrogant sod he appears on the pitch.' Thanks for that, Mum. Seriously though, it has taken a lot of effort. And I admit that I have not always helped myself because I have not always let people in.

About 18 months before the World Cup I decided to do something about it. Fined by the Lions, dropped by England, in the doghouse at Northampton and out of love in my personal life, I was pretty close to rock bottom. I was completely miserable. Inspired by Wayne Smith, the new head coach at Saints, I arrived at the conclusion that if people didn't understand me I would work harder to help them get to know me. Smithy told me that while it probably was no more my fault than that of other people, I needed to be the one who went out and made more of an effort.

A team-mate had described me as a lost soul who seemed happier away from people. Goodness knows what others were thinking. I had been neglecting my family, to the point where I could not be bothered to pick up the phone and speak to Mum and Dad and see how they were, or to tell them when I was injured. My attitude was that they would find out soon enough on teletext.

I like people to be comfortable, but I hadn't made the effort to make those around me feel that way. Fortunately I realised before it was too late. Fortunately those around me stuck by me: my family, my friends – particularly Paul Grayson and Nick Beal – and my girlfriend Joanne. Which is why as I stood in the middle of the pitch inside the Olympic Stadium, my thoughts were not for me and for what I had achieved. The medal around my neck was for all those who had contributed to getting me there.

My story is a tale of ups and downs, of triumph and despair, of happiness and sadness, of being revered and reviled. Looking back it feels like I have lived nine lives, rather than just the one. But I wouldn't swap it for the world; nor the people around me.

1
Growing Up

They didn't hear the first knock. The radio was on and Dad was up a ladder. Mum was up to her arms in wallpaper paste, her stare locked on the pattern taking shape before her eyes in the upstairs bedroom.

It came again. More urgent this time. *Ra-ta-tat-tat*. Dad looked at Mum for a clue as to who it could be. We had only been in the house a week. We didn't know anyone. Mum crept to the window and peered down. All of a sudden she froze.

'Oh my God, Ron. It's Matthew.'

Dad shot down the stairs to the hall where packing cases stood piled on top of one another, still half full after the move south from Birkenhead to Blackfield in Hampshire, where Dad's new job had brought us. He opened the front door, and there, standing on the doorstep in front of him, was a lad wearing a motorcycle helmet. But this was no pizza delivery; in his arms was a distraught five-year-old. Me.

Our new home was at the end of a little lane on the edge of the New Forest. The day was warm and bright, and my sister Emma and I had been playing on our pushbikes up and down the leafy lane. You could not imagine a safer place to be. At least until the scooter hit me.

The shaken rider handed me over to Dad. I had a broken collarbone and a gashed head. He was all apologies, insisting I had come out of nowhere and he'd had no time to react.

By now Mum, who'd followed Dad down the stairs, was frantic with worry. As we were new to the area neither of my parents knew where the hospital was. Still, they laid me across the back seat of the car and set off, hazard lights flashing and Dad waving a white handkerchief out of the driver's window. It must have been quite a sight, as must the expression on Dad's face when we arrived at the local hospital in Hythe to find a notice pinned to the entrance which stated that they were shut and that we needed to go to Southampton, a further half an hour away.

We laugh about it now, particularly at the memory of the lad on the scooter returning to our house a week later to present me with a Tufty Road Safety board game. But it was not remotely funny at the time. My career could have been over before it had even begun.

I was born to Ron and Lois Dawson on 31 October 1972, and almost from the day I arrived kicking and screaming into the world at Grange Mount Hospital in Birkenhead I was a worry to them. They did not know then that I would go on to have lumps knocked out of me for a living, but based on the early evidence they might well have guessed. As a toddler I never used to walk anywhere; I was always running around on my toes and falling downstairs. One day I tumbled into a wrought-iron gate and emerged with a lump on my head and the clearly visible imprint of one of the gate's bars. Another time, I got a wine gum stuck in my throat and stopped breathing.

Dad worked shifts at Mobil Oil, and my problems always seemed to come in the evening when he was away on the two till ten beat, so it was Mum who often had the traumatic task of scooping me up in one arm while using her free hand to point Emma, three years older than me, in the direction of the car for yet another mercy dash.

He was at work the day I performed a disappearing act which so alarmed Mum that she called in the police. Mind you, I was only two and a half at the time. She had left me playing barefooted with my first girlfriend, Elspeth, on a patch of grass at the end of the cul-de-sac in which we lived. But by the time she next turned round to check on us we'd decided to walk to our nursery school, through the estate and up and over the main road using the footbridge. Mum swears she realized we were missing within seconds of us leaving. Whatever the truth, she had the police around pretty smartish. They searched our house and then Elspeth's before combing the neighbourhood, eventually spotting the two of us walking hand in hand on the other side of the main road.

Mum nearly suffocated me with her hug when she got me home. Then she lost it a bit. She was embarrassed that so many policemen had been called out to look for me. And there was another reason for her red face: her dad, Sam Thompson, was a chief inspector with the Birkenhead Police. The following day, Grandad went into work to find a note pinned to the noticeboard with his name on it: 'Would C.I.

Thompson please keep his grandson under control and stop providing extra work for half the Birkenhead police force!'

It didn't get any easier for Mum and Dad as I grew older. Two days before my seventh Christmas Mum was wrapping presents in the upstairs bedroom when I charged through the door with my best friend, Spencer Tuckerman, in tow to ask if we could go sledging on a snow-covered slope down the road. So keen was Mum that I didn't see my unwrapped gifts that she nodded straight away, without thinking through the possible consequences. Half an hour later, Spencer's mum was on the phone. 'Lois,' she said, 'bad news I'm afraid. Matt's had an accident. His face has been run over by a sledge.' Mum arrived at the scene of the head-on smash to find Mrs Tuckerman crouched over me trying to hold my nose together and staunch the flow of blood. I was once again rushed to Casualty where I had to have 16 stitches.

In a desperate attempt to keep me out of mischief, if not harm's way, Dad turned to rugby union, the sport he had played as a centre for the Old Boys team at Rock Ferry High School during his younger days in Birkenhead. He took me along to the Esso Social Club where a shortage of lads of my age resulted in me being thrown in with the under-10s. I was very small for that age group, so in an effort to make me look mean Dad wrapped a towelling bandage round my head. They then stuck me out on the wing in the hope that I wouldn't get involved too much (Mum still thinks that's the best place for me during a match).

I enjoyed the rugby, but I also loved football, which I started playing when we moved to Marlow in 1980, and it was the only sport on offer at the Holy Trinity primary school. My grandfather on Dad's side had played for Garston Gas Works, later to become Liverpool. I supported Everton. I continued to play rugby on Sundays at Marlow RFC, where Dad coached me (he'd initially just come along to watch, but after a while standing on the touchline someone asked him to help out; he agreed, he worked hard for his certificates and coached for the next 11 years), but football was my main love and before too long I was picked up by Chelsea Boys. A Chelsea scout had seen me and Spencer playing locally for Flackwell Heath, and the pair of us were invited to play for the baby Blues. To this day, Spencer's dad, Alec, is convinced I would have gone all the way had I stuck with it. I was a right-back, 'fearless yet quite skilful at the same time' in Alec's opinion – which, of course, I value. The reports coming back to my parents also suggested I had a good chance of making it. I was very dedicated and I wanted it badly.

But by that time I had left primary school and started at the Royal Grammar School, Wycombe, where rugby was the main sport, and I had only played a handful of games for Chelsea when I got the nod from RGS that I needed to concentrate on my work and rugby rather than go to Chelsea twice a week. I was reluctant to give up football, though, even when Dad told me I had more chance of making it in rugby because 'every kid wants to play football'.

As far as I was concerned, it wasn't as simple as that. I was a typical teenager and I wanted to break away from Dad's rugby coaching. We got on, but we were often at each other's throats. 'God, why are you always having a go at me?' was the sort of attitude I'd quickly developed. He worked so hard, getting up at five o'clock every day to fight the M25 en route to either Heathrow or Gatwick and not getting home until seven or eight o'clock in the evening. And then he would have me to contend with. I had no appreciation at all for what he was trying to do for me. On Sundays I just wanted to enjoy myself playing, but he was the coach and we did things his way. It always seemed to me that he spoke to me in a way he didn't to the other boys. Whenever I'd had enough of it I would walk off and tell him to leave me alone; he would then get angry with me. Football, however, was a totally different experience. Mum would come and watch while Dad was busy with the rugby team.

My cause with Dad was not helped when I was arrested for petty theft. I was kicking around with a dodgy bunch of boys who were teaching me bad habits. One was that you save money if you don't pay for goods. So there I was in a shop on the high street in Marlow, stuffing one of those party streamer sprays into a pocket in my jeans, when I felt a tap on my shoulder. The two lads I was with bolted out of the shop and got away but I was banged to rights. The police were called, and I was ushered into the back of their car and driven all of 200 yards down the road to the police station. I thought the world was going to end. Mum, who was working part-time at the local post office, got the call to come and get me, and I felt so ashamed that I could not look her in the eyes.

I was given only a warning by the police, and was grounded by Dad, but neither hurt me as much as the reaction of Mum, the daughter of Chief Inspector Thompson, someone I had an unbelievable amount of respect for. 'What is your grandfather going to think?' she sobbed. She made me feel about two feet tall. In fact, the experience would haunt me for years. When I turned 18 I applied to join the police force but panicked when the application form asked for any previous convictions. It was only when Mum and Dad assured me that I didn't have a criminal record that I put it in the post. (In the end I was turned down on medical grounds as I had just undergone a knee operation and they felt I wasn't fit enough.)

Being grounded was an annual feature of my childhood. I would take my summer exams, my report would follow me home on the last day of term and my first week's holiday would be spent paying for my poor results alone in my room.

'This is not good enough, Matthew,' Dad, it seemed, always said on opening the envelope. 'You're grounded. Go to your room.'

'Right. Whatever.'

I was under orders to read for an hour each morning, but that was way beyond my powers of concentration. So I waited until my parents had both left the house for work and then jumped on my bike and went to meet my mates. It required military precision to get back home, return the bike to exactly the same position I'd found it in the garage, then to jump onto my bed and open the book 50 pages on from where I'd left it before Mum's car turned into the drive.

As I got older I gradually began to realize what a fool I was being, in my rebellious attitude towards Dad in particular. He was my biggest supporter; nobody wanted better things for me than him. But that realization took time to dawn on me; initially I agreed to go back to rugby only if he stopped coaching. With time, though, I welcomed his support and indeed sought his approval, even if his vociferous backing wasn't to the liking of everyone. In assembly one day at RGS he was named and shamed for over-exuberance on the touchline during a school match. I was so proud of him. I thought it was hilarious. It was the one and only time my name was read out during assembly without me being told off as a result. On another occasion he was warned for shouting at a referee. He liked to tell them why they were wrong (and you wonder where I got it from!).

When I played rugby during my teenage years I could always hear Dad's voice. Whenever I passed the ball from the base of a ruck I'd hear him bark, 'Follow the ball!' I would have thought something was wrong had I not been able to pick out his voice. And, being a coach, his enthusiasm extended beyond the playing field, so keen was he that I got the most out of myself. When I was selected for England 16 Group Dad felt I was too much of a couch potato at home, so he organized 'training' sessions in our back garden. He would try to get me doing press-ups and shuttle sprints. I would go out for five minutes to humour him, then return to the sofa. Happily, certainly from Dad's point of view, I became more committed once I turned 17. Two or three times a week I would go on an eight-mile run, up to the M40 roundabout, back down a little lane, then all along Marlow Bottom. I'd get home from school, change into my kit and set out. The best times were always in the summer when I could wear a vest and run past the girls coming home on the school buses. It was both a pleasure and a pain.

Dad wasn't the only guiding light during my formative rugby-playing days. From the age of 13 through to the first XV my coach at RGS was Colin Tattersall, and he had a huge influence on my game. We were a successful school side, losing only two or three games a season, but when I was in the sixth form we played against hardly any public schools. They wouldn't take our fixture because we were a state school, albeit a very good one with a strong set-up. That has since changed. RGS now plays against the likes of Radley, Millfield and Harrow, but at that time we only got to play against those sides in the Daily Mail Cup.

It was probably a good thing that I showed promise in sport because my academic accomplishments were average, as most of my tutors never tired of telling me. How I ever got into the Royal Grammar School in the first place I will never know. We had to take a 12-plus to secure a place, and how I passed that remains a mystery to me. Me and exams don't get on. To this day I hate the words 'exam' and 'test'. I managed to scrape four GCSEs first time round, adding another four later on, but I failed all my A levels, primarily because I was away playing with the England 18 Group for six to seven weeks during the lead-up to the exams. I came back not much more than a week before my first paper, so it was hardly perfect preparation. And believe me, I needed perfect preparation. Fortunately, the school allowed it, but mine was a poor show academically. It's not something I'm proud of, but at that time of my life I was just not tuned in to working, be it homework or writing essays. All I wanted to do was play rugby. Or football, or snooker, or golf, or cricket . . .

I played all five matches for England under-18s in that 1990–91 season, forming a half-back partnership with Epsom's soon-to-be-Irish Paul Burke. We narrowly lost to the touring Australians 8–3 at Twickenham (no disgrace as they won all 12 matches they played), but we beat Ireland, France and

Scotland in successive matches, conceding only 16 points in the process. However, our campaign ended on a depressing note in Colwyn Bay when we lost to a Wales side that had been thrashed 44–0 by the Aussies. We had seemed on course for a Junior Grand Slam when we led 10–4 well into the second half, but we let them back in, gifted them a really soft try and Chris John's boot did the rest. Wales won the match 13–10 and with it the Triple Crown.

The following season I moved up to the England under-21 side, leaving behind scrum-half Andy Gomarsall to captain England 18 Group to the Junior Grand Slam we had missed out on. My debut came at centre in a 21–21 draw with the French Armed Forces in a match at Twickenham played as a curtain raiser to the Pilkington Cup final between Bath and Harlequins.

It was my first game at Headquarters, and Mum and Dad were in the stands. They have barely missed a game since, a habit born out of Mum's fear that she should always be on hand in case I suffered a bad injury. It dates back to when she used to make the sandwiches at Marlow. If any of the kids were injured she would accompany them to hospital in the ambulance, and the first thing they would always say to her was 'I want my mum', and that stuck with her. I know she'll be an awful lot happier when I retire from rugby. She finds the whole experience torture, and it has never become any easier for her. But she feels that if she misses a game, I'll get injured. I can only guess at the number of games she and Dad have missed throughout my career across the world – less than 10 certainly. I am unbelievably lucky, because although the majority of parents support their kids, very few do to the extent mine have. Dick Greenwood, father of Will and a former England player and coach, once told Mum that he knew exactly how she feels. 'It's like a little spotlight follows Matt around the field, isn't it, Lois?' he said. He couldn't have put it better. Because of the position I play I am often trapped under piles of players while play carries on. Mum keeps watching me rather than following the ball, which she leaves to Dad. She feels that if she takes her eye off me something bad will happen. She doesn't usually have a clue about how the game is going, but if I go down because I've got a fly in my eye, she'll be the first to know.

All this support at times made for a difficult relationship between me and my sister. As kids, Emma and I lived very different lives. Socially we had different sets of friends: she went to a school in Maidenhead and had friends in Marlow whereas mine tended to be more in High Wycombe and Aylesbury. She saw her brother playing for England and getting the odd write-up in newspapers and her Mum and Dad following me everywhere. Looking back, it must have been hard for her, and I can fully appreciate her frustrations. I'm sure she would have welcomed some of that attention herself. It was only later, after we had both left home, that I consciously tried to make up for lost time. Emma is now married to Martin, with two children, Daniel and Ellen, and we often meet up for barbecues.

At the end of August 1991 I was invited to join Northampton Rugby Club. I accepted, and this marked the point at which my relationship with my parents changed. Up until then they were my support group; any problems I had, I turned to them. But at Northampton I met Keith Barwell, a wealthy local business-man, and he took me under his wing.

Northampton had approached me after seeing me play at scrum-half for England 18 Group against France at Franklin's Gardens in April. When I returned from a tour to New Zealand with Marlow, it was to a message from Saints' youth-team coach Keith Picton asking me to call him. I had already had a look at Wasps and there had been interest in me shown by Harlequins and Saracens, but I liked what I saw at Northampton.

Within weeks I was an 18-year-old commuting to the East Midlands to play for Saints under-19s. It was an expensive business, but Keith sorted me out with a job, working as a security guard for one of his companies, Firm Security. I was what is known in the trade as a 'flyer', which meant I had to be ready at the drop of a hat to go anywhere and offer security back-up. For example, one evening they phoned me up to say I was needed in Worcester by 10 o'clock the following morning to patrol Littlewoods.

Keith and my parents have since become the best of friends, but after I moved up to Northampton in January 1992 Mum and Dad felt a little bit left out. An awful lot of things were being sorted out for me by Keith during this period, things which parents would ordinarily do, like helping to arrange mortgages. My new place was about an hour and a half from home, which I didn't think was all that far, but as far as Mum and Dad were concerned I could have been on the moon.

By August of that year I had moved into the head office of Firm Security and was being paid £10,000 a year. I stayed there until September 1993, when I went to work for the *Milton*

Keynes Herald, another of Keith's interests, selling £15 adverts over the telephone. From there it was on to a career of sorts in teaching, a fact that will amuse my tutors at RGS who wrote me off as intellectually challenged. At the time I was sharing a house with clubmate Brett Taylor, and he was teaching at Spratton Hall prep school in Northampton. I had spent a lot of time at RGS coaching junior teams, so when an opportunity came up to help out with PE lessons and generally to be an odd-job man around the school, I jumped at it. It was obviously good for the school to have me around for the rugby and PE, but I was keen to do more, so they allowed me to teach basic geography and maths to kids up to the age of 10. I surprised myself with how smoothly it went. I got on well with the kids, made them understand the subjects and found it easy to teach them.

I was at my happiest, however, when I was outside, and one summer I was asked to strip the paint off all the school's football and rugby posts, sand them down and then rust-coat and paint them. Many saw it as a thankless task as it was a three-week job, but the weather was gorgeous. I finished it in two months, and I've never been so tanned.

Brett and I, known as the 'terrible twosome' (or 'pretty boys' to Keith Barwell), were very sporty and quite fit and athletic with all the training we did. As soon as the first ray of sunshine appeared we would be out in our shorts and sleeveless T-shirts to volunteer for car-park duty. It was no chore at all. You wouldn't believe how many mothers turned up in open-top cars, fully made up and wearing short little skirts. We of course thought we were God's gifts to the world.

Nothing altered that view when we were roped into taking

part in the summer production of a Victorian music-hall show. Our particular scene required us to pretend to be two weight-lifters, complete with big moustaches and all-in-one leotards, lifting black balloons disguised as cannonballs on the end of a weight bar. Half an hour before we were due on stage we pumped ourselves up with circuit weights and clap press-ups in the dressing room, and then covered ourselves in bronzing lotion and got fully oiled up. The looks we got from the mums as we took off our dressing gowns on stage in the music hall were truly memorable.

Life was good for me in the early 1990s, and it was about to get a whole lot better.

Defence in football, midfield in rugby. That seemed to be my fate when, after joining Saints as a scrum-half, coach Glen Ross picked me at centre. Having been selected for the bench as a scrum-half for a second-team game, I'd come on in the centre and scored a couple of tries. Before I knew it I was in the first team, making my debut at Gloucester and playing quite well in a Northampton victory.

That night, I went out with Ian Hunter and Brett Taylor and got so wrecked that I ended up sleeping in the wardrobe of a room in the Richmond Hill Hotel. The next morning I woke with a very stiff neck and rushed out to get the papers, expect-ing huge 'Dawson is fantastic' type headlines. I was rather taken aback to find no such thing. The only reference to me in any of the reports was that I had missed a 22-man overlap! But the England selectors took a more positive view, and picked me to represent the under-21 team at centre for the game against the French Armed Forces. Kyran Bracken was scrum-half that day, but this time I did make the headlines, snatching the draw by scoring and converting a last-gasp try.

I still saw my future in the game as a scrum-half though, and that summer Glen Ross set me up with a spell in his native New Zealand, playing scrum-half for a club called Te Awamutu in Waikato. I spent my first two weeks living with Glen at his place in Hamilton; then, once I'd found my feet, I moved on to a farm deep in Waikato country which was owned by Te Awamutu coach John Sicilly. Also staying on the farm were two Scots boys from Melrose, Rob Hule and Stewart Brown, and together we just had the greatest time. Every day would be spent driving quad bikes up the mountain and then erecting fences. We had this big ram hammer with which to drive in the fence posts, but I was barely strong enough to pick it up let alone ram it down.

After a couple of weeks our job descriptions changed from fence erectors to tree surgeons. John needed all his pine trees trimmed, explaining that while the top third has to be branches and leaves, the second third has to be clean so that when it gets cut there are no knots in the wood. He then sent three muppets into the forest and left us to get on with it. Ladders against trees, taking no safety precautions at all, we took massive saws and secateurs up into the branches with us. It was extremely dangerous, and every quarter of an hour or so one of us would fall a good 20 feet to the ground. But there were no serious injuries, and as the days turned into weeks my body got stronger.

Life on a farm at the end of a long single-track road miles away from civilization was simple but wickedly good. One day the three of us were driving home with John and he got to a corner where he knew there would be wild turkeys sitting on the fence. On went the headlights, the turkeys froze in the beam, and out got John with a crowbar. The next day we were instructed to dunk the carcasses in water and pluck them.

'Why?' I asked.

'Try plucking one without wetting it first,' came the reply.

I did, and within seconds there were feathers absolutely everywhere. By the time we'd finished plucking this turkey, John's front lawn was obliterated. The wind had picked up and blown the feathers all over his house too.

'Wet them and they stick. You can then grab them and throw them in a bag,' he explained. 'Got it?'

We stayed on that farm for a month, the three of us living in a little annexe. After that we moved into a house in town and went from one labour job to another. We laid a resin concrete floor in a factory one day, landscaped a garden on another. No two days were the same.

All the while I was developing as a rugby player in general and as a scrum-half in particular. I learned some hard rugby lessons in New Zealand, the most important of them never to make the same mistake twice. New Zealanders are passionate rugby people and they want you to do well, but they are very unforgiving. If you make a mistake, they'll tell you all about it.

When Te Awamutu failed to make the end-of-season play-offs I said my goodbyes, but not before meeting up in Hamilton with the touring England B squad. I also took the opportunity to hook up with Wayne Shelford, the former All Blacks captain who was playing for Northampton but had flown home during the off-season. We went to the B Test together at Rugby Park and an amazing thing happened. As we walked into the stand and up to our seats the whole place stopped to look at Buck. Talk about a national icon.

No rugby player has impressed me more than Buck. I have played rugby with some hard men, but Buck was in a league of his own, to the point of being slightly mental. He came into the changing room one day at Northampton with really long hair tied in a ponytail, having vowed not to get it cut until Phil Pask's wife Janice had given birth. He was late for the pre-match meet and in a hurry. He took off his shirt to change into a training top, and we saw that his back and arms were covered in scars. There must have been hundreds of them, each with a couple of stitches in. He explained that that morning he had been to hospital to have surgically removed all the bits of gristle and scar tissue that had built up over the years of his playing career. His back was like a bloody road map. It was horrendous. He then put his shirt on and went out and played.

Another time Buck played in a game against Rugby where he got the most almighty shoeing – real proper stuff in the days when a player would really get it if he was on the wrong side of a ruck. Most people would have got up and started throwing punches, but Buck just clambered to his feet, looked at the fella with the guilty feet and smiled. I swear the guy shat himself. We didn't see him for the rest of the game. We knew Buck was just biding his time until opportunity knocked, and so did he.

That stay in New Zealand was a crucial time for me, because when I got back to England my scrum-half apprenticeship was complete. I was selected by the Midlands at number 9 and was set on a course which would soon lead me to a place on the full England bench and a World Cup winner's medal.

'England,' said Andy 'Prince' Harriman, 'were a scratch side who hadn't played together before, an unknown quantity even to ourselves.' Then he went off to collect the Melrose Cup as captain of the winning side of the inaugural World Cup Sevens. The day was 18 April 1993, and according to those present at Murrayfield, at the time the half-built home of Scottish rugby, it should be remembered as one of the greatest in English rugby. Not only was I there, I was a member of the triumphant squad.

Over the course of three extraordinary days that April the 10-man England squad lived out a Cinderella-style fantasy. Unloved and unrated, we took on the world's best in a format of rugby barely recognized by the powers-that-be at Twickenham and came out on top. We had been given so little chance by the Rugby Football Union that they hadn't considered it worth sending us to the Hong Kong Sevens beforehand. Unlike Scotland, who had warmed up for the tournament by globetrotting around the sevens circuit and promptly fell at the first hurdle, we just turned up in Edinburgh that spring. I wouldn't say that we gave ourselves as little chance of winning as everyone else, but it did start out as a bit of a jolly – until it dawned on us that we were actually good enough to go all the way.

To this day, few people remember who played for England in that tournament, other than Andy Harriman and maybe Lawrence Dallaglio. It was not that we had a weak squad, because we didn't, despite the fact that only Prince and Tim Rodber had been capped. It was more that we had relatively little experience of sevens at the very highest level. I had made the squad because I was naturally fit and could keep running all day. I could also play anywhere in the back line, as well as kick goals. Nick Beal, Ade Adebayo, Dave Scully, Chris Sheasby, Justyn Cassell and Damian Hopley completed our squad, and we were put up in the George Hotel in Edinburgh, which was the nicest hotel I had ever stayed in. I shared a room with Hoppers. There was a Playstation plugged into the television, we had all our laundry paid for, and we ate some lovely seafood. I was there for the ride really, a wide-eyed 20-year-old not really able to believe that I was playing for my country in a World Cup.

In the days preceding the tournament all the other teams seemed to be locked into the sevens mentality. We were more likely to be locked in bars. We had a bit of a tour mentality, and that was how we bonded, from the first evening when Prince declared, 'Right, boys, we're going out to have a good night.' A good night? It was carnage. But when we eventually woke some time the next day we were all mates. Then, all of a sudden, we were a really good team.

In Prince we had the fastest man in the tournament and, as it turned out, its outstanding player. He was extraordinary in every way. Our training drill was one-on-one over five and ten metres, trying to step your man. Andy would be skinning people. It was phenomenal. You just couldn't catch him. He was more elusive than Jason Robinson. Jason has very small steps, but Harriman was bang, bang, gone – big steps like Iain Balshaw, very explosive and powerful. Awesome, actually.

After the first and second days we started to believe. Drawn in Group D, we made light work of Hong Kong (40–5), Spain (31–0), Canada (33–0) and Namibia (24–5) with me playing in all but the Canada game. We lost to Western Samoa (10–28), who had come into the tournament on the back of winning the Hong Kong Sevens for the first time, but still went through to the quarter-finals, which were contested in two round-robin groups of four. We were drawn in Group 2 with New Zealand, Australia and South Africa, while Western Samoa joined Ireland, Fiji and Tonga in Group 1.

The Samoans surprisingly lost two of their three matches, the Irish pulling off a major shock by beating them 17–0 before Fiji edged them 14–12 to put the tournament favourites out. No such problems for England: we began the second phase by scoring three tries against New Zealand in the first seven minutes, through Harriman, Scully and Beal, and won the game 21–12. Against South Africa we had to come from behind following Chester Williams's early score for the Boks, but managed it with Prince and then Hoppers crossing and Bealer converting for a 14–7 win. When the Aussies were wiped out 42–0 by New Zealand in their last game before we met them, conceding six tries in the process, the omens looked promising, but against us David Campese escaped for an early try and the Wallabies led by 14 points before we got on the scoreboard. Despite tries by Justyn Cassell and Dave Scully, we went down 12–21.

Annoyed at a result which meant Australia topped the group even though we'd both finished on seven points, we went into our semi-final with Fiji determined to regain our momentum. We decided to introduce some real physicality, and to get hard with it. Sheasby, Rodders, Hoppers and Lawrence outscrummaged the Fijians from the outset and they didn't really react to it. We started to press them and put them under pressure, and opened up a 14–7 lead through tries by Prince and Lawrence. Fiji came back at us and threatened to draw level when Rasari went on the charge, but Dave Scully planted a spectacular tackle on the big man which knocked him backwards. The ball sprang loose and Ade put Prince away for the try which settled the issue in our favour (21–7). Dave was awarded the Moment of the Tournament for that tackle, and he deserved it.

That said, it could have gone to Andy Harriman for his opening try in the final against Australia, who had come so close to losing to Ireland in their semi before stealing victory in the last move of the match through a try by Willie Ofahengaue. Prince absolutely flew past Campo and his mates as if they were wading in treacle. It was his twelfth try of the tournament which, not surprisingly, made him top try scorer.

I was not involved in the final; instead, I played the role of cheerleader on the sidelines. And there was much to shout about as tries by Lawrence and Rodders, who outran Campo to score under the posts, extended the England lead to 21 points before half-time. It seemed too good to be true and, sure enough, the Aussies powered back after the break, scoring three tries as our legs went. Critically, though, Nick Beal had converted all three England tries, whereas Michael Lynagh managed only one for the Wallabies. After a frantic final minute in which they threatened our line again, the whistle brought blessed relief, and the small matter of a World Cup winner's medal.

2
Losing Ground

Anything and everything seemed possible when I returned from Edinburgh in triumph with the Magnificent Seven. I was even talked about in some quarters as a candidate for the forthcoming Lions tour to New Zealand. I had never even heard of the Lions. As it turned out, that summer of 1993 I was named in the England A squad to tour Canada, and I flew out to Vancouver as first choice ahead of Kyran Bracken. With 16 Englishmen on Lions duty, including scrum-half Dewi Morris, it was an opportunity to really put my name in the frame. It turned into a nightmare.

The tour opener was a game against British Columbia in Victoria. Ahead of us were four further fixtures including two non-cap Tests, and if things went well there was always the possibility of a call-up to join the Lions (as happened to Martin Johnson when Wade Dooley came home early following the death of his father). But things did not go well. Not for me, at any rate. I had felt a hamstring twinge in training before the first game, and we were only 10 minutes in when it tore and my tour was over. Worse still, Kyran took full advantage. Although England went on to lose the first 'Test', they bounced back to tie the series, and *Rothmans Rugby Union Yearbook* was in no doubt who was responsible. Its tour review read: 'Kyran Bracken was the only tourist who really enhanced a claim for a full international place. In the chase for Dewi Morris's scrum-half shirt he leapfrogged Matt Dawson. Bracken's distribution and vision in the second international definitely gave the tourists the necessary edge to tie the series.'

At the time I didn't think too much of it. I still thought I was the bee's knees. I returned to Northampton with Tim Rodber, whose tour had also been cut short by a wrecked hamstring, and we had a cracking time for the rest of that summer, playing golf and drinking beer. Only later did I really look back on that period as a missed opportunity. It could have been a big turning point in my career; instead, it proved to be exactly that for Kyran as his really took off.

Kyran had been to university and had done the 'wild' phase I was now in, so while I was forever thinking about which mate at which university I could go and visit next, he was far more tuned in to the rugby. On his return from Canada he was sent to Australia to join up with the England under-21 tour. Kyran went straight into the 'Test' team and scored two of England's three tries in a 22–12 win over Australia. There was now no stopping him. A few months later, when the South-West narrowly lost out to the touring All Blacks at Redruth, he again caught the eye, and when he followed that up with another smart display for England A against the same opposition seven days later the selectors knew he was ready to step up. What they didn't know, however, was that Dewi Morris would be forced out of the Test team to face New Zealand on 27 November 1993 with a bout of flu after he had been named in the starting line-up. As the next in line, Kyran was handed his full international debut. I was summoned on to the replacements' bench for the first time, but by now there was clear daylight between the two of us in the rankings. I was still talking a good game, but I was half the player I had been earlier in the year. I was away with the fairies and I didn't really understand why.

Kyran enjoyed a startling England debut. It had everything, including an England win over an All Blacks side that had gone into the game as 1/6 favourites. Kyran had his ankle stamped on after just two minutes by New Zealand flanker Jamie Joseph but refused to come off, ending the day on crutches as one of the heroes of the 15–9 triumph. Afterwards his profile was massive. All of a sudden, from having been in the box seat months earlier, I watched him sail over the horizon. He was a big star, appearing on the *Big Breakfast* and being pictured in the newspapers walking out of a hotel with his girlfriend. I thought, 'Holy shit, what about me?' Kyran was the only show in town, and it hurt. I felt that the number 9 shirt should be mine and that I should be getting all the attention. I was still a young lad and I just didn't know how to react. Rather than earn it, I wanted it given to me. It was just an immaturity within me. I had a lot of work to do to get the shirt back, but I didn't know how to go about it. I tried to get on with playing rugby but I couldn't find any form. I tried to force everything, lost my way, and ended up getting dropped by the club.

And yet I'd come within a whisker of winning my first cap at the age of 21 against the All Blacks. From the moment Joseph's boot had come down on Kyran's ankle I'd thought

I was on. I'd warmed up for the whole bloody game expecting Kyran to hobble off any minute. There is no way in this day and age he would or could have carried on; the instruction would have come down to 'get him off'. But that day there was no budging him, even though when he did come off the pitch he was on crutches for months afterwards. At the time, I didn't understand why he had been so obstinate, why he'd showed so much doggedness and determination. Only later did I come to appreciate what an outstanding effort it was. It was Kyran's way of saying, 'This is my shirt and I'm not giving it up.' I don't know whether he realized the sort of precedent he was setting for us both, but from that day on I knew he was going to be a major factor in my career.

It was probably a blessing in disguise that Kyran did not leave the field that day at Twickenham because I now know I wasn't ready, in the same way that I can now admit to myself that for two years, until December 1995, when I finally made my full debut, I thought I was a lot better than I was. The season before that All Blacks match I was flying, really flying, but then I started to believe my own publicity. Even when I came back from Canada early I consoled myself with the thought that I was still the best scrum-half around. I simply didn't realize how much work was needed. I am naturally a confident sort of person, fortunate to have been born with great self-belief. But there was probably too much an element of arrogance in my make-up when I was younger. I didn't get the balance right.

That was how I was in 1993, riding on the seat of my pants, giving thought to only what was right in front of my eyes. So when England called me on to the bench for the New Zealand game I took it all in my stride. I wasn't particularly nervous, because in those days you never saw a replacement unless there was a major injury, so I didn't expect to play. I joined up with the squad on the Thursday and didn't know any of the moves. On Friday there was a light team run. I think I probably had 30 seconds' running, one scrum and one lineout. That was it. But so what? It wasn't as though Kyran was going to get injured.

Come the day, cue Jamie Joseph and the instruction from England coach Dick Best to me to go down and warm up.

'You know the moves, right, Daws?'

'Dick, I don't know any moves, or any calls. What's going on?'

It would have been laughable had it not been so serious. There I was, sitting in the tunnel with Dick Best, and he was telling me the lineout calls. I was totally crapping myself. I did some stretches and nervously laughed to myself.

'I haven't got a clue here, Dick. I haven't got a clue what's going on here, mate.'

'Don't worry,' said the coach of the England rugby team. 'Just give it to Rob Andrew.'

Sometimes I wonder what would have happened to my career had I got on the pitch that day. Never mind 50-plus England caps, I would have needed a miracle to win a second. I would have been toast. That said, after the way Kyran played that day, I thought my England career might be brown bread anyway.

The first lash caught me by surprise. I was not tensed, my body was relaxed. Then he hit me again, and I cried out.

Blood poured down my legs as a gang of rugby players stood around me laughing.

It had always been a dream of mine to play for the Barbarians, probably more so even than for England, because they had such an aura about them. The history of the club, the players who had worn the shirt, the great games, The Try Gareth Edwards scored against the All Blacks in 1973. Everything seemed magical. As a youngster, my black and white hooped replica shirt was my pride and joy. I wore it everywhere.

But I will not play for the Barbarians again. Not after my experience in Zimbabwe in May and June 1994. Not after what happened on that tour. Not after being assaulted by a Welshman wielding a cactus leaf.

I was very much a social animal at the time. My attitude was that all my success in rugby was purely down to natural talent and I didn't have to work at it. Despite having lost ground to Kyran Bracken in the previous 12 months I was still a World Cup winner enjoying life to the full. I had a prima donna attitude in training as well, basically thinking that because I'd got close to an England cap it was just going to happen for me sooner or later. Lording it about Northampton on nights out with pretty girls was pretty much par for the course. I had some wild times. I was 21 years old, so who could blame me? So when the invitation arrived from the Barbarians it sounded like another good crack with another good bunch of lads, as well as the chance to fulfil a lifelong ambition to wear the shirt. There was a club tour to Chicago scheduled for the end of the season, but that wasn't even a consideration for me.

Not too many big names went on the tour. Neil Back,

Richard Cockerill and Darren Garforth went from Leicester, but otherwise the squad was mainly composed of Welsh boys, really good lads. We played three games, beating Zimbabwe Goshawks 53–9 and Matabeleland 35–23, and losing to Zimbabwe 23–21 in Harare. But my memories are not of the rugby, nor of the sights and sounds of a country I had never before visited. Rather, they are of what I took at the time to be the 'Barbarian way'. It was a case of old boys treating us like schoolchildren. And then at the end of the tour, to top it all off, we had a session 'in court' which was just horrendous.

Nick Beal, one of my best mates, was also on the tour and we spent quite a lot of time together. So of course we got fined for being mates.

'Yeah, fair enough. I'll down half a pint of tequila.'

But that wasn't what they had in mind at all. I was told to take my trousers down, bend over a chair and prepare to be spanked by a massive cactus leaf.

'What? What are you talking about?'

As the youngest player on tour I expected them to have a bit of fun at my expense, even if standing in front of the whole squad with my shorts round my ankles, leaning forward over a chair, preparing to be hit by a seriously spiky object, was not exactly what I had in mind. Still, Bealer played along with it and waved the leaf close to my backside. But that was not good enough for the others. They wanted pain. Derwyn Jones, the towering Cardiff and Wales second row, grabbed the leaf off Bealer and whacked my arse. The blow cut me, blood started to ooze from my cheeks, and I exploded in rage.

'What the fucking hell do you think you're doing?'

My backside was full of cactus splinters and it hurt like hell. And still the ordeal wasn't over. It was now Nick's turn to feel the pain.

'No,' I said. 'There's no way I'm doing that. I'm the first to enjoy a bit of a giggle but no, I'm not having any of that.'

There and then I switched off. I lost interest in the Barbarians. I hadn't minded the other stuff – the drinking games, and the Circle of Fire challenge where toilet paper is rolled up tight and you have to clench it between your bum cheeks, set a light to it and run around the room before the paper burns out. That was okay, but the cactus lark I thought was well out of order. I swore to myself there and then that I would never play again. If I was asked now, almost a decade later, my answer would still be no because I promised myself that I wouldn't and I am a man of my word. Not only physically, but mentally I was scarred by that experience. It was very, very odd indeed. It upset me. They didn't treat me with any respect at the time. Nick's a little bit more forgiving, but then he didn't get whacked so it's easier for him to be that way. You don't easily forgive or forget after having to lie on the bed in your hotel room while your mate pulls splinters out of your arse. I was angry, really mad. I had thought it would be good for a few photos, that everyone else would wet themselves, and that the cactus leaf would just skim my backside. But Derwyn, who was basically a good lad but due to his size was employed as 'the enforcer', got carried away. I didn't want to show any pain but I couldn't help it. There was blood running down my legs and onto my shorts.

If that wasn't bad enough, when we got home it was a real battle to keep my Barbarians shirt. They wanted to take them all back. I couldn't believe it. We didn't receive a bean for going; the only reason I went was to get the shirt and to be able to say I had played for the Barbarians. I got one in the end, though, so at least I have a shirt to go with the memory.

Back in Northampton I wasted no time getting back into the swing of things, even if my backside was still too sore to plonk on a barstool. People were starting to recognize me around town, so it was always easy to be out, even on a Friday night before a game, when I would head to Aunty Ruth's in town for a cup of coffee. But I was always out for out's sake; my focus was not on rugby. Saturday night I would always go out to get hammered and just be a boy.

The game was still amateur in 1994, let's not forget, and this sort of behaviour wasn't particularly frowned upon. But, with hindsight, it hurt my career. England were preparing to change the guard at number 9; the selectors were looking for the player to take the scrum-half baton from Richard Hill and Dewi Morris and carry it into a new era. I had played in England's two A-team victories over Italy and Ireland, yet Wasps' Steve Bates was selected for the summer tour to South Africa. I was absolutely gutted. The alarm bells should have rung then. I should have realized that I obviously wasn't good enough. Instead, I chose to believe it was the selectors who were at fault. Jack Rowell, the new England manager, had simply got it wrong.

Both my fitness and my attitude to rugby were slack. There was no structure to my training. I'd do a bit, but I was always naturally fit so I didn't push myself. I was dogged and determined and brave, and because I'd cause a little bit of havoc at the base of the scrum, making breaks and scoring the odd individual try, I got more than my fair share of attention. I got away with it because I was still something of an unknown quantity, but that all changed in the 1994–95 season when the rest of the First Division wised up, saw that I wasn't a bad player and decided to get on my case. I thought I could weather the storm, but I got battered. I was frequently injured and lost my form pretty quickly. Over the winter I needed someone in my life to say to me, 'The 1995 World Cup is there for you if you really work at it,' but I didn't have a mentor on the playing side in that way until I'd formed a relationship with Ian McGeechan, who replaced Glen Ross as head coach and director of rugby at Northampton midway through the season.

I wasn't alone at Northampton in being a prima donna; there were probably three or four of us who thought we were above it. Even to the point that we didn't bother going to the final league game at West Hartlepool. I didn't travel with the team; I played golf instead. I look back now and think it's no bloody wonder we got relegated. It was a predicament all of our own making. We were a good-time club, cruising around town like big fish in a small pond. The alcohol-and-party lifestyle we led was symptomatic of an attitude problem which brought about our downfall. Because we thought we were too good to go down people failed to work on the little things which seemed minor but, when added together, amounted to a big problem. I know I didn't work hard enough. We didn't make sufficient effort with the supporters, or in training, or in preparation for a game. We just expected every-thing to happen. Nobody said how we were going to go about staying up in 1995, just that we would.

Our fate was sealed on the final day of the season when Harlequins won at Gloucester, which rendered irrelevant our victory over West Hartlepool. I saw the result in the clubhouse after finishing my round. Finally, the penny dropped.

There were a lot of very embarrassed people within the playing staff when we assembled for a meeting the following Monday, because there was no one else to blame other than ourselves. Ian McGeechan was scathing in his criticism. 'You lot are living in a comfort zone,' he said, and we were. It was too comfortable playing for Northampton. We had good crowds and good facilities, we were well known in the town, and we could get in as many bars as we liked. But, of course, when you're in a comfort zone you don't see it. It's not until somebody comes along and points it out to you that you twig. After Geech had spoken it was the turn of club captain Tim Rodber to have his say. 'This comfort zone disappears now and it never returns,' he said. 'None of us are going to walk away from this. We put the club in this mess and we are all going to get it out, right? We are going to blitz the Second Division. We are not going to lose a game. Right?'

A few days later I was sat at home, no longer so keen to go out given that the whole of the town seemed to be asking the same question ('How the hell did you lot manage to get relegated, then?'), when the post arrived. It was my Saints' end-of-season report, penned by coach Paul Larkin. 'A very frustrating and eventful year you have had,' he began.

Inevitably you must have suffered the full range of emotions, but there is always some consolation. After the previous season when you had supposedly suffered loss of form, you were able to concentrate your efforts in order that you regained your confidence as first-choice scrum-half. Frustrated with injury at least you were still able to achieve this. And despite injury, you were able to grab consolation with England A selections.

Next season you will have to contend with different problems, but if you are able to shrug off the injury doubts then you will be ready psychologically. I also feel that with Dewi Morris retiring from the England scene there is much to prove. Kyran Bracken may have the edge, but I feel that nothing is definite. You need to concentrate your efforts and work on your range of skills. That means non-stop passing practices prior to sessions and kicking drills. Because we are in the Second Division you will have to be at the top of your game to get the recognition.

Our gameplan will continue to expand next season. We must take on board the wider game through the hands; the mobility of our back row will legislate for any breakdown. You should be looking to snipe and penetrate from third, fourth and fifth phases etc. Inevitably you will be involved in the occasional back-row move to keep the opposition occupied.

The most important factor is that we are confident. Not complacent, but prepared to win through hard graft. Prepared to accept that the team will win the championship, not the individual. Prepared from the onset for every possibility.

Larkin ended his report with the words, 'You have it all in your grasp.'

Little did I know, but in the early summer of 1995 I still had a place in England's World Cup squad within my grasp. In March, on the same weekend that Kyran Bracken helped England to a 24–12 Five Nations victory over Scotland at Twickenham, I had been sent on a mission with England A to South Africa to check out the World Cup facilities in Durban. We played one match, against Natal, and I played the full 80 minutes in a 33–25 defeat at King's Park. Although England opted for Dewi and Kyran as their World Cup scrum-halves, Kyran picked up an injury during the tournament which meant Jack Rowell needed to send for a replacement. I was next in line, but I was touring Australia and Fiji with England A. Jack's Mayday call coincided with a game against Queensland during which I was boomed by a big Fijian centre and suffered major-league concussion, and as I was away at the races, so to speak, England were forced into a decision. With me out of the reckoning, they plumped for Andy Gomarsall, my understudy on the A tour.

Even though Andy would actually play no part in the tournament, I was beside myself when I heard. Fortunately that was not for a while, thanks to a combination of a friend's sensitivity and a case of mistaken identity. Paul Grayson, my Northampton and England A half-back partner, had heard the news while I was under observation, suffering from impaired vision and various other side effects and thus unable to travel on to Melbourne with the rest of the squad. For the best part of a week he sat on it while I recuperated in Manly with Tim Stimpson, who had also left the tour having gone down with glandular fever. When we were given the all-clear by the doctors to fly home we headed for Sydney airport, only to discover that I was attempting to travel on Grays's passport. I phoned him to say that he must have mine as I had his, and that I couldn't leave the country. We then chewed the fat about rugby and about life, which gave him ample opportunity to say, 'Oh, and by the way . . .' But being the mate he didn't, suspecting that I would have gone walkabout had I heard about Gomars.

He was absolutely right. It was a nightmare end to what had been an utterly forgettable season.

3
Return of the Artful Dodger

The whistle blew and my head started to spin. The game was over and I was running on empty. As I reached the dressing room I slumped on a bench and closed my eyes. Then it all went blank. Moments after playing my first international for England, I passed out.

When I came round, I would reflect on an upturn in fortune which had brought me my first cap only months after I'd been relegated to the Second Division with Northampton, and transformed me from rugby-playing schoolteacher with casual attitude into fully professional England international.

But now wasn't the time. It wasn't the time either to admit to myself that I had a virus which was invading my body and would confine me to bed for a fortnight after England defeated Western Samoa 27–9 at Twickenham just nine days before Christmas, with Matthew James Sutherland Dawson at scrum-half and his best mate, Paul Grayson, wearing the number 10 shirt.

Weeks earlier rugby union had become a professional sport, but there were still amateur traditions to observe, one of which was that new caps go out and get as drunk as skunks. It is a proper initiation, with no cactus leaves involved. Each of your team-mates selects a drink and you share it with him. The outcome was inevitable, especially when Ben Clarke and Phil de Glanville came over. Clarkey had a bottle of red wine which he insisted Grays and I polish off with him, then DG ordered us each a vodka martini, which went down like paint stripper. I turned to Grays and said I had to go. He laughed at me and called me a pussy. I went to the loo and chucked the lot up. It was 10 minutes of pain, but I got rid of most of the alcohol before it had even got into my system. Then I was back at the bar sipping a beer, feeling on top of the world.

England have had some good chunderers, none better than Bath's Steve Ojomoh, who puked into the wine bucket in the middle of the table at the Hilton Hotel in London just as he was asked to go up and be presented with his cap. He didn't hear his summons because he had his head buried in the bucket.

At least I discharged my cargo in private. But Grays was unimpressed. He had kept it down and was still going strong when I returned. Moments later his colour changed, and his missus suggested she take him up to their twin room. What happened next wasn't pretty. Grays puked in his bed, got out of it, got in with Emma, then puked in hers as well. From there he stumbled to the toilet, saying how sorry he was, and puked again. He didn't know where he was, other than that he was in a world of pain. The pussy.

The morning after the match I woke in the Petersham Hotel feeling deathly. I saw a doctor who confirmed that I was not well and had not been for a while. I had got through my England debut on pure adrenalin, much as James Simpson-

Daniel would when playing against the All Blacks with glandular fever in 2002. But it didn't matter. I had my cap.

That summer I had seen no reason to circle Saturday, 16 December 1995 on my calendar. When pre-season training began at Northampton, ahead of us lay a year playing Second Division rugby away from the public spotlight. Ian McGeechan wanted to remind us of the hard work that had earned us membership of the Saints' playing squad in the first place, before the good times took over and softened our edges. So, a year after spending pre-season in Lanzarote, Geech took us training in parks around Northampton, the town we had taken out of the top flight of English rugby. He ran us into the ground, he watched us spill our guts, and after every session he would walk around saying, 'It's gold in the bank, boys, it's all gold in the bank.' And so it was, for having spent pre-season backing up the pledges we made the day after we were relegated, we proceeded to go unbeaten through the league campaign.

It was a vital period for me and my rugby because I was not the most popular player at Northampton at the time. I was seen as very arrogant and cheeky, which I probably was. I didn't know where the line should be drawn. I thought I could get away with saying things because of who I was and who I played for. If I was sitting having a drink with my friends and someone came and plonked themselves down and started joining in, I would look dismissively at them and say, 'I don't need this.' I was blind to my obligations as a player representing the town's major sporting team. Winger Harvey Thorneycroft used to be the one to pull me aside.

'Daws,' he'd say, 'that person thinks you're a little bit out of order.'

'What you talking about?' I'd reply. 'He's a nob.'

Geech drummed most of that out of me. He was interested in actions, not in smart-arse talk. Who were we, any of us, to lord it about when we were playing Second Division rugby? And where Geech really got it right was that he mixed this criticism with encouragement. I have always responded to people who have confidence and belief in me; show me that and you'll get the best out of me. It is doubt which breeds distrust in me. Geech said he believed in me, that I would reach the top if I was prepared to work with him to unlock my potential. He devised a gameplan which he said would help me achieve my ambitions; he got me working one day a week with Nigel Melville, the former England scrum-half and captain, and he gave me this single piece of advice which transformed my game: 'Think "There's a hole!", not "Where's a hole?"' Before every game he would come up to me and say, 'Don't force it.' It became a trigger phrase for me. He had seen what I'd gone through in 1994, when I was trying to create holes and was getting smashed all the time, to the detriment of the team. He could tell I needed to become more patient. 'Keep passing it,' he said. 'Get rid of it, bide your time, and then, when you see a hole, go and take it.'

As the 1995–96 season wore on I began to gain the reputation I wanted for Matt Dawson. I took risks, I was a bit ballsy, I made the right decisions and I took control. I was helped massively by Geech's ban on us kicking the ball whenever we were awarded a penalty. Unless we were right in front of the posts, 20 yards out, I was under orders to tap and go, forcing the team to go with me. Sometimes this was comical. One point behind or ahead with 20 minutes to go, we get a penalty 25 yards out and 10 yards wide of the posts and I'd be off. You could hear the crowd groaning, 'What the bloody hell do you think you're doing?' But we'd score – maybe not in that very play, but it would always come. We were playing at such a pace that we would congratulate a team if they stuck with us for 60 minutes. We were so fit and strong and so determined that we knew no team could last the full 80 with us.

By the time newly crowned world champions South Africa came to Twickenham in November, Northampton had won their first 10 league games, only once failing to top 40 points, and I had already scored more tries than I had in the whole of the previous campaign. My resurgence was too late to force England's hand for the clash with the Springboks, but my time was approaching.

It helped that England were beaten far more comprehensively than the 24–14 scoreline suggested, and also that Kyran did not enjoy one of his better afternoons. Consequently, by the time Western Samoa touched down at Heathrow my cause was again being championed. 'If England are to find the missing link, a pivot for their game,' wrote Mark Reason in the *Sunday Times*, 'they need a scrum-half who can provide fast ball and the hardness to run at defences. With Dewi Morris retired and Kyran Bracken failing to deliver, the man who is increasingly recognised as having the best credentials is Matt Dawson.' Geech added his weight to the push for my inclusion in the side to play the Polynesians by saying, 'If he does make it through into the international field he'll make a significant impact. He will be one of those players who will be involved all the time.'

A week later I was on the team sheet, in the same back line as some of the all-time greats of English rugby: Will Carling, Jeremy Guscott and Rory Underwood. And not just me, either, as Grays had also got the call. England had decided to roll the dice and blood two half-backs in the same game.

It was difficult for Grays and me to come into such an experienced team in such influential positions, to play with authority and to run the game as you need to at 9 and 10. Nobody seemed to appreciate that except for one person, the England captain. I thought Will Carling was a really good lad. He was a big kid and liked a similar sort of banter to me; he was a real cheeky chappy. But what impressed me most was that he always looked after me and Grays. Will was obviously a big name, a big star, the first genuine rugby celebrity. But he was great with us, referring to us as his 'sons' (Grayson and Dawson). He knew it was crucial for us to have his support, and it was unequivocal.

But that could not calm my nerves in the days leading up to the game. I didn't really venture much outside my bedroom. I was bricking myself, spending half the time on the toilet with acute stomach aches. I didn't realise that I was genuinely ill, as sick as a dog. On the big day itself Grays and I sat together in a room in the Petersham Hotel doing anything to try to take our minds off the ordeal to come. We were just mucking about when we were suddenly brought back into the here and now by the theme tune for *Grandstand* on the television in the corner.

'Oh quality, Steve Rider from Twickenham,' I said. 'That'll be us later.'

Within a minute I was on the toilet and Grays was pacing around the room impatiently waiting to follow. From that point until I came round in the dressing room after the game to find Bill Bishop, president of the Rugby Football Union, waiting to present me with my senior cap and tie, everything is a blur in my memory.

People warned me that I wouldn't remember any of it, and they were right. I still haven't got a clue. I can't even tell you the final score. I think Lawrence Dallaglio and Rory Underwood scored tries, and that we played left to right in the first half, but I can't be sure. I do know that the game was quick – obviously a step up from what I'd been used to as in the last 10 minutes my legs were heavy and my lungs started to burn as the adrenalin ran out – and that we won, but more than that I have to rely on press clippings. I have never watched the game on video.

Experience brings with it a greater awareness and an ability to slow down pressure situations in your own mind to a manageable speed. It has also enabled me to manage my nerves. I no longer worry myself stupid that we are on television, or that there are 70,000 watching in the stadium. I don't even give it a second thought. As soon as the whistle goes there could be no one in the stadium. The only thing I still get nervous about is making mistakes. I've done all my homework, I know I've got it in my head, so there's nothing actually to get nervous about other than execution.

That does not mean I am completely dispassionate. To this

National Anthem gets me every time. Whenever I sing it I try to pick out Mum and Dad in the stand. I watch Dad take his cap off, throw his head back and belt out the words. I feel pride in the fact that they are proud of me. I will only sing the opening couple of lines because I know if I go on I'll start blubbing. After that I let Mum and Dad take over while I run through my key notes and trigger thoughts – which in plain speak are shorthand reminders of what is required of me in the England number 9 shirt. Why am I doing this? What am I going to get out of it? How much effort am I going to put in?

Back at Northampton the wins continued to pile up, but the complexion of the season, and indeed the Game, had changed. Rugby union, for so long the most Corinthian of sports, had thrown open its doors to professionalism.

I was at my local gym at Dallington, with Brett Taylor, Paul Grayson, Tim Rodber and Ian Hunter when the news broke. We had just finished a session and were sitting in the bar having a sandwich and a glass of orange juice. My initial reaction was that the game wasn't ready for such a move; only later did I think of the financial repercussions. Fortunately for Northampton, Keith Barwell had cut straight to the chase. His view was that once the game was 'open' it would be a race between the clubs and the RFU to sign up the players. So he called an emergency meeting at which he made a presentation, and promised that the club was going to look after its players. No one asked any searching questions because no one really understood what it all meant. I had no reason to doubt Keith anyway, as in many ways he had been providing a livelihood for me for the past five years. He had opened a couple of doors for me in terms of employment, and I knew I could trust him. So when he offered me the opportunity of doing as a full-time job what I had spent a large part of my life thinking about or doing anyway, I became very excited.

At that time it wasn't a question of money for me – the thought of playing professional rugby as my job was enough of a dream to be going on with – but Keith had that sorted as well. He handed me a five-year contract in which Northampton agreed to pay me an annual salary of £15,000. It was double what I had been earning the day before as a school-teacher at Spratton Hall. I grabbed the pen out of Keith's pocket and signed the contract there and then. No lawyers, no agents, just thank you very much.

Keith had divided the squad into three tiers: A1s, As and Bs. The top tier, in which I was included along with the likes of Tim Rodber, Martin Bayfield and Gregor Townsend, were deemed to be established internationals and offered an annual salary of between £12,000 and £15,000. Next came the fringe internationals, then the club players. The total wage bill for 40-odd players was £240,000, with a £3,000 bonus available if we won two-thirds of our matches, and Keith signed up all his men – except for one.

Dear Martin,

Would you consider a move down the road to Northampton Rugby Football Club? We know you are a world-class player already playing for an excellent team in Leicester, so why should you consider a move?

Let me put one thought in your mind. Northampton

are going to be a great club. In Rodber, Bayfield, Grayson, Dawson, Townsend, Dods and Bell we have seven established internationals. Ian Hunter will also shortly be available. We intend to strengthen the side by recruiting two world-class players to supplement our front five. We would like you to be one of them. With Ian McGeechan as our coach and with currently £1 million in the bank we intend to 'go for it' during the next two to three seasons.

It wouldn't do you any harm to have lunch with me. During the next few weeks players will have to make big decisions that will mean them signing contracts and agreeing wages for the next one to five years. We could offer you a financial package that is unbeatable.

Warm regards, Keith Barwell.

It is testament to his ambition for Northampton that Keith went fishing for Martin Johnson. He offered him a £15,000 salary and listed him as A.N. Other on his budget for the season. It is Keith's biggest regret that he did not raise his offer by £5,000 as he is convinced that he would have lured the future England and Lions captain away from Welford Road.

But no one really knew then what amount of money was too much or too little. All sorts of figures had been bandied about in the months after South Africa had upset the form book by beating New Zealand to win the World Cup. Rupert Murdoch had signed a 10-year deal worth £366 million for exclusive rights of an annual 'Tri Nations' series between the Boks, the All Blacks and the Wallabies. Then another Aussie magnate, Kerry Packer, wanted to start a global circus to challenge Murdoch's deal. The England and England A lads attended a meeting down in Maidenhead at which Ross Turnbull, Packer's representative in Britain, promised us the world if we signed with him. I hadn't yet made my debut against the Samoans and was a little bit starry-eyed in the company of Will Carling, Dean Richards, Jeremy Guscott and the like, but as thousands of pounds were being offered we all agreed that it was too good an opportunity to turn down. It was so far above my head that I didn't even see it. If it all happened now I'd probably have the likes of Steve Thompson and Ben Cohen hounding me to explain what's going on, because I did the same in 1995 to Kyran, Martin Johnson, Tim Rodber and Phil de Glanville. I didn't have a clue. Everything was so far removed from anything I'd ever experienced. I signed a letter of intent which Kyran, who was a solicitor, kept in the safe in his office. We were told that contracts would be put in the post to our club representative, and that the quicker we got them signed and returned the sooner the 'circus' would be up and running. It was literally as quick as that, and then, as quickly again, nothing happened and it was never heard of again.

But there could be no holding back the tide of professionalism. Since my days playing with the Marlow under-16s I had thought that the game needed to become more professional. And when Will Carling was stripped of the England captaincy in the spring of 1995 for saying that the English game was run by '57 old farts' my view was only confirmed. I was not alone in thinking that the players were professional in attitude and physical ability, but that everything else was totally amateur

– the set-up, the financing, player welfare and so on. The administrators couldn't seriously expect the players to continue to become better and stronger, and therefore to make more and more money for the game, yet not go professional. Sooner or later something had to give.

I don't believe that the way the game went pro was right. The Blazers just announced that rugby union was 'open' and effectively washed their hands of the situation. It was like, 'You wanted it, you have it, you deal with it.' The transition needed to be managed skilfully. Had it been, then maybe the gulf between the haves and have-nots might not have been as big and the likes of Richmond and London Scottish would still be around.

I had no problem supporting Northampton in the ensuing club versus country wrangles. By then I had a mortgage and day-to-day security, all of which had come from Keith and Saints. The RFU had assumed they would get control of the players, but they faffed about with different contracts and how best to move forward. I preferred to be paid by someone I trusted and felt loyal to, so there was only one option for me. The Union was not at that time a body I felt I could trust. Relations between the two parties became increasingly strained and reached a head when the England squad boycotted a training session at Bisham Abbey. The situation had become so confused, and the players were the most confused of all. We were all geared up for the start of the season and then it all blew up. One of the lads referred to us as bargaining chips, and it did feel that way. It was a deeply worrying time. At the click of a finger we could all have had our England dream taken away. We were looking for middle ground but there was none; we were loyal to our clubs but we didn't want to snub England, which is every player's ultimate goal. The Union made it very awkward for us to choose between club and country when we shouldn't have been put in the position of having to choose anyway.

The day of the boycott, when we skipped training to attend a meeting at the Heathrow Hilton, there was a sense of nervous anticipation among the squad. There were going to be offers, decent offers too, on the table to side with the clubs, but there was also unease at the ramifications of us signing an agreement and breaking away from the RFU. I thought the chances that I would not play for England again were about 70–30. That bothered me because that was what I wanted to do, and I know the club also wanted me to do it. I just couldn't understand where the problem lay. It seemed so simple to me: you play for your club, with whom you are contracted, and if you get selected by England they pay you a fee to represent them. Rob Hardwick, a prop forward from Coventry, was the one player to turn up at the England session that day at Bisham. He would get his one cap, but the general view among the squad was that he wasn't thinking of the other people involved. We were all desperate to play for England, but had we allowed ourselves to be rolled over by these guys then that would become the norm for the next generation.

The Union had their chance to avert such a conflict. We as a group gave them every opportunity to sign us all up on RFU contracts very early on, and they decided not to do it. They were so amateur in their approach. I'm sure there was plenty of business acumen among the members of the committee, but as a committee they were still very much old school operating under old-school rules. Yet while they wanted us to play for the honour of representing the jersey, they were quite happy to sell all the catering rights, up the prices at Twickenham, and generally make a load of money on the back of the professional era. They became perturbed that we had some bright guys in the squad who decided it was very wrong that the players, who make the occasion what it is, were not receiving a decent percentage of the income.

The game is about the players. It's about youngsters from all walks of life aspiring to play for England and dreaming that one day they will make it and be recognized as the best in the land. No matter what people might say, you can't mess with that dream. When we went on strike four years later, coach Clive Woodward threatened to pick a team of junior league players to wear the Red Rose. It wouldn't have worked. They wouldn't have been England. That wouldn't sell out Twickenham, and that is where the RFU make their money. Eventually, the Union realized that.

Keith Barwell is a good man, one I am proud to count among my very best friends. Whether it's going for a beer, to a barbecue or to his shoot in Bradden, we are mates. And as with all my good mates I feel a loyalty to him which I know he reciprocates. Over the years I have turned down lucrative offers from Gloucester, Leicester and a number of French clubs to leave Saints. In return, he has always looked after me. For instance, when I became a Lion in 1997 he didn't dance around Franklin's Gardens screaming, 'Happy days! I've got Daws on a five-year contract and now he's a Lion!' He simply upgraded my deal, without me even broaching the matter.

I once asked him why he got involved. 'I sometimes ask myself the same question,' he replied. 'Sometimes I look in the shaving mirror and have a little honesty session with myself. Part of it, at the time, I think, was to show off, to try and be involved with these young bucks. But, on reflection, I was more keen to make the club successful.' I believe that, because first and foremost Keith is a supporter of the club. If there is one thing he has learned throughout his business career and his life in general, it is that he is one of the lads. He was originally a telesales man, and he's never forgotten it.

Keith's ambition for the club has never diminished. He has always wanted to bring in the best. Many players from other clubs use him a little bit because of this. They know that if they sniff around Keith when they're coming out of contract, their club will get a bit edgy and may bump up their own money. But Keith is nobody's fool, and when the game went professional so his attitude to achieving success hardened. 'I was not that paranoid about winning in the early days,' he admitted to me. 'The game was always the thing. I wanted Saints to win, but if we didn't I'd simply have two pints rather than one. But I began to realize once I took the club over and started raising people's expectations that I had to deliver.'

Northampton certainly delivered in the 1995–96 season. We finished the season as champions, six points clear of our nearest rivals London Irish, having won all 18 of our games and averaged nearly 50 points a game. It was some record:

Division 2: P18 W18 D0 L0 F867 A203 Pts36

(a) v. London Irish, won 65–32

(h) v. Moseley, won 50–7

(a) v. Nottingham, won 43–7

(h) v. Wakefield, won 23–0

(a) v. Bedford, won 49–17

(h) v. Blackheath, won 69–14

(a) v. Newcastle, won 52–9

(a) v. Waterloo, won 69–3

(h) v. London Scottish, won 54–11

(h) v. London Irish, won 52–24

(h) v. Nottingham, won 35–5

(a) v. Moseley, won 46–16

(h) v. Bedford, won 48–0

(a) v. Blackheath, won 24–10

(h) v. Newcastle, won 26–5

(h) v. Waterloo, won 69–5

(a) v. Wakefield, won 34–21

(a) v. London Scottish, won 59–17

I played in 17 of those games and finished the campaign with nine tries. I could not have been happier, and I eagerly awaited the end-of-season verdict of coach Paul Larkin. When it arrived I was not disappointed:

In my summary last season I stated that with the retirement of Dewi Morris it was possible for you to come to the fore because I wasn't convinced by Kyran Bracken. I merely emphasized that such an achievement would take a concentrated effort all season, more so since we were in

Division Two. So imagine the pride of everyone who had helped you aspire to that pedestal of honour in England v. Western Samoa.

However, the accolade is all yours. You had the mental strength to overcome the psychology involved in shrugging off your lingering hamstring doubts with the help of Phil Pask, but more importantly you had the self-belief and confidence not only to grasp, but to establish yourself as the number one in the country.

If ever there was an Artful Dodger in our side, then it's you. The Artful Dodger at the base of the scrum or ruck, always chirping, always cheeky, always ready to nick anything and, most irreverently, always prepared to make a fool of his opposite number by sniping at his heels. These are the traits of character that personify an outstanding scrum-half. You have developed them precociously. It is now time for you to review the progress you have made and decide the best way forward.

Inevitably our gameplan makes decisions easy for you. You need to concentrate on the basic skills and I am convinced that you will not neglect the drills. Everything you do should be based upon moving the ball away from the breakdown with speed, bearing in mind that the presentation of the ball is not always what it should be, especially from second-, third- and fourth-phase rucks. The game we play demands your speed of thought; you initiate everything that happens; it is important that you dictate to those around you what you want. The new laws play into your hands and I am sure you will exploit them to their fullest.

It has been a fantastic season for you. It has been an achievement that you will relish and one which you won't relinquish easily. I feel you have the dogged determination of character to make that England berth yours, right through to the next World Cup [in 1999] and beyond. The important thing is to maintain your focus and allow your self-effacing qualities to help deal with the distractions. You are in good company at the club. The success of the club will help you secure your future. I look forward with great excitement to watching your development.

The 'England berth' had been mine throughout the 1996 Five Nations Championship, and my domestic success was replicated on the international front: I ended up with a winner's medal after we pipped Scotland to the title on points difference. I only wish the campaign had been half as enjoyable as playing for Saints. It was not exactly thrilling stuff, from a spectator's point of view or from mine: we scored only three tries in our four matches. But given Jack Rowell's reaction whenever I tried to show any flair, it didn't come as the greatest surprise to me. 'Daws,' he would say, 'I know you like to do all those sorts of flip passes when you play for Northampton, but you never ever do one of those in an England shirt. Do you understand?'

Paul Grayson has always said to me that the part of my game he appreciates the most is that however the ball comes out I will get it to him. It's not always pretty. I can be slapping it, kicking it, overheading it, whatever, but I will get the ball to him. Jack didn't want any of that. Consequently, during the

1996 Five Nations, whenever I saw a bobbling ball I just fell on it or hacked it clear. It went against the grain and it started to eat away at my enjoyment of playing for England.

I actually really like Jack. I get on well with him and have very good banter with him. But as a coach he didn't coach me. I didn't go to England and learn anything. He wanted me to play like a robot. He wanted me to pass and kick. No wonder I got dropped in the autumn of 1996. I wasn't playing well because I wasn't enjoying it. I wasn't enjoying playing for my country. How shocking an admission is that? Having learned to let my rugby do more of my talking for me, I didn't make a huge fuss about it. In hindsight that was probably a mistake, because I didn't raise any eyebrows with the way I played, whereas I'd spent all my career with Northampton, Midlands and England A making the odd mistake but making breaks and putting people in holes too. Always doing something to catch the eye. That's what got me into the England side, yet when I got there I wasn't allowed to do it. It was very frustrating, and thank God I had Geech coaching me at the club, otherwise I would never have made the Lions squad for South Africa. It was not that I was one of his players, it was that he knew what I could do but wasn't being allowed to do for England. Take the 'Solo' try I scored in the first Test for the 1997 Lions in Cape Town – Jack Rowell would never have sanctioned it. He would have gone mental had I gone it alone from the base of one of his scrums.

Jack's decision, out of nowhere, to drop me from the England squad in November 1996 shocked me to the core, and it could have had even more serious consequences as it set in motion a sequence of events that left me clinging to life.

England decided to pick Andy Gomarsall for the match at Twickenham against Italy, and decided against explaining their reasoning to me. To this day I have no idea why, and I still feel unhappy about it. I fell out with Les Cusworth, Jack's second in command, over the way the situation was managed, or rather mismanaged. Les had rung me up to make sure everything was all right and given me all the vibes that I was in the side. Then, literally five minutes before the team was announced, they dropped me from the team and the bench and stuck me in the A team to play Argentina at Franklin's Gardens. I confronted Les and asked if he could give me a reason why so that I could go away and work on it. 'I don't really know,' he said. 'It was Jack's call.' So I buttonholed Jack. 'You don't need to talk to me about that,' Jack said. 'Speak to Les.' I took a deep breath and bit my lip. I was disappointed, gutted even, but I decided to stay calm. What good would me getting angry do? It was a rational reaction to an irrational situation and I was pretty proud of myself for the way I handled it. As I drove back to Northampton from Bisham Abbey, I vowed to show them what a big mistake they had made by starring for the A team.

Of course it didn't work out that way. After 19 minutes of the game I buggered my knee and was out for 10 weeks; meanwhile, Gomars scored two tries against the Italians. Now I was angry. It seemed I had lost a chance to get myself into contention for the 1997 Five Nations, the shop window for Lions selection the following spring. But things were about to get far worse.

I was in hospital the following day for a scope on my knee, and I had a drip line inserted into the back of my hand by needle, through which they then injected the anaesthetic. As is routine in these instances I was asked to count to 10.

'One, two, three, four . . . five . . .'

Then, just as I was drifting off, I heard raised voices.

'Holy shit, his heart rate!'

Then I was gone. Out cold. And I woke up none the wiser after the procedure had been completed. Until, that is, the specialist came and sat down beside me to explain that my body had totally shut down. For some reason my heart rate had dropped to two beats a minute and they had had to get me back. Had I ever had a problem with anaesthetic before? No. Did I have any medical condition I had forgotten to tell them about? No. All right, have you ever experienced any blackouts before?

'Er, yes.'

I recounted the story of the day I went for my jabs prior to flying off to Zimbabwe with the Barbarians in 1994. How I had gone to Dr John Raphael's surgery in Northampton the morning after a dinner party for which I had made a very good banoffee pie and at which I had got wasted. Brett Taylor and I were sitting in chairs chatting with Raph about the night before when he said, 'Right, Daws, let's get this done. Drop your trousers.' I stood up, turned around and pulled down my boxers. But as the needle went into my bum cheek I felt myself going.

'God, Raph, I feel a bit faint,' I said.

'Yeah, yeah, all right, Daws.'

There was then another jab and the room started spinning. I turned round to sit down, and just before I hit the seat I passed out. However, because I was slumped in the chair it looked as though I was sleeping. Brett and Raph carried on chatting away and talking to me.

'Daws, I know you're listening, you prick,' said the ever sensitive doctor. 'Why are you being such a nob?'

Right on cue the colour drained from my face and I slid down the seat. It was then that Raph realized I had completely gone. I came round in a cold sweat, but because it was the first time I had experienced anything like that I didn't really think anything of it. It wasn't until now, two and a half years on, that I put two and two together. In both instances it must have been the needle I reacted to. After that I was instructed to declare my needle phobia whenever I needed medical attention. But even that did not save me from another frightening incident in 2001.

Austin Healey and I had been playing golf in Spain, and then we'd met up with Iain Balshaw and a couple of other lads in Sotogrande. During light training I jarred my foot on the artificial surface and turned my knee. When I got back to Northampton the club put me in for an arthroscopy and the doctor asked me if I wanted an epidural so that I could watch it on video. I'm well into that sort of thing and took him up on his offer. They gave me a pre-med – no problem. I then pointed out that I had a phobia about needles and had previously passed out. The doctor advised the anaesthetist who told me not to worry, she was just going to put a bit of local in my back before giving me the epidural.

'You do remember what I said about me and needles?' I said again, not having a clue about what was going on.

'Yeah, no problem, it's the tiniest of pricks in your back.'

I had this drip lead going into my hand and I could feel it

pulling, so I was already feeling a bit ill. Then the 'tiny prick' went into my back.

'I'm really not feeling well,' I gurgled.

Just as one of the nurses started to say 'It's no problem', I passed out. When I woke up I had these electrodes all over me. They wouldn't tell me exactly what happened. All I know for sure is that when I went into the room there were two people and when I awoke there were seven and a lot of shouting, screaming and running around.

Why I am vulnerable to this I really don't know. I'm told that my phobia of needles and a sensitivity to medications is caused by an excessively low heart rate. All I know for sure is that when I don't like things, when I get nervous and afraid, I get very tired and just want to slow down and sleep. I suspect these incidents are a hugely exaggerated version of that. But now I take no chances.

When I went for a scan in Wellington before England played New Zealand in June 2003 they planned to put dye into my leg so they could see exactly what was going on. I told the England doctor, Simon Kemp, about my phobia and asked how big the needle would be. He turned around and quipped, 'Don't worry, it's only about that big,' indicating six inches.

Did I laugh? Did I hell.

4(i)
Heaven and Hell

LION CUB TO KING OF THE PRIDE

I can still see it now. The look on the faces of those Springboks as I feigned to pass infield that night in Cape Town. South Africa knew best. They were going to mash the Lions, send us home with our tails between our legs. Yet here they were buying perhaps the most outrageous dummy in rugby history.

South Africa, the world champions, were 1/5 favourites to win the series. A whitewash was the popular bet. In the eyes of the home media we were pussycats, not Lions. We could not buy respect. 'There are only 47 people and their close family who believe that we're going to win,' said our coach, Ian McGeechan, and that was the size of it. None of the media thought we would, no one across the world thought we could. And as for me playing a pivotal role . . .

There were just seven minutes left on the clock in Cape Town when Tim Rodber turned to me and called the 'Solo' move which would change my life for ever. We were down by two tries to nil and the 'told you so' headlines were being prepared, even if there was only one point separating the sides on the scoreboard due to a combination of South African indiscipline and Neil Jenkins's golden boot. Rodders was always 'picking and going' because our gameplan revolved around setting close targets. But he was getting munched all the time. So when we were awarded a scrum 35 yards out from the home line, he came over to me and said, 'Daws, just go, mate. I'm getting bashed. Do a Solo. Do a Solo.' It was a move we had rehearsed in training. The scrum-half would break blind and then have the option of feeding the winger on the outside or the number 6 inside.

To this day I remember the whole move in slow motion. Flanker Ruben Kruger had been constantly breaking his binding on the short side and I had been pointing at it all match to try to get referee Colin Hawke to penalize him. This time, perhaps sensing the ref's stare, Kruger held firm. I saw my chance and went. I like to think I am a little bit quicker than Rodders, and I got round Kruger and then past their number 8, Gary Teichmann. Ieuan Evans was on the right wing, and he cut inside on a run I didn't even see. He always ribs me that he would have been in under the sticks, but he went so early that I had no chance. Nor was Lawrence Dallaglio in position to take a pass. On my own, my only chance of avoiding being smashed into touch by either Teichmann, scrum-half Joost van der Westhuizen or full-back Andre Joubert was to throw a dummy and give myself a couple of yards to work with.

So I threw it – a theatrical, over-the-top number – to precisely nobody. As I did so I started slowing down, and to my amazement the Boks stopped. Even Joubert, coming across, hitch-kicked. I couldn't believe they'd all bought it, the suckers. It was a score which won us the match, which convinced us all beyond doubt that we could win the series, and which, quite simply, stands as the single most memorable playing moment of my career. Even now people ask me about it. They know exactly where they were when I touched down, what pub they were in watching the game, how they reacted, even how drunk they got. And that is very special. To be involved in a game and then to create that one moment which triggers a memory that will stay with people for life is very, very special. I feel very privileged to have done that.

Yet at the time I scored that try it felt no different to scoring for Marlow under-8s. I had no perception of how big the game was, I think because I had been third choice, then second choice, then thrown in. It had all happened so quickly. I hadn't had time to think 'Oh my God, this is the biggest game of my life'. I was even quite relaxed and chilled before kick-off because I had very simple jobs to do and there was no weight of expectation on me.

My critics, particularly Austin Healey, will tell you I only made the tour party because Geech was my club coach at Northampton. I had been dropped by England the previous autumn, then ruled out of the 1997 Five Nations campaign by injury. By my reckoning I was at best third-choice scrum-half behind Wales's Rob Howley and Austin. But as South Africa were to find out, Lions tours throw up tales of the unexpected.

I had known little of the British and Irish Lions until 1989 when a friend of mine, Phil Chamberlain, somehow got himself on a four-week trip to follow them in Australia. It sounded a good crack, but I didn't really know what he was on about. I was a spotty teenager, mad for rugby, playing it all the time, but because you never saw Lions rugby on television in those days I didn't really understand the concept. I thought it must be something like the Barbarians. I can't even recall watching the matches in 1989. But I did rip a page out of *Rugby World* magazine which had the Lions motif on it, and stuck it on my pinboard.

By the time the next Lions tour came round in 1993 I was living with Tim Rodber, Paul Grayson, Brett Taylor and Nobby (Ian Hunter). Amazingly, given that I had never seen a Lions Test, even on TV, my name was bandied about as a possible tourist. There was quite a bit of press saying I should be New Zealand-bound, and I couldn't believe it. I hadn't even been capped at that stage. Anyway, it didn't happen, and while Nobby was selected, Rodders and I went to Canada with England on a non-cap tour, both of us returning early with hamstring injuries.

Fed up, the two of us went ever so slightly crazy. We spent pretty much every night of the summer in a bar in Northampton called Aunty Ruth's. The night before Nobby's first game, against North Auckland in Whangarei (a game in which he would last only 38 minutes before dislocating his right shoulder and being packed off home), we both went to bed battered only for Rodders to wake me up with the tune of the house, 'Remedy' by the Black Crows, blaring in my ear. He had rigged up the sound system in order to ambush me and had a speaker under each arm. 'Come on, we've got to watch Nobby!' he yelled. That was my introduction to Lions rugby.

Looking back now, I wonder whether 1993 would have caused the same furore as the 2001 tour to Australia had rugby been a professional sport. There were a few murmurs of dissent coming back. Will Carling, for one, didn't really seem interested. Wade Dooley returned home following the death of his father and was then barred from rejoining the tour. If you do happen to have players who are unhappy, it does filter through. But 1997 was very much like 1989: everyone got on famously and it was just the most fantastic of tours on and off the pitch.

From the moment my name was linked with the Lions in 1993, I decided I wanted to be on the 1997 tour. The love affair had begun, and it has never gone away. For all the unhappiness in 2001 (more of which later), I would go on another one tomorrow. The Lions is the ultimate rugby dream. Playing for England is probably the greatest honour I'll ever achieve – certainly captaining my country was – yet the Lions is the best of the best. It's the history and the tradition, as Geech said on the eve of the 1997 tour: 'What we have got is four countries playing as one. The mantle that you carry and the challenge that you have is to put a marker down in South Africa about the way we can play rugby. A Lion in South Africa is special. The Lions are special. The legends go with it.' The Lions mean everything to me. That's why I would stand by what I said in 2001. I'm that kind of person. If things upset me or I feel they could affect my squad, my family or my friends, I'll speak out.

The 1997 tour passed by in a huge blur. I do remember having my head shaved bald by Keith Wood. He was only supposed to give me a number two, but sneakily he removed the grating and ploughed a stripe down the middle to leave me no choice but to have the lot off. I remember also Paul Grayson return-ing home with a groin injury after playing only one game.

Grays's injury was a big disappointment, and I did miss him. I'd lost my partner, and it was a cue to go and find myself a little bit. I was 24 and a little bit too reliant on the friends I had. It was time to stand up for myself if I wanted to make any impact at all.

I started only one game before the Test series began and assumed I was battling it out with Austin for a place on the bench, as Rob Howley was quite rightly in the number one spot. My aspirations were no more lofty than that, because at the beginning of the tour I had a feeling, from the way the practice sessions went and from his selection for the first mid-week game, that Austin was ahead of me in the pecking order. Sometimes you just have to accept that. On tours like this you can't get above your station and assume you're going to be in, even that you're going to be fit. That was the mistake Graham Henry made with the 2001 Lions, pencilling in his Test team before he left Britain. Look at the Test team in 1997. Paul Wallace – no one in their right mind would have put Paul in that team. Absolutely nobody. Jenks at full-back, Alan Tait on the wing, Jerry Davidson and Richard Hill in the pack ahead of Eric Miller and Simon Shaw. You have to stay open-minded. Yes, Geech played certain combinations, but he mixed things up so that at no time did the squad feel divided between the Test team and the midweek dirt trackers. From start to finish we were all in it together. We trained well, and there was great respect among not only the players but between the players and management. You're never going to be best mates with everybody, of course, but the whole party was prepared to do absolutely whatever it took to make things work. If that meant Rob Howley wearing the number 9 shirt, so be it. A place on the bench would still be a massive achievement for me.

Then Rob dislocated his shoulder against Natal on 14 June, just seven days before the first Test. All bets were off.

It came down to being in the right place at the right time. Austin had made two starts to my one, in a 64–14 win over Mpumalanga on 4 June. I felt I'd played well in that game, done all the things I was supposed to do, been very busy and organized. I'd even scored a try for good measure. And I was on the bench in Durban when Rob's shoulder went. One man's misfortune is always another's opportunity. And it was a huge opportunity. I had most of the game left to play. If I came through all right I would probably be playing in the Test team a week later. I was on trial as never before.

Rob's wife, parents and in-laws had flown out to see him play in a Lions series, and he was inconsolable in the dressing room afterwards. 'Rob dissolved into a fit of despair' was how Dr James Robson described his immediate reaction to the news that his tour was over. But at the time he left the field I had no way of knowing how bad his injury was. I just had to get on with it; there wasn't any time for me to get emotional or to flick two fingers in the direction of Jack Rowell and Les Cusworth for dropping me from the England side without explanation. I was playing against Natal with a Test jersey at stake.

This was another match the Lions were expected to lose, yet we ran out 42–12 winners, which made the reference to us as 'pansies' on newspaper flyers in the Cape Town area on the day of the opening Test all the harder to fathom. Funny that they weren't reprinted for the Monday edition. All of a sudden the debate was about whether a 2–1 series win for the Boks could really be termed a success.

Geech had said at the start of the tour that the 13-match itinerary was akin to playing ten Five Nations games and three World Cup finals. His lieutenant, Jim Telfer, used another analogy. 'This is your Everest, boys,' he whispered. 'Very few ever get the chance in rugby terms to go for the top of Everest. You are privileged. You are the chosen few. Many are considered but few are chosen. It's an awesome task you have, an awesome responsibility. They do not rate us. They do not respect us. The only way to be rated is to stick one on them. There's no way we go back. We take every step forwards. Nothing, nothing stops us hitting the fucking maximum.'

We did that at Newlands. We stuck it to them. The downside was that the second Test in Durban a week later would be nothing short of ferocious. The Boks knew that, Geech knew that. He primed us for the onslaught but assured us that if we absorbed the best they could throw at us and stay patient, our time would come, and we would go for the kill. 'We have proved that the Lion has claws and teeth,' Geech said. 'We have wounded a Springbok. When an animal is wounded it returns in frenzy. It does not think. It fights for its very existence. The Lion waits, and at the right point it goes for the jugular and the life disappears. Today, every second of that game we go for the jugular.'

What unfolded at King's Park was probably the toughest encounter I've ever experienced. But it did not cross the line between fair and brutal, unlike the way South Africa played at Twickenham in autumn 2002. They weren't cheap-shotting, but they were certainly throwing their bodies around. The surge of power that came our way was unbelievable. As had been the case in the first Test, the home side lost it in the fourth quarter through indiscipline. Amazingly, given the end result, we didn't threaten their line once. In fact, we got nowhere near it. They scored three unanswered tries and Jenks kicked us to victory from our own half. Yet tactically we were fantastic, not only to amass 18 points with the limited ball we had, but to shut them out in the last half-hour. Admittedly their goalkicking was so shocking as to be almost unbelievable, but let that not detract from one of the greatest defensive displays of all time.

We knew the home side would be like men possessed after blowing up in Cape Town, and that if we got too loose they would punish us. So we set out to frustrate them. We had John Bentley and Alan Tait chasing my box kicks down the touchlines and smashing into the receivers, while on the occasions we did run it, Scott Gibbs blasted up the middle. Time and again South Africa would let frustration get the better of them; we would then kick the penalties to touch and drive upfield from the set-piece, where the Boks would kill the ball and Jenks would kick the points.

With four minutes to go, and the scores locked at 15 apiece, Gregor Townsend drove for the line and the ball came back to me. The last thing on my mind was a drop goal. It hadn't been mentioned. You tend to either hear the call at the previous set-piece, or a trigger call from your fly-half in behind you. But we were driving and driving and I thought it had to be on out wide. Someone must be open. So I was looking for a wide ball to a first receiver. Instead I found Jerry Guscott getting ready for the money shot. It was a case of, as he would say, make it or break it. He made it. After a score I'm usually the first to yell 'Concentrate!' but when that ball soared between the posts we all went absolutely nuts. We had to somehow regroup, slow our pulses and refocus on defending our line. There was still plenty of time for the game to be lost.

It was then that we drew on the inspiration provided for us by the midweek boys, who had scored 52 points at altitude against Orange Free State four days before. The Test team had not travelled to Bloemfontein for the game, and I watched it in the room I was sharing with Gibbsy back in Durban. It was an awesome display, described by our team manager Fran Cotton as 'one of the all-time great Lions performances', and it gave us all a massive lift. The feeling was that if they were playing rugby like that we had to live up to their example. Here was a team that had flown to altitude on the day of the game, had endured the sickening loss of Will Greenwood to an injury which could have cost him his life ('James Robson thought he had lost him,' Fran admitted. 'He thought he was going to die on the field. He was unconscious, fitting. He'd swallowed his tongue and was biting on his gumshield. He could not get any reaction from his pupils at all for a minute. He thought he'd gone'), yet had still managed to score six tries. As we dragged one another into position to repel yet another Springbok assault on our line, we tapped into that defiant spirit. Our bodies cried out for mercy, but we held firm. Against all odds, the series was ours.

Ellis Park, the spiritual home of South African rugby, was supposed to host the party to end all parties. And so it did, but the hosts had anticipated Johannesburg celebrating a Springbok series triumph rather than a Lions drink-up which left the management with a £3,000 bar bill and me nursing the mother of all hangovers. South Africa won the third Test, having finally realized that it pays to play a goalkicker. A combination of injuries and a couple of days on the piss after the second Test proved our undoing. We were still desperate to win, though; there was no feeling that it was just a jolly. Even though we had won the series there had been the usual southern-hemisphere bleat of 'at least we scored tries' and a feeling around the place that they were better than us.

But try telling that to the record books. History will not remember it that way.

1997 Lions to South Africa: squad and results

Forwards: Jason Leonard (England), Dai Young (Wales), Graham Rowntree (England), Tom Smith (Scotland), Paul Wallace (Ireland), Mark Regan (England), Keith Wood (Ireland), Barry Williams (Wales), Simon Shaw (England), Martin Johnson (England, capt.), Jeremy Davidson (Ireland), Doddie Weir (Scotland), Richard Hill (England), Neil Back (England), Rob Wainwright (Scotland), Lawrence Dallaglio (England), Eric Miller (Ireland), Tim Rodber (England), Scott Quinnell (Wales); replacements: Nigel Redman (England), Tony Diprose (England).

Backs: Neil Jenkins (Wales), Tim Stimpson (England), Tony Underwood (England), Nick Beal (England), John Bentley (England), Ieuan Evans (Wales), Allan Bateman (Wales), Scott Gibbs (Wales), Jerry Guscott (England), Alan Tait (Scotland), Will Greenwood (England), Paul Grayson (England), Gregor Townsend (Scotland), Matt Dawson (England), Austin Healey (England), Rob

Howley (Wales), Kyran Bracken (England); replacements: Mike Catt (England), Tony Stanger (Scotland).

(P13, W11, D0, L2, F480, A278)

Eastern Province Invitational XV 11 Lions 39 (Port Elizabeth, 24 May)
Border 14 Lions 18 (East London, 28 May)
Western Province 21 Lions 38 (Cape Town, 31 May)
Mpumalanga 14 Lions 64 (Witbank, 4 June)
Northern Transvaal 35 Lions 30 (Pretoria, 7 June)
Gauteng 14 Lions 20 (Johannesburg, 11 June)
Natal 12 Lions 42 (Durban, 14 June)
Emerging Springboks 22 Lions 51 (Wellington, 17 June)
1st Test: South Africa 16 British Isles 25 (Cape Town, 21 June)
Orange Free State 30 Lions 52 (Bloemfontein, 24 June)
2nd Test: South Africa 15 British Isles 18 (Durban, 28 June)
Northern Free State 39 Lions 67 (Welkom, 1 July)
3rd Test: South Africa 35 British Isles 16 (Johannesburg, 5 July)

4(ii)
Heaven and Hell

THE MAKING OF A CAPTAIN

Sitting on the sodden turf at Newlands, it was hard to believe I was back at the scene of my greatest moment in rugby. The blindside break, the dummy pass, the try that had decided the first Test for the Lions against South Africa a year earlier seemed a lifetime away. England had just lost to the Springboks, our seventh defeat in seven matches on what will forever be remembered as the Tour from Hell. Much had changed since my last time in Cape Town. Then I hadn't been able to get into the England side; now I was captain of my country.

The call had come two months earlier as I walked my springer spaniel, Freddie, in the fields around Tim Rodber's home just south of Northampton. My mobile phone rang and I immediately recognized the voice. Clive Woodward wanted to know if I would meet him the following day at the Compleat Angler, a hotel on the banks of the Thames in Marlow, a couple of miles from my parents' home. He wouldn't say why. Weeks earlier he had threatened to drop me and my Northampton team-mates from his squad in response to Saints' owner Keith Barwell withdrawing us from England tour duty, claiming the summer trip to Australia, New Zealand and South Africa was a 'tour too far'. My England career might have been over there and then had not Ian McGeechan saved the day by persuading Keith to back down.

Clive, who had succeeded Jack Rowell as coach the previous autumn, had picked me for the last two games of England's 1998 Five Nations campaign, but even so, after what had gone before, making the tour squad rather than leading it was my only thought. Then, as we sat sipping coffee looking out over Marlow Weir, Clive popped the question: would I captain the tour?

Blimey, I thought. Of course I will.

There is no greater honour in all of rugby. It makes no difference what team you've got or who you're playing. I believed that then and I still believed it as evening turned to night on the southern tip of Africa and we could at last bring the curtain down on a tour which none of us who experienced it shall ever forget.

I'd be lying if I said I hadn't recognized the potential for a disastrous trip from the moment Clive and I went our separate ways that day on the riverbank. England faced an itinerary of four Tests in five weeks over three different continents, and I had charge of a squad containing 20 uncapped players as a result of a mass withdrawal by many of the senior players. Reaction to this came thick and fast from Australia, our first port of call. Dick McGruther, chairman of the Australian Rugby Union, described the England tour party as 'probably the most under-equipped group of Englishmen to be sent to Australia since the First Fleet' (referring to the 11 ships that sailed from Portsmouth in 1787 bearing the first European settlers, mostly convicts). He accused the RFU of treating the southern hemisphere with contempt, saying that England had broken its word to send its best team. Australia was insulted, McGruther maintained, by what he described as the 'biggest sell-out since Gallipoli', and he added, 'I think England will have their own fatal landings in Australia and New Zealand over the next few weeks.' He then invited all Australians to come and enjoy a 'Pommie thrashing'.

His inference was clear: that England's missing stars were not injured but had instead been persuaded not to tour by their clubs, who were in dispute with the Union over who controlled what in English rugby. I won't have that. There were a lot of England players who had played a lot of rugby through 1997 and 1998 and had picked up niggles which, had they played an extra summer, would have turned into chronic injuries. I could fully understand what they were doing by pulling out; I was more interested to know who had organized this type of tour after a Lions year. Where was the thought for the players? I, too, had thought of pulling out because we were fast approaching World Cup year and I wanted above all to be right for that. It seemed that nobody was thinking about what was best for the players; it was all about what was best for the clubs, the RFU and England. I didn't have a problem with being a little bit selfish in that respect. It came down to the question of whether the benefits of a summer of rest would outweigh the loss, in the short term at least, of my England shirt.

Four years later I would opt out. I spoke to Clive and Wayne Smith at Northampton and said I felt I needed to rest rather than go to Argentina. Clive made the call for me not to go, but

I don't think I would have done so anyway because my body was telling me I had to have some time off, away from rugby. I did lose my shirt, England won the Test match and everyone was singing and dancing about my replacement, Andy Gomarsall. But I swallowed it and got on with it, and I believe my form the following season vindicated my decision.

But in the summer of 1998 I was swayed by the offer of the captaincy. It was an opportunity I could not refuse, an honour I would never turn down. For all I knew it would not come my way again. It was a priceless chance to enhance my rugby education, and, boy, during those five weeks did I learn things.

On arrival Down Under in late May it was impossible not to take McGruther's insults personally, even if his words were aimed at the RFU rather than us directly. We quickly became hacked off with reading the papers because everyone seemed to be laughing at us, but I believed we could use it to our advantage and show them that we were not a second or even a third team. Nobody had given England a chance in the World Cup Sevens in 1993; no one had given the 1997 Lions a chance either. We had won both. So why not again?

Actually, there were a number of reasons why not, not the least of which was that only six of the tour party – me, Austin Healey, Ben Clarke, Graham Rowntree, Garath Archer and Steve Ojomoh – had more than 10 England caps to their name. The average across the 37-man party was less than four, and there were 20 debutants – 10 in the backs and 10 in the forwards. But I had to stay positive, I had to keep faith, even if I knew in my heart of hearts that we were on a hiding to nothing.

On the day we departed I wrote a column in the *Daily Telegraph* in which I remarked that 'there is a great depth of talent in English rugby. What we may currently lack in experience we make up for in enthusiasm and raw skill. Every player is keen to prove himself.' That was fairly true. Some of that squad are not only still playing for England but playing bloody well for England, Jonny Wilkinson, Josh Lewsey, Phil Vickery, Lewis Moody and Danny Grewcock among them. It was unrefined talent at that point, very unrefined. We were one or two players short of giving the back line the necessary experience required, but, despite the absence of Martin Johnson, Lawrence Dallaglio, Jason Leonard, Richard Hill and Tim Rodber, the forwards were definitely competitive. In the first and second Tests against New Zealand later in June we matched them up front for more than half the game, and at some stages we were better. The first half in Dunedin, for example, we were on fire, even after Danny had been sent off. Likewise, up until half-time in Auckland our forwards obliterated the All Blacks.

Ultimately, however, the tour will not be remembered for those cameo performances, rather for the record defeats we suffered at the hands of Australia and New Zealand, and for the pledge from Clive that never again would England plumb such depths. It was straight after the tour that the gloves came off. Clive told us straight that we had to stand up for ourselves. 'The players have to be their own people now,' he told the *Sunday Telegraph*. 'I hate it when people say the players are the meat in the sandwich, stuck between club and country. That's crap. They're all big boys, all over 18. They have to stand up and be counted.'

This was not an off-the-cuff remark. Right at the start of the tour he had batted the ball into our court, saying that it was up to us to be fit for England. He would no longer pick on reputation. Unfortunately, his outburst coincided with me aggravating a knee injury, having to pull out of the Test match against the Wallabies in Brisbane on 6 June, and having to pass the armband over to Tony Diprose.

I'd picked up the injury in a freak diving accident during a pre-tour break with Austin Healey in Lanzarote. Austin had this ability to bounce unbelievably high on the springboard and then, like a trampoliner, kill the bounce on landing by bending his knees. I gave it a go, but as I landed my knee turned out and I tweaked it. I cursed him, but there was nothing new in that. I fully expected it to be fine, but 48 hours before kick-off I had to concede that it wasn't strong enough to get through an international game.

The upshot was that I spent the match in the BBC Five Live commentary booth at the Suncorp Stadium, trying to find words to describe a 76–0 defeat. I had to analyse 11 Australian tries, which by the end was proving painful. I'm sure the listeners at home could sense my tone. John Mitchell, our forwards coach, had said beforehand that the team was 'shit scared . . . it's the fear of being wiped out which motivates us'. And wiped out we were by the future World Cup winners, even if we didn't concede a try for more than half an hour. I could hear the Aussie commentators absolutely digging it in and there was nothing I could do about it. It became so embarrassing that the Aussie crowd started leaving long before the match was over. But we couldn't go home. There was nowhere to hide. It was an horrendous day and a harsh, if valuable, lesson to learn.

I didn't say it then, but sometimes you need experiences like that. Those who were in the side and got severely shown up – and there were a few of those – realized they weren't up to it and needed to go away and do some work. It made everyone open their eyes, because there was a feeling among some that they were young and as good as their potential hinted they could one day become. I went into the dressing room afterwards and it was a shocking scene. As tour captain it was just a matter of trying to raise heads, pick up the pieces and point out that we were in for a torrid month and that it was going to be a severe test of character. 'Some of you are going to come through and some of you are not,' I told the boys. 'Where do you want to be?' I couldn't come on any stronger than that because it was the first match of the tour and I knew it wasn't going to get any easier. What hurt most of all was that all the press, the outrageous predictions and comparisons with Gallipoli, had come true. We needed to stick together, the whole squad, cop the flak and try to move on.

There was a difference in opinion as to the best way to do that. Clive, who admitted he got it wrong in selection and that he should have injected more experience into the team, packed us off to Surfer's Paradise the following day, saying, 'It's not a question of being soft, it's a question of doing the right thing. The players need a break.' Mitch had a different take on it. He said that had he had his way the squad would have spent the day running round the paddock hitting tackle bags and being reminded of who they were representing. Sports medicine, he called it. He added that had he played in that match he would have been indoors hiding, not sunbathing on a beach. Most forwards and backs coaches don't see eye to eye, to be honest, but it was a bit naughty of Mitch to talk out of school – if that's not the pot calling the kettle black! While I agree with him that humiliation is not easy to accept, the fact is that some players had given their all. It wasn't good enough, but they had still given everything.

From that point on we pretty much shut ourselves away from the papers, as every Tom, Dick, Sheila and Bruce had something to say about us. England are everyone's favourite enemy so there was no shortage of people to rub our noses in it. There were people all over the world absolutely loving it. But you've got to be bigger than that. It was humiliating, yet we took it on the chin, learned the lessons and came back better for the chastening experience. In fact, it turned out to be a huge turning point in England's development; never again will there be such a weak England side. We have now developed from having one competitive fifteen to the point where England's third XV would probably be better than the team that played against Australia that day.

A week later we were in New Zealand, the Land of the Long White Cloud and, potentially, even longer nightmare, especially when first up, in rain-lashed Hamilton, was a New Zealand A team coached by Graham Henry and featuring one J. Lomu. But we really got stuck into them and restricted them to an 18–10 win. I wouldn't say it was a moral victory for us, but it was definitely an improvement. And that's the path we needed to follow. The pressure on us all was immense as the public and media were waiting for us to fall flat on our faces in the mud. To defend as we did deserved credit, and the forwards turned in an heroic performance in horrendous conditions. The Gloucester boys, who made up five of the pack, felt right at home. I was proud of the grit and determination shown by the team. 'We can progress with this type of display,' I told them afterwards.

To then ship 50 points against the New Zealand Academy team three days later in Invercargill was devastating. It had quickly become clear which players were going to be involved in the Test team and which were not. In fact, the wheat was being separated from the chaff at an alarming rate. Some of the boys found it very hard, not just in terms of the physical pounding on the pitch but the relentlessness of playing and living rugby in a country where the game is king. With hindsight, the Academy fielded a pretty fair team: Daryl Gibson at full-back, Bruce Reihana and Doug Howlett on the wings, Pieta Alatini at centre, Byron Kelleher at scrum-half, and up front more future All Blacks in Greg Feek, Kees Meeuws and Reuben Thorne. By contrast, England's team contained few players who would go on to have international futures. There's the story.

It may seem strange, but even at this low point no parallels can be drawn with the 2001 Lions in terms of failing squad morale. Talk to the boys of '98 who are still in the England squad and they will tell you it was one of the best tours they have ever been on. We had a magic time. The initial part in Australia wasn't too hot, but in New Zealand we really gave it our all. Mitch did get stuck into us and Phil Larder made us do some mindless tackling drills, but we worked hard and played hard.

By the time we arrived in Dunedin for the first Test on 20 June I could sense which of the players were not up to it and which were resigned to being a little bit out of their depth. Yet, as I said, the other side of the coin was that people were really rising to the challenge. For the weekend games, one forward after another was saying, 'I might not be a Lawrence Dallaglio or a Martin Johnson, but I'm going to give it my all.' To do that going backwards is proof positive that attitude was not a problem.

As captain, I had to decide how best to spend my time. Should I spend it encouraging individuals who were not going to be making an impact on the team in the very short term, or should I concentrate on the top 25 players and really build competition for places? It was a difficult balance to strike. For the most part I played a pastoral role, picking people up, lifting heads, boosting confidence. But there were some players we needed to get right on board because they were going to be an integral part of the Test team. Austin Healey, for instance, will go down as one of England's great players, but at the time he wasn't performing and he needed bringing on board.

We lost that opening Test to New Zealand by a record score and margin, but the 64–22 scoreline doesn't begin to reflect the way we played. The forwards were nothing short of heroic, especially after Danny Grewcock was sent off on the half-hour, supposedly for kicking hooker Anton Oliver. Danny's dismissal was significant, as were the double standards preached by All Blacks coach John Hart, which sickened me. On the one hand, Danny got his marching orders for an alleged kicking offence for which there was no clear television evidence; on the other, All Black lock Ian Jones escaped punishment for blatantly stamping on the face of Graham Rowntree at a ruck, his studs getting caught in Wiggy's headguard as he tried to withdraw his boot. At the dinner afterwards I made a speech which went down like a lead balloon. I said I thought it was fairly poor that New Zealanders were going on at us about discipline. It was unfortunate that Danny had been sent off, I continued, before adding, 'Unfortunately, there should have been another second row sent off, shouldn't there?'

I don't retract that remark because the situation was farcical – as Mick Cleary put it in the *Daily Telegraph*, a 'staggering betrayal of fair play'. Playing in New Zealand is like being a visiting team at Old Trafford. You never get a decision in the Manchester United box, but if Ruud Van Nistelrooy goes down you know he's more than likely to get a penalty. There seems to be an angelic aura around the All Blacks, one that allows them to get away with committing the same offences again and again without getting penalized. It is so frustrating for the teams playing them. Everyone in New Zealand thinks that England players slow the game and wind scrums and delay passes. Try using the other eye.

The following day a disciplinary committee – two New Zealanders and an Australian – handed Danny a five-week ban and rejected the allegation of foul play against Ian Jones after the referee, Wayne Erickson of Australia, was shown the video and stated that he 'would not have imposed a penalty for what he considered to be legitimate rucking as opposed to trampling'. But Ian Jones could clearly be seen rucking on Graham's face. How can we condone this in the rugby world? Because of the way the tour in general, and the weekend in particular, was going, we just knew that nothing was going to come of it, though that did not prevent the RFU from later lodging a formal protest.

It was an even more difficult time for Clive Woodward, as on the morning of the match he'd received news that his father had died. He was under a lot of stress at work, and then, with him on the other side of the world, comes the most appalling news about his father. To his immense credit he didn't let it affect the side, and he left soon after the final whistle to concentrate on what he needed to do at home. Coincidentally, one of my close friends – Mick Owen, my managing director when I worked at Firm Security in Northampton – had been diagnosed with cancer only days earlier, and Clive was aware of that, so he knew I had a rough idea how he was feeling. Both of us were very sensitive with each other as we parted, wishing each other well.

By the time Clive's plane headed skywards he was angry as well as upset over what we all saw as the childish carry-on in and around the players' tunnel by John Hart, and his attempts to distract and intimidate the referee. Hart claims he spoke to Erickson in the tunnel at half-time only out of concern for the safety of the scrummage in light of Danny's red card; he didn't, he said, want to be responsible for an injury occurring. But Erickson said he considered Hart's approach 'inappropriate'.

The hostility did not end there. Later that evening Richard Cockerill was involved in a brawl with New Zealand hooker Norm Hewitt. In true captain's form I knew as much about the spat as anybody else – bugger all. I only caught wind of it when we got back from a night out with some of the other All Blacks. It was described to the press as 'play fighting', and I only learned the full truth when Cockers brought out his autobiography, *In Your Face*, after the 1999 World Cup. It contained the following extract:

> John Mitchell, Graham Rowntree and I go into town for a beer. We enter this bar, it must be two or three in the morning by now, and find Hewitt in there, badly pissed up. He starts slagging English rugby, saying how shitty we are. I ask him how his arse feels with all those splinters in it from sitting on the bench. Then I really get to work on him. I start doing the Haka in front of him, slapping my thighs and sticking my tongue out. He seems to take it all right, considering he's got a reputation for being as much a handful as I am. It's agreed we'll all move on somewhere else and we call a cab. Hewitt gets in first, ahead of me, and as soon as I stick my head through the door to follow, he leathers me. Suddenly it all kicks off in the van, him and me going at it for all we're worth. My eye swells up straight away and is a right mess. He's had a good cheap shot at me but it's far from over. When we reach our destination I'm the first out of the taxi, and I'm waiting for him this time. When he gets out I smack him one and we end up brawling again, right down the street.

Doubtless Cockers would regard this as normal Leicester activity, a bit of harmless rough and tumble. Whatever it was, it was definitely not a sign of the tour going off the rails. As I would discover with the 2001 Lions, when a tour goes off the rails you don't go out for a beer with your mates, let alone the opposition. All right, what went on shouldn't have, and everyone wishes it hadn't because it was unnecessary, but Cockers, like me, had been an amateur rugby player in the days when you could indulge in rough and tumble without coming under scrutiny.

As skipper, I tried to refocus minds on the solid performance the Test team had produced in so many areas, little knowing that the tour was headed for rock bottom in Rotorua against the New Zealand Maori. They were well up for the opportunity to give England a good thrashing, but that could be no excuse for what unfolded. England lost 62–14 and missed 24 first-up tackles along the way. Mitch ripped into the midweek players afterwards, saying that they had had their chance, had blown it, and England would never see them again.

His words echoed a warning I had issued prior to the game. I had felt the need to warn the squad that certain individuals were in danger of kissing goodbye to their England careers by the way they were behaving – going out all the time and regarding the trip as a bit of a jolly. 'Look,' I told them, 'if you don't get serious we will get home and Clive will never pick you again. It's quite simple. You've made a rod for your own back really.' It is no secret to whom I was referring; you only have to look up which players last wore an England shirt on that tour. Whether they were already resigned to never being picked again anyway is for them to say. Clive's maxim, except in extreme cases, has always been that if you are good enough you will play, and in my experience he has stood by that.

The good news for our hopes against the All Blacks in the second Test was that the mood among the first-choice players was upbeat as we swept into Auckland. We had taken a lot of confidence from the Dunedin game and we thought that if we could keep the ball for a bit we would actually be in with a chance. Our hunch was right. At half-time at Eden Park we trailed 14–7, and it should have been all square. I scored a try inside the first half-hour which gave me immense satisfaction, breaking from a ruck and beating Taine Randell and Christian Cullen to the line, and Ben Clarke had a perfectly good score disallowed. Given that we bossed the Test for an hour, the final scoreline of 40–10 in favour of New Zealand certainly felt cruel; we'd conceded four tries in the last quarter as our resistance finally waned. Nonetheless, the game, without question, was the highlight of the tour. For once, all the heroes were dressed in white, and I would pick out Dave Sims, Rob Fidler, Graham Rowntree and Ben Clarke. Stephen Jones, writing in the *Sunday Times*, noted, 'England's rag-bag collection of second, third and even fifth choices, derided all around the country, had the temerity to stay in contention for an hour and even raise serious question marks over the current All Blacks. The plain and heroic fact is that England's forwards outplayed the New Zealand pack.' He also described me as a 'massive force' at scrum-half, which was very flattering, especially when Clive, who had returned from attending his father's funeral shortly before kick-off, added his own praise. 'I am seeing Dawson in a new light,' he said. 'I've got to know him very well over the last five weeks. He's really impressed me as a player and captain.'

I don't actually remember an awful lot about the day because I was as tired as I've ever been on a rugby pitch. And that was at half-time. The second half was too knackering to describe. I remember sitting in the changing room at the break and Mitch coming over to talk and me not being able to say anything. It was as though I'd already played a full 80 minutes. I was absolutely screwed. I was not alone either, and that state of physical exhaustion contributed to us leaving the gameplan behind in the last 20 minutes.

Jonny Wilkinson's tour had finished the previous weekend at Dunedin when he was stretchered off the field, and Josh Lewsey, who'd played centre that day, was moved up to partner me. It was in fact an eventful tour for Josh from the moment we met up in England. The backs were doing some fitness work when, much to Josh's horror, Clive came over and asked him to take off his shirt and show the rest of the lads his physique. 'That's what you've got to aspire to,' said Clive, pointing at Josh. 'You've all got to get into that sort of shape.' At the same time, on the other side of the field, the forwards were being drilled by Mitch, who instructed prop forward Duncan Bell to remove his shirt. He then absolutely abused him. In the minds of the management, Josh and Duncan offered two extremes as to what an England player should and should not look like. They say you've got to be cruel to be kind . . .

I have since had even more feedback about that second Test. Wayne Smith, my coach at Northampton, has referred to it a number of times, saying that I gained a huge amount of respect from that game as an individual. I never thought of that at the time. The New Zealand public are very critical of their rugby, but they do applaud individual talent. Mitch was also generous with his words. After becoming All Blacks coach in 2002, he said I would be in his team were I a Kiwi. Blimey. It means an awful lot to me that I am respected in New

Zealand. There are no people in the world more knowledge-able about rugby, with the possible exception of South Africa. To be respected there will always give me cause for pride. And for that game to have coincided with the birth of my godson, Paul Grayson's son James, made it a very special day.

The tour should really have ended then and there. There was no desire whatsoever to embark on a 28-hour journey to South Africa after those two Test matches against the All Blacks. All that extra travelling across goodness knows how many time zones, and for what? The only good news was that Austin and I managed to blag a couple of first-class seats, which was nice. We get so much crap for talking too much, but sometimes chat can get you into good places.

The most memorable happening in Cape Town in early July, apart from another towering display from the pack in an 18–0 defeat, was Clive checking us out of the three-star team hotel and into the best gaff in Africa, known locally as the Pink Palace, which was about six times the price. Not only that, but he picked up the tab on his own credit card. That one act spoke volumes for the ambition Clive had for England. It said he would no longer put up with second best. It also said to me that he wanted sole charge from now on (manager Roger Uttley knew nothing about the change of plan). Here, I thought, was a man unafraid to speak his mind. He said what we were all thinking when lambasting those responsible for organizing the tour. 'This was something I inherited,' he was quoted as saying in the *Daily Mail*. 'Unfortunately, the people who put it in place are still on the RFU. They keep their heads down and hide while we travel round the world to play Tests on successive Saturdays. I wish they would say why they did it.

What I cannot seem to get through their thick heads is that we don't control the players. This means they cannot go around arranging fixtures, telling people what strength of teams we will be sending.' He stepped up his attack on his Twickenham bosses in the pages of the *Daily Telegraph*. 'Anybody who could organize a Test match in New Zealand one Saturday and then another Test halfway round the world in a completely different time zone the next Saturday is somebody who doesn't know about playing the game.'

It was not until later that Clive's position really strengthened, but at that time he certainly gained the respect of his senior players because he was genuinely looking after our best interests. When he moved us out of the Holiday Inn Garden Court and into the Mount Nelson, it was because he considered the former an unsuitable environment to prepare for a Test match. It was not a case of wanting a bigger bedroom or more luxuries. The food was poor, there were no meeting rooms, and we were sharing the hotel with a couple of other international teams as well as the rugby media.

The precedent he set that day ensured that now England want for nothing in their accommodation. At home we are based at the luxurious Pennyhill Park in Bagshot, where our privacy is guaranteed. We even have a training pitch within the grounds. When we have down time, it is exactly that. You can wander around and you can sit and play backgammon or cards and speak freely without being worried someone is around the corner listening. Your time is your own. Some journalists have told me they need to be close to the squad because they feel certain information is slow to be released to the public domain. My own view is that you have to have a certain respect for the process. I don't think when things go wrong you can expect the first thought to be, 'Oh, we've got to tell the press about it.' Whether it be injuries, selection or de-selection, we must be allowed time to get it right first, and then make it public.

On the Tour from Hell England patently did not do the business yet, as I sat on the pitch at Newlands at the end of our final game, soaked to the skin and comparing a record of played seven, lost seven to the elation of Lions victory on the same pitch a year earlier, a peculiar thought crossed my mind. For all the problems we had encountered, for all the defeats we had suffered, for all the insults that had been hurled in our direction in three different countries, I would not have swapped the experience for the world. It was an absolutely essential building block to where I am now. During those five weeks I gathered a huge amount of knowledge on how to communicate with players and management, and the openness and honesty that are central to the person I am now can be traced back to that voyage of discovery in June and July 1998.

England tour to Australia, New Zealand and South Africa 1998: squad and results

Forwards: Darren Crompton (0 caps at start of tour), Will Green (1), Duncan Bell (0), Phil Vickery (1), Graham Rowntree (15), Tony Windo (0), George Chuter (0), Phil Greening (3), Richard Cockerill (9), Garath Archer (10), Rob Fidler (0), Danny Grewcock (5), Dave Sims (0), Ben Sturnham (0), Lewis Moody (0), Steve Ojomoh (11), Ben Clarke (32), Pat Sanderson (0), Tony Diprose (7), Richard Pool-Jones (0)

Matt Dawson

Backs: Tim Stimpson (6), Matt Perry (7), Austin Healey (11), Matt Moore (0), Nick Beal (2), Tom Beim (0), Spencer Brown (0), Dominic Chapman (0), Steve Ravenscroft (0), Stuart Potter (0), Jos Baxendell (0), Jonny Wilkinson (1), Alex King (1), Josh Lewsey (0), Matt Dawson (capt., 11), Scott Benton (0), Peter Richards (0)

(P7, W0, D0, L7, F88, A328)

Test: Australia 76 England 0 (Brisbane, 6 June)
New Zealand A 18 England 10 (Hamilton, 13 June)
New Zealand Academy 50 England 32 (Invercargill, 16 June)
Test: New Zealand 64 England 22 (Dunedin, 20 June)
NZ Maori 62 England 14 (Rotorua, 23 June)
Test: New Zealand 40 England 10 (Auckland, 27 June)
Test: South Africa 18 England 0 (Cape Town, 4 July)

5(i)
Misunderstood

HATE MAIL, HATED MALE

'Dawson, you're a prick!'

The opening line hit me between the eyes.

'You're a disgrace to your team, to yourself and to your country. I'm glad you lost. In fact I couldn't be happier. Thank God I'm not English.'

There was no signature on the letter, which had been penned in scruffy handwriting. Only a South Wales postmark on the envelope offered any clue as to its source.

I took a bite of toast and shuffled through the rest of the pile. A couple of bills, a flyer offering deep-pan pizzas delivered within 30 minutes of ordering 'or your money back', and another letter addressed by hand to Matt Dawson, England captain. It was from an elderly gentleman who got straight to the point. He had fought in World War Two and he was disgusted by the way I had led my team. Back in his day, he wrote, I would not have survived as the leader of a platoon. The language was more acceptable, but the sentiment was the same.

And so they continued to come. In first and second post, for days and days. Literally hundreds of letters from the Celtic countries, many of which were extremely abusive and offensive. There were others, too, from English people who wanted to say how much they had enjoyed watching us play and congratulating us on illuminating the inaugural Six Nations Championship with our adventurous style of play. But they were the exceptions to the rule.

A week earlier, England had been on the verge of a Grand Slam. Four successive wins had soothed the pain caused by our premature World Cup exit the previous autumn. There was a new spirit of hope, and as captain I was partly responsible for it. As I soaked up some spring sunshine at our Dalmahoy base on the outskirts of Edinburgh, there was no sign of the storm brewing.

By four o' clock on the afternoon of Sunday, 2 April, however, I could not feel my fingers. The sunshine of midweek had been replaced by frozen squalls, and England had lost a game of rugby, and with it a Grand Slam. After being one of the few England players to observe the post-match courtesy of shaking hands with the opposition, all I could think about was getting warm. I turned away from the Murrayfield pitch and headed up the tunnel and into the visitors' dressing room. Without pausing I walked straight under a shower with my full England kit on and stood there, my body and mind numb. But for the sound of water splashing, there was silence. Nothing was said. There were team mates all around me, but in a steam-filled room I could have been alone.

When feeling finally returned to my limbs I stepped out of the shower, stripped off and wrapped a towel around my waist. I walked out of the shower room and back towards my locker, where I was confronted by Richard Prescott, director of communications for the Rugby Football Union. There was, he said, 'a problem'. We had lost the match against the Scots, but we were still champions, and as such I should have picked up the Six Nations Cup.

'Is it too late now?' I enquired.

'Yes.'

They loved that, my poison pen pals from the Celtic fringe. At a stroke I was condemned as the face of arrogant England. The leader of a side so sure they would win that I hadn't bothered to read up on what contingency plans were in place should the unforeseen happen. Well, that is bullshit. To my knowledge no one had said anything at all to the England camp about what the arrangements were for any presentation. There were no details of what would happen in certain scenarios on any of our schedules. To make matters worse, the guest of honour was Her Royal Highness the Princess Royal. While I had forced the cold from my body with the help of jets of steaming Scottish water, the patron of the Scottish Rugby Union had stood in the biting chill of the most unforgiving of Edinburgh evenings waiting for me to come and shake her frozen hand.

'Why didn't you tell us we had to do this?' I asked a Scottish official in genuine bemusement. I was wasting my breath. The Scots lost no time in making out that we had refused to front up because we were sulking after our 19–13 defeat. 'It was their decision not to receive the trophy,' a spokesman for their union was quoted as saying, and within an hour of the final whistle the episode had become a full-blown royal snub, forcing Jeff Addison, president of the RFU, to issue what the press termed a 'grovelling apology'. 'We unreservedly apologize,' said Addison, 'for what has obviously been a break-down in communications to Her Royal Highness, the sponsors and England supporters who had travelled to the game.' Still the SRU fanned the flames by claiming we had been made aware of the post-match drill three days before the match and then immediately on the full-time whistle. I don't know about a breakdown in communication within the RFU; all I can say, hand on heart, is that I knew nothing of such matters.

Why didn't the SRU remind the England players of the protocol straight after the final whistle? It would have been the easiest thing in the world for them to do. It happens all the time. After most of the cup finals I've been involved in – and I've lost them all with Northampton – somebody has told us to hang around for a presentation. Of course it can be annoying when you're on the losing side, but we do it. At Murrayfield, though, no one said anything. I can't help but wonder why. It is tiny things like this that give England rugby the bad name it has within the home unions, and maybe that suits some people. We're always depicted as this arrogant bunch of rugby players, and there is absolutely no justification for it. We're humble when we talk to the press, respectful of our opponents. We have enjoyed success, but we don't gloat. Then we miss a presentation we know nothing about and, bang, the stereotype is reinforced.

The same sort of thing happened at Lansdowne Road in March 2003 when we lined up on one side of the red carpet prior to the Grand Slam decider and Ireland claimed we were in the wrong, then went ballistic about it afterwards. Donal Lenihan, erstwhile Lions manager, concluded that 'England make it very easy for other people not to like them.' Oh please.

It's farcical, it really is, but I'm sure the storm in a teacup had its effect. A week or so later England returned to Dublin to hear whether they or France had won the right to stage the 2007 World Cup, and learned that they had lost out by 18 votes to three. Guess who Ireland and Scotland didn't vote for.

I would like to think that we are all adult enough to move on from such minor issues. But that perishing April day at Murrayfield the SRU made things into a big deal. And that is one thing that will really piss me off when I look back on my career. I've been involved in five Five and Six Nations title wins (1996, 1997, 1998, 2002 and 2003), which is a bloody fine accomplishment, yet the memory is tarnished by pathetic little incidents away from the game involving trophies and carpets. Why can't we be treated with the same respect as our home union rivals? When Scotland won the Five Nations in 1999 they had so much praise heaped on them it almost suffocated them. Why does that never happen with England? Why do we always have to be totally squeaky clean, totally humble and 100 per cent successful to get any credit? It really is a shocking state of affairs.

Murrayfield was empty when I finally got my hands on the Lloyds TSB Six Nations Trophy. Clive and I were invited to attend a private ceremony at Twickenham some days later at which the silverware was presented, and a lone photographer recorded the moment for posterity. It wasn't ideal, but hey, I was still England captain going to pick up the first ever Six Nations Trophy. Once again we expressed our 'deep regret' over the misunderstanding, and once again we meant it. But inwardly both of us felt a greater annoyance at the lost opportunity on the field than the one off it. England had won the championship outright for a record twenty-third time, moving one ahead of Wales, and had set a record for points in a season of 183, yet history would not mark us down as anything special. That pained me when I reflected on how much we had accomplished in the six months since the World Cup.

The 1999 World Cup had not gone according to plan. We had home advantage, and provided we kept winning at Twicken-ham the route to the last four was well within our range. But we didn't. We lost a pool match to New Zealand and were thus condemned to play three games in nine days. The third of them was a quarter-final against South Africa in Paris on 24 October. We lost 44–21.

It was ludicrous that teams were so heavily penalized for losing one pool game. Making the runners-up play off in midweek for a quarter-final place effectively ruled them out of the competition. The resulting itinerary was simply too pun-ishing. While England played Fiji within five days of being knocked about by Tonga, South Africa put their feet up for the entire week. It was little wonder we ran out of steam in the French capital.

Personally it was a huge thrill to play in a World Cup, especially as I'd missed out in 1995. I was annoyed that people said I was only in because Kyran Bracken was injured as I had no doubt I was selected on merit. I scored a try in our opening 67–7 win over Italy and added another in our 101–10 demo-lition of Tonga. But in the match in between, against New Zealand on 9 October, I drew a blank and we lost 16–30. As in the 1995 semi-final between the nations, it was Jonah Lomu who was the difference. With the scores tied at 16–16 the ball headed in his direction, and before it even reached him I had this feeling of impending doom. It was one of those moments when you look up and your heart sinks. I could tell he was going to skin Jerry Guscott on the outside, and then it would be me in his path. I tried to go high and generally get in the way. He swatted me off, but I stayed on my feet. Then Matt Perry went in and got boomed, then I tried again by jumping on his back. He didn't break stride. Even Lawrence Dallaglio could not stop Jonah, who went over the try line with three of us clinging to him.

The game was lost, and so, effectively, was the cause. Playing three Test matches in a week was too big an ask, given that South Africa, the world champions, were resting up. More-over, we suffered significant collateral damage during our 45–24 win over Fiji. I strained my shoulder and hamstring, Austin Healey hurt his back, Jonny Wilkinson ran on to a swinging arm to the head from Greg Smith, and Matt Perry and Dan Luger were also crocked. That was on a Wednesday before a Sunday quarter-final. It made the format of the tournament a nonsense. There was no thought for the people playing the game. You cannot expect international-quality rugby players to play three games in just over a week. At that level it is dangerous. You are asking for injuries. Sure enough, against South Africa I tore my hammy and was ruled out of rugby for six weeks.

Despite our problems we still thought we could beat the Boks, at least until Joost van der Westhuizen scored a dubious try for which I blame myself. I gave Paul Grayson a really crappy pass, he had his kick charged down, and they went over. From there they locked the game up, booming the leather off the ball, and we didn't have the gameplan to turn the tide. We lacked a little bit of Test match experience, which was disappointing. I was really upset with myself because it had been a good opportunity for me to come to the fore and take the game by the scruff of the neck, along with Grays and Martin Johnson, but we didn't. People have said that because Jannie de Beer dropped five goals we were destined to lose. But I don't believe in destiny.

Afterwards we sat in a room and had our caps presented to us. I remember Clive getting quite emotional and briefly summarizing what we'd been through and what we'd missed out on. At the time I didn't know whether or not it would be his farewell speech, bearing in mind his 'judge me on the World Cup' remark prior to the tournament. In truth, at the end of October 1999, nobody knew what the new millennium held in store.

We went into the 2000 Six Nations Championship determined to put an end to the uncertainty that had plagued us for the previous three months, demanding of ourselves that we win the title to make up for the disappointment of Paris. Anything less and we had a pretty good idea that more heads would roll. I had already seen my good mates Tim Rodber and Paul Grayson fall victim to the post-World Cup cull, and Clive himself must have had a few sleepless nights before he clung onto office. It would have been totally the wrong call for him to have gone or been shown the door, and I thought that at the time. But then he had boxed himself into a corner by being asked to be judged on the World Cup and there were those of the opinion that England's worst World Cup campaign since 1987 was reason enough to show him the door.

Not only did Clive survive, he appointed me his captain, albeit in the absence of Martin Johnson who had a damaged Achilles tendon. Becoming England's first Six Nations skipper was a huge honour. More than anything else I relished the responsibility. I had no delusions that I was going to be in the post for the rest of my life because it is imperative to have someone like Johnno in the team and captaining the side, but there and then I saw it as a chance to implement some ideas I thought could benefit the squad, and which I knew had worked for previous teams.

Coming out of the World Cup, I felt we hadn't had an open and honest team spirit or a really genuine team ethic. There were still cliques within the set-up, a split between the senior and junior players. There were some very senior players – guys like Tim Rodber, Jerry Guscott and Phil de Glanville – around whom I think the new internationals felt uncomfortable. Not because they were being nasty, just because they didn't realize that by being approachable other players would find it refreshing and the team as a whole would benefit. The Bath boys would get on very well with Jerry because they obviously knew him within a club environment, but someone like Ben Cohen didn't know him from Adam, and to my mind, because there wasn't a lot of time there wasn't a lot of effort made to build those bridges. I set out to change that. My philosophy was that it should be all for one and one for all. Obviously you can't force people to be friends, because we're all different. And I didn't try to do that. I didn't say, 'Right, you lot, we're all going to be best mates.' That was a matter for the individual. What ultimately is imperative in a team environment is respect. We had to be able to respect each other 100 per cent.

I had reached this view early in my international career. When I first came into the England squad during the Jack Rowell era I didn't say boo to a goose, either in team meetings or on the training park. I would have ideas for moves that might work against certain opponents, but I would keep them to myself. I didn't dream of speaking up for risk of being branded a smart arse. Jack never wanted to hear what I had to say anyway. I had no experience and I was under 25.

It was a mistake on his part, I am convinced of that, and I had no intention of repeating it now that I was captain for a Six Nations campaign. It was a question of trying to get everyone onto the one level. So, whenever I hosted a team meeting I would invite the quieter players to talk. I wanted total participation. And if certain players didn't speak up I would talk to them individually, seek out their opinions and, if appropriate, convince them that the whole group would benefit from hearing them. You can't go too far in this direction, of course; you can't have all and sundry talking all the time. But if someone, anyone, had something to say I would encourage them rather than blank them and just go with the coach's and captain's views all the time. I wanted open dialogue. It was a lesson I had learned from Pat Lam, the great Samoan forward who was captain of Northampton at the time. When Pat joined Saints from Newcastle nothing was too much trouble for him. It was so refreshing to have someone who had time for everyone and made everyone else equally considerate.

Looking back, I have little doubt that this philosophy sped up the development of guys like Iain Balshaw, Mike Tindall and Ben Cohen. England now have some fantastic players who have done some fantastic things at the top of the game in a very short space of time. To see the likes of Matt Perry, Mike Catt and Austin Healey giving these youngsters, as they were then, the benefit of their experience and then listening to them in turn was hugely satisfying; to then see the likes of Ben, Tinds and Balsh put what they had learned into practice was even more so.

In a very short space of time we really did start to change the way England played. We had employed a fairly forward-orientated game during the 1999 World Cup and I felt it was time for a breath of fresh air. We were fortunate we had the type of players available we needed to bring about this change of emphasis, from piano shifting to piano playing. Having come close to losing his job, I believe Clive approached the 2000 Six Nations with a nothing-to-lose attitude, taking risks and making all the selections he really wanted to make. His game-plan combined razor-sharp attack with rock-solid defence. We had previously tried it in other games, but when it had come to the crunch in the big games we'd always shut up shop. Now we were committed to it, and our opening game against Ireland on 5 February really set the tone for the championship. The three young backs made their debuts and scored three tries in a resounding 50–18 victory. Ben claimed two and caught the eye of the snappers by celebrating as if he was a professional footballer; Tinds, partnering Catty in midfield for the first time, scored the third. That day, with me leading my country at Twickenham for the first time, we clicked.

It was not simply that we all bought into the gameplan. Going into the World Cup we had done an unbelievable amount of fitness training which personally I felt undermined our challenge as I thought we were knackered. But now we were harvesting the fruits of that labour. We came into the Six Nations as probably the fittest team in the world. And we played like it. We were relentless. Speaking to the Irish boys afterwards, it was obvious they were very down, but they had to admit they had been run ragged because we attacked from all areas of the pitch.

I had spent the week prior to the game thinking about leading England out at Headquarters. What was I going to say in those last few moments before we left the dressing room and headed towards the roar of 75,000 fans? I remember sitting in my room on the Thursday and phoning Paul Grayson. There was a captain's meeting the following day and I told him I was struggling to pitch to the players exactly how much the game meant for England. Grays has always been there for me as a sounding board and someone to lean on for advice and support. This occasion was no different. When I put down the phone I was clear in my mind. 'This is a new era for England,' I told the players the next day. 'Draw a line in the sand and move forward. This is our time. Express yourselves out there. Don't come off the field with any regrets.'

As a kid I never played at being England captain, though I know Jonny Wilkinson, for one, did. From the early days, when my dad used to take me to Twickenham, I had it in my mind that I wanted to play for England, but nothing more precise than that. Most years Dad and I went to one or both of the home internationals. I remember parking up by the fish and chip shop on the Whitton Road, walking down past the barracks and into the ground. Walking through the West Car Park to meet up with friends. Dad sneaking beer into Twickenham. Sitting in the old North Stand. Just fantastic memories. And now I could add the one of me captaining England in that very arena watched by the proudest Mum and Dad in all the world.

Not that pride was restricted to my family. The father and uncle of Ben Cohen cried tears of joy as they watched his try-scoring debut from the stands. Peter, his dad, and George, a member of England's 1966 World Cup-winning football team, were thrilled to bits for Ben, and with good reason. As was the family of Mike Catt, who marked his fortieth appearance for his country with a terrific performance. Catty, who had never been fully accepted by the Twickenham public, later took an emotional swipe at his critics who had dogged him for so long. 'Put yourself in my position,' he said. 'Imagine yourself getting slagged off for two or three years. I haven't enjoyed my international rugby for ages. I'm happy now, but it's only one game.'

Perhaps, but it was the game he had waited all his career for. He had always been a player who wanted to express himself and try things, but he'd never really had the players around him to complement that ambition. Great players, yes, but none of them wanting to take those sort of risks. He was way ahead of his time. Even now that he is the wrong side of 30 he would still be my number one pick in midfield, because he offers so much vision and class. Catty is one of the most talented all-round rugby players I have ever played with. He's got absolutely everything. He can kick, he can run, he can pass, he's got great hands and he's got genuine speed. But England didn't play to his strengths for years. Internationally, I don't think he ever professed to be a fly-half, yet he was thrown in there on the basis that he would get loads of ball. He was given a job description which wasn't natural to him. With someone like Mike Catt you've got to play to his strengths, put him in certain areas and give him an opportunity to do what he's good at. Instead he was put at 10 and told to play the same as Rob Andrew at times, and then a bit like Stuart Barnes. Jack Rowell made the same mistake with him as he did with me. Just as I was not Richard Hill, so Catty should have been allowed to be Mike Catt.

It wasn't until Clive Woodward, Andy Robinson and Brian Ashton took charge that they realized he was so much more effective in midfield. By that time he'd been cowed, to an extent, by the reaction of the Twickenham set. The crowd only respond to what they see, and they'd seen a number 10 who came on and didn't give them what they were used to. Someone who wasn't executing team strategy as well as, say, Rob Andrew did. They were a bit miffed by it. Most people, I believe, now acknowledge that Catty was being played in the wrong position for too many years. Had he represented England at centre from the start I believe he would now have over 70 caps. Certainly Clive considered that he 'had his best game for England by a mile' that day against Ireland. And it was good timing. This was the first game in the post-Guscott–de Glanville era. England needed a guy to step up to the plate in midfield. That day at Twickenham, benefiting from the flat positional play of Jonny Wilkinson on his inside, Catty stepped up.

Conquering home turf with our virgin soldiers was one thing, repeating the feat in the backyard of World Cup finalists France was another altogether. England's previous experiences in the Stade de France had been wretched: a handsome defeat in the opening round of the 1998 Five Nations and the quarter-final loss to the Springboks the following year. Only Jason Leonard, among the whole squad, had ever won a game in Paris. As captain, however, I wasn't about to dwell on the past. For one thing, England had swiftly moved into a new era. For another, England sides tend to go into their shell when they worry too much about the opposition. My focus was on what we had to do to develop as a team.

It was one of those weeks when everything went according to script. Great hotel, great facilities, great training. And then, on the Saturday, we went out and absolutely battered them physically. It was, without doubt, my biggest win as captain, before or since. A triumph built not just on what we did on the field, but off it too.

Take the Friday, for example. The day before home games the England squad always like to have bread and butter pudding. But there we were sitting in France moaning about how we weren't going to have it. So I spoke to our liaison officer, and he called his wife at home in England, who just happened to speak French and to be an exceptional cook. She then phoned the chef in our hotel and described to him the recipe for bread and butter pudding. Later that evening he emerged from the kitchen with an enormous full-fat bread and butter pudding. The boys absolutely loved it. Little things like that might have no direct bearing on the game whatsoever, but they do make a difference to how you feel. And for the next hour or so the boys didn't feel as though they were in France in hostile surrounds.

That feeling arrived soon enough as we emerged from the bowels of the Stade de France the following afternoon. But we got off to a good start; Phil Vickery put in a couple of massive hits and that really set the tone. We showed a toughness that day which had maybe not previously been associated with England teams. We were at times cynical – Simon Shaw and Austin Healey were sin-binned as the French laid siege to our line in the closing stages – but we refused to lose the game.

I recall being struck by how remarkably cool and calm the younger professionals were. In fact, I still get absolutely blown away by it. They saw that contest as a game of rugby, nothing more. It didn't matter to them where we were playing or how many people were watching. All that mattered was who we were playing and what the threat was. They just got on with it, all smart and streetwise. Jonny kicked all our points and we won 15–9.

In our moment of triumph Clive was complimentary to me, saying I had been fantastic and revealing that I was the first captain to have actually told him to back off and calm down. He said that was great, and he couldn't speak highly enough of my captaincy. It must be unbelievably frustrating to be a coach, to work so hard with a group of players all week and then to go and sit in a stand and cross your fingers. But that is the way it is, so I simply said, 'Look, Clive, you've done as much as you can, now leave it. We'll deal with it. I'll take that responsibility.' My feeling was that I couldn't go through a pre-match week preaching coolness and calm if there was going to be shouting and screaming from the coaching staff in the dressing room. For me it was a question of setting the right tone, and in the build-up to *le crunch* we had a group of England players who were utterly calm and focused.

When we beat Wales 46–12 at Twickenham a fortnight later it was clear to me that the team was making real strides. We scored five unanswered tries, one of them from Phil Greening, who had a magnificent game. He really caught the eye and at the time seemed sure to be the hooker who would progress with England into the 2003 World Cup. I was genuinely sad to see him fall off the radar 18 months later, after he moved to London. He was a good friend and a lot of people tried to help him, but having initially been a little unlucky to be dropped he then didn't pull out all the stops to get back. I know what it takes because I've been there myself. You have to eat a bit of humble pie, get your head down and sacrifice a few bits and bobs for a while in order to do the right thing. Unfortunately Phil didn't do that. He just carried on doing what he was doing in London. He is a very big character, as we all know, but life in the bright lights didn't help his rugby, and before he knew it Steve Thompson, Mark Regan and Dorian West were being rewarded for their dedicated professionalism. And that was a real shame for Phil because that day at Twickenham he was rampant, absolutely awesome. He was probably one of the first real quality lineout throwers, with a genuine talent to pick people out. Around the park he was even more sensational, all speed and fast hands. I can pay him no greater compliment than that he redefined the role of the hooker.

It was after the Wales game that I began to realize what a very special bunch of players I was with. I was so pleased they had gelled so well. But there was no huge secret to it other than that we were thoroughly enjoying what we were doing. We went to Italy in buoyant mood and stuck 59 points on the Azzurri.

In the build-up to Rome I had gone public with my view that we had played too structured a game in the World Cup. We had been accused of being 'Robocops' by Brad Johnstone, who had coached Fiji for the tournament and was now in charge of Italy, and he was probably right. Looking back at the videos I think we probably were a bit too predictable, and as a decision-maker I have to put my hand up and take my share of the blame for that. It was a harsh lesson to learn, and one we'd rather have learned before the World Cup, but by the time we renewed acquaintance with Johnstone we had come to appreciate the need to be less rigid. Even now, we still refer to the 'Robocops' remark in the dressing room because the last thing the coaches want of us is to be pre-programmed. Anyone who comes into the team is always told to go out and express himself.

Nobody enjoyed the way we played in 2000 more than Austin Healey, who had a fantastic season and, in the view of Stephen Jones, rugby correspondent of the *Sunday Times*, became the key player in the England team. Austin scored a hat-trick against the Italians, the first ever by an Englishman in a Six Nations match, as he constantly reminded us. Given a free rein to pop up anywhere, he was lethal. He reads the game fantastically well and opponents were unable to keep tabs on him and his electric pace. He is so much more effective when he's allowed to do whatever he wants to do.

I scored two tries myself in the Italian capital, yet ended

the game in anguish having dislocated my shoulder when Italy scored their try right at the start. Someone hit me and my shoulder popped out. Although the doctor put it back in I had to leave the field two minutes from time and I was less than happy. As captain, I wanted to finish the game. That, however, should have been the least of my worries. Little did I know at the time, but my shoulder would become a real problem, causing me to miss the biggest game in Northampton's history and to give up my England shirt, the captaincy and my place on the summer tour to South Africa. But all that was ahead of me. Uppermost in my mind at the end of March was the forthcoming Six Nations clash with Scotland and the chance to exorcise the demons of Wembley nearly a year earlier.

The feeling was one of total shock. When the final whistle blew it was as though there had been a bereavement. It was the first Grand Slam game I'd been involved in, and victory had been snatched away from us right at the death. In the shadow of the Twin Towers, the trophy was out of its box awaiting collection – but not by us.

Successive victories over Scotland, Ireland and France had put England in sight of a first Slam in four years. Wales, beaten by the Scots and the Irish and forced to play their home games at the home of English football while the Millennium Stadium was being built, were given little chance. But on 11 April 1999 the Valleys emptied and Wembley became the Arms Park for the day, complete with Tom Jones and Max Boyce.

Still, England dominated the game and led by three tries to one when we were awarded a penalty. Lawrence Dallaglio, then the captain, directed Jonny Wilkinson to kick for touch rather than for goal. Our momentum was halted there as Tim Rodber was harshly penalized for what appeared a fair tackle and Neil Jenkins kicked Wales upfield for one last crack at our try line. What happened next I can still recall in vivid detail, in the same way I remember my Cape Town try for the Lions in 1997. Scott Quinnell moved the ball away from the lineout and found Scott Gibbs to an almighty roar of anticipation from the crowd. I remember Gibbsy going in between Rodders and Richard Hill, powering along like the pocket battleship he is. Then me running at his ankles and attempting the tap tackle from five yards away; I remember diving and getting a handful of thin air. Then another roar as Steve Hanley came across and Gibbsy stepped inside him. By the time I picked up my head to see what was going on he was under the posts with red shirts jumping all over him. Jenks's conversion gave Wales a 32–31 victory.

Walking to the tea room afterwards was an experience I would rather never repeat. We had abuse thrown at us by every Welshman not singing 'Flower of Scotland' in celebration of the fact that the Scots, not us, were champions. I couldn't stand to be near anybody, Mum and Dad or anyone else. I needed time to fester. I worked my way out onto a balcony with Rodders and Paul Grayson and the three of us stood there forlornly, each feeling sorry for himself, each unable to find any words to make sense of what had just happened. It was like a bad dream only I was awake. I wanted to pinch myself and clear the nightmare from my mind. But I was stuck with it.

I cannot imagine a worse memory than that. The combination of it being my first Grand Slam game and its being played at Wembley Stadium, a mecca for every Englishman. It had been such an inspiring place to be, even though it was full of Welshmen. Earlier in the day I had walked around almost open-mouthed, thinking, 'Oh my God, this is Wembley.' Even in my days as a promising right-back for Chelsea Boys I'd never thought in my wildest dreams that I'd get to play on the hallowed turf. My mind shot back to all those FA Cup finals I had watched as a kid, to the 1985 final I had been to with Dad when my team Everton lost to Manchester United and that goal by Norman Whiteside. During the warm-up I had looked across to exactly where I'd sat that day, 14 years before. I was totally inspired by the setting, blissfully unaware of the emotion I'd be feeling come Sunday night.

I have been scarred by that experience to the extent that if someone mentions Wembley Stadium to me now I don't think of all those May Saturdays of my youth watching cup finals. I don't think of England winning the World Cup there in 1966, or of Stuart Pearce converting *that* penalty against Spain to put us in the semi-finals of Euro '96. I don't think of any of that. I think of Scott bloody Gibbs running through us and breaking my heart.

Later that evening the England squad went back to the Petersham Hotel in Richmond for dinner and a few drinks. Clive stood up and said, 'I believe good things come out of bad days. In time, this will do us the world of good.' At the time I believed him, largely because, I suppose, it was a consoling thought on a night when my mind was a painful place to be.

*   *   *

As I led England out at Murrayfield 12 months on I remembered Clive's words. The experience of Wembley had not done us much good in the World Cup, so this was the day we would harvest the benefits. That is what I told myself. And when England led Scotland 10–3 midway through the first half on a crisp and bright early April afternoon, I had no reason to think differently.

Bad weather had been forecast, but it had been due to arrive before the game. By half-time, as we headed for the dressing room with a one-point lead and the game's only try, scored by Lawrence Dallaglio, there was still no sign of it. It was then that the ambush was sprung. Down in the dressing room, cocooned from the elements, we did not detect the sudden and dramatic drop in temperature outside. While nature's scene shifters got to work, we assessed how we had played with a dry ball and plotted our second-half strategy based on the conditions before the break. As we ran back out it began to sleet and snow.

With hindsight, of course, we should have had someone out there during the interval gauging the change of weather and relaying the news to us. But we didn't, and as captain I've got to blame myself for what happened next. You take the credit when things go well, so you must accept the flak when it doesn't. We needed to manufacture a stoppage and the chance to regroup and reassess our options; instead, we ploughed on. For five or six minutes we played some good rugby and we thought we had, literally, weathered the storm. But this was no ordinary storm. The rain fell in such quantity that the pitch flooded, and in the icy chill we froze in every respect.

While we fannied about, Scotland wised up. They booted the leather off the ball and made us play in our own 22. Frankly, we capitulated. I hold myself responsible for our failure to adapt to the conditions and the change in the nature of the game. I was in a position, not only as captain but as scrum-half, to get us back into the right areas of the field. I should have recognized that it was no longer a day for playing pretty rugby. Instead we got carried away with chasing the game. The weather got worse and worse, and so did we. Duncan Hodge, the Scotland fly-half, kicked a fourth penalty goal and then, five minutes from time, pounced on a loose ball to claim the decisive try.

Fair play to the Scots lads. They played a very canny game. They targeted us at half-back and smashed the shit out of me and Jonny. They also targeted some of our forwards and niggled away very effectively at the likes of Garath Archer. Our discipline was desperately poor. From 1 to 15, everyone lost his cool at various times. They outplayed and out-thought us, and it hurt.

As, of course, did the postbag I received in the ensuing days. I am not the first England captain to be abused and I very much doubt I will be the last, but it was disappointing. I can't hide the fact. For a game which is meant to be watched by gentlemen I was pretty disgusted by some of the letters that were sent to me. I had not experienced it before, and I honestly didn't think we, as players, had done a lot to deserve it, as the criticism was not of our performance but the trophy presentation cock-up.

I later asked my dad what he made of the episode. He had watched the game from the stands and then come inside to hear his son make his speech. 'From where your mother and I were you seemed to do all the right things,' he told me. 'You stayed on the pitch afterwards to congratulate the Scots, you paid tribute to your hosts in your speech and, to be quite honest, we did not know there was a problem. If somebody had been "snubbed" I certainly heard no word of complaint from any of the Scots I was around.' All the same, I decided to write a personal apology to the Princess Royal. I wanted to reassure her that what had happened had been a genuine misunderstanding and that there was no intention whatsoever on the part of England to snub either her or the ceremony. I said that I hoped our actions hadn't caused any offence and added a personal wish that one day I would play against Scotland again and get the chance to formally apologize to her in person. Some days later I received a reply from her private secretary thanking me for my letter, saying that no offence had been taken and agreeing that there must have been a breakdown in communications.

That 1999/2000 season went from bad to worse for me personally. I played in the Tetley's Bitter Cup final against Wasps, and not only did Northampton lose but the left shoulder I had originally dislocated on England duty in Rome clearly wasn't right. In fact, it was fairly buggered. A week earlier Saints had beaten Llanelli to reach the Heineken Cup final, during which game I had gone to take a tap penalty; Scotty Quinnell, who was on the floor, had pulled my shirt sleeve and my arm had come out of its socket. I'd shaken it and it had gone back in of its own accord, so I'd carried on. Then, with about five minutes to go, I'd made a tackle and it had popped out again. That had been the end of my afternoon. With it strapped up I somehow survived the Tetley's Bitter Cup final, but I needed a rest and there was none to be had. All season long Saints had been chasing the treble, and now we were paying the price with a fixture pile-up. No sooner had we come off the field at Twickenham than we had to shake off the disappointment and the fatigue and go again, this time to Saracens in the league in midweek.

It would prove to be a game too far for me as my shoulder finally broke down completely. Ironically, it went as I tried to fend off Kyran Bracken, the player who had most to gain from my absence from the national team. As I reached out I jolted my arm, it came out of the socket, and that was that. I was wearing a brace under my shirt, a wet-suit material covering half my torso with Velcro strapping my shoulder in place. As a result my movement was fairly limited anyway, but as my shoulder dislocated within the strapping it was pulled and ripped in all sorts of directions. The scan confirmed what I privately suspected: my season was over.

I was sick to my stomach to have to miss the final of the European Cup on the last Saturday of May. Northampton had never won a major trophy, and now the biggest one of all was within tantalizing reach. But I could neither help them beat Munster nor conquer the exhaustion running through the club. I am a bad spectator at the best of times, but this was the worst of times to be seated high up in the stands at Twickenham. Of course I was overjoyed for my team-mates when we triumphed 9–8, and particularly for Paul Grayson who kicked all our points. But I can't pretend I wasn't desperately disappointed to miss out on playing anything more than a supporting role, which included getting permission from Clive Woodward for the lads to use the England changing room. I sat there feeling hollow. Elated yet gutted.

I still feel the burden of not having won a trophy on the field with Northampton, and I have to say it is starting to really piss me off. If I don't pick up some form of silverware with the club before I retire I won't feel I've served the club as well as I should have done. It really will disappoint me. But that is a personal thing which I must deal with. For my team-mates, that glorious day at Twickenham provided a great sense of closure. Unlike me, they have something other than frustration to show for all their years of effort at club level.

5(ii)
Misunderstood

STRIKING PROGRESS, STRIKE IN PROGRESS

Lying on my bed, I was surrounded by luxury. Not for nothing is the Pennyhill Park Hotel the 'official pre-match venue and training facility' of England rugby. As with Clive Woodward's set-up, the hotel's pledge to its customers is 'to strive for perfection'. It is a rare day indeed that you want for anything there. The twenty-first of November 2000 was that rare day.

On the BBC evening news I had seen myself standing in front of a phalanx of microphones. I'd switched over to ITN and there I was again, this time illuminated by the flash guns triggered by Fleet Street's finest. 'Bloody hell!' I'd thought. But that was earlier. Midnight had now come and gone. I was in need of sleep and sanctuary from the crisis that had engulfed the England rugby team.

It was a day that will not easily be forgotten by anybody with even half an interest in our sport. Indeed, given the treatment it received on television at the serious end of the news bulletins, it was immediately apparent that the extraordinary events had transcended the game of rugby union. For the first time since William Webb Ellis unwittingly created a whole new ball game, England were out on strike.

The decision had been taken to withdraw our labour in protest at the failure of the Rugby Football Union to offer us what we considered a fair financial deal. We had wanted two-thirds of our fees guaranteed, with the rest dependent on results; the RFU's offer was weighted in favour of the win bonus. After months of prevarication by the Union we had reached a point of no return. Just a few days after beating world champions Australia at Twickenham, the players voted for industrial action.

It was hard to take on board what we had done, and I didn't want to think about where we might be headed. There are no signposts to international oblivion. You just arrive there. I lay awake working through all the possible scenarios in my mind. All lines of enquiry prompted one basic question: were we doing the right thing? The answer always came back the same.

Since that fateful day at Murrayfield back in April the fortunes of the England team had again taken a turn for the better. While my shoulder went under the surgeon's knife, the squad headed down to South Africa for the summer. It was a short tour, five matches in all, but with two Tests against the Springboks it offered an ideal opportunity for England to silence their growing band of critics.

The claim after Murrayfield was that England did not have the bottle for the matches that mattered most. There had been Wembley, then defeats to New Zealand and South Africa in the World Cup, followed by Scotland. It had been conveniently forgotten that we had won in Paris, but what the hell. Back-to-back Test matches in Pretoria and Bloemfontein offered up a chance to prove that England could win big games, and win them on the road too.

The first Test on 17 June ended in narrow defeat, by 18–13, although how the video referee did not allow the try scored by Tim Stimpson, which would most probably have won England the game, remains a complete mystery to me. The following week England set the record straight with a 27–22 triumph. It was only the second time in 15 Tests against one of the southern hemisphere's big three that a Clive Woodward side had come out on top, the first having been at Twickenham in the winter of 1998 when we denied the Boks a world record eighteenth successive victory by winning 13–7. I had played a leading role that afternoon after being made goalkicker for the day and doing the business, but this time I was sitting in front of the television at home once again trying to deal with mixed emotions. Delight on the one hand, self-pity on the other. That was until Martin Johnson rang from the jubilant dressing room. It was great to hear his voice. It gave me a huge lift. The biggest lift of all, though, came from the result itself. The lads returned home cock-a-hoop, convinced that England had achieved a significant psychological breakthrough and could use the result as a springboard to autumn success against the Wallabies, Argentina and South Africa.

Behind the scenes, though, all was not well. The players and the RFU had not seen eye to eye for a while on financial matters. We always seemed to be signing contracts halfway through seasons, the amounts would always be changing, they would always be trying to scrape a bit off here and put a bit on there. Nothing was ever set in stone, and we were getting more and more frustrated. Our view was that there isn't a business in the world that pays its performers 5 per cent of the turnover, so why should we accept it? Everyone was making money out of the England rugby team except the players. It's not as though we were even asking for the earth. We were just asking to be treated like anyone else at the top end of their profession. If you ask the top 22 lawyers in the country to work for you and win big cases, you know you will have to pay big money. The same with surgeons. Because they are the best in the field, and the best can command larger fees. It's the same in any profession. Yet in English rugby, I repeat, we were being paid less than 5 per cent of the turnover. It was just ludicrous. All we wanted was fair recompense. We didn't want to be like Premiership footballers earning millions of pounds a year and bankrupting the sport, but neither were we prepared to undervalue ourselves when we have probably got not even 10 years at the top. England players are not set up for life; after rugby they're still going to have to go out and work. But while they're at the top of their tree they should earn a wage that reflects that. That was our contention.

Martin Johnson, Lawrence Dallaglio and I represented the squad as we were the three main captains of the team and had been over the previous two or three years, during which time the matter had slowly come to a head. Every time we met with RFU chief executive Francis Baron we hoped it would be the last, and that agreement could be reached. But there was just no movement. A successful businessman he doubtless is, but Baron seemed to us to have no feeling for the game, or for what the players were risking in an environment where every collision could be your last.

We had only signed the 1999 World Cup contract on condition that the next contract, for the Six Nations, would be sorted out well in advance. Of course it wasn't. Nor did the lads sign any deal for the tour to South Africa. And so the dispute reached the autumn of 2000, still no closer to a resolution on the matter of intellectual property rights (the use of the players' images) and match payments. The rights had been sold by the RFU to its sponsors, but they were ours, not theirs, to sell.

With Australia in town, we decided that enough was enough. The RFU seemed to have no sympathy with our position and were patronizing in their attitude towards us. We wanted £4,000 per man to play with £2,000 riding on the result; their offer was the reverse: only £2,000 up front, with £4,000 for a win, in a game where a bounce of the ball can be the difference between winning and losing no matter the amount of effort put in by the players. We felt this was the wrong way round. Five days before the tie with the Wallabies we met with Baron and said that the England squad would honour the RFU's commitment to their sponsors in the week of internationals if he reversed his offer. Three hours later he offered us £4,000 and £1,750 respectively. Close, but not close enough. It had become a matter of principle, and when we rejected his offer he withdrew it. In response, we decided to turn our training shirts inside out to hide the Cellnet and Nike logos. Johnno telephoned Clive Woodward to tell him, and Clive went ape, vowing to drop any player who did so from his team to play Australia. Later, he called back with a compromise arrangement which we accepted: he would set up a meeting between the players and the RFU management board to resolve the dispute once and for all, providing we did nothing to upset the sponsors.

There is always electricity in the air at Twickenham when the world champions are around. Add the Ashes rivalry which exists between England and Australia, and here was a match to savour. As we lined up for the anthems it was the try line rather than any picket line that sharpened our focus.

I was more than happy to be named among the substitutes after five months of inactivity, with the promise of getting on and being right in the thick of the action for the last 30. By then we trailed 15–19. The lads had not adapted that well to what they were playing against in the first half, but had fine-tuned at half-time and were now making a game of it. Not that the Aussies thought they were going to lose. From the way a couple of them were sledging us it was clear they could not envisage a scenario in which Iain Balshaw came off the bench to post the chip that Dan Luger touched down for the match-winning try eight minutes into stoppage time. When video ref Brian Stirling confirmed the score I went loopy and apparently upset the Australians with my histrionics. My response to that is that they shouldn't have been giving us all the banter until the final whistle had blown. My celebrations were my way of saying, 'How do you feel now, boys?'

Their scrum-half, Sam Cordingley, was particularly culpable. 'You're too old for it, Johnson,' he told Johnno. 'Give it up. The young brigade are here.' Hang on a minute, mate, wind your neck in a little bit. The air was blue when I came on, and I thought, 'Holy shit, what's going on here?' They quickly tried it on with me, but I didn't bite, well aware that those things have a habit of backfiring. The Aussies are very good at sledging and it can break teams and individual players. That's why they do it. But with the game so finely balanced they were taking a risk giving it the big 'un on our home patch. I reminded them of that at the end. I know they didn't like it, but if you're going to dish it out you've got to accept a bit. Those are the yard rules.

That victory was one of the defining moments in English rugby history. We had beaten the best in the world and posted successive wins over southern-hemisphere opposition for the first time. 'This weekend,' considered former South Africa coach Nick Mallett, 'we saw the start of the emergence of the new world order in rugby. England and France are now unquestionably right up there.'

'But for how long?' I wondered as I stared up at the ceiling of my hotel room at Pennyhill Park. I took a couple of deep breaths and tried to slow the thoughts racing through my mind. It was past 2 a.m. but I couldn't sleep. Over and over I replayed the events of the evening: the meeting with the RFU management board, our attempt to persuade them that we were worth £4,000 per man no matter the result, and the Union's final offer of £3,500 plus a £2,250 win bonus. We again said the offer was unacceptable, but agreed to put it to the squad.

The management board left the room and the players were summoned from around the hotel. Each of them was totally aware of the potential consequences, and the decision was left to them. There was no bullying by senior figures. Johnno, Lol and I were unanimous that that couldn't possibly be the case. The votes were cast and the decision was taken to strike.

Our critics said it was ridiculous that we should jeopardize the future of the English game for the sake of an extra guaranteed £500 per man per game, but there was a principle at stake and it was worth fighting for. Sometimes you have to stand up for what you believe in. I felt so strongly that I was prepared to sacrifice my career if that's what it took to improve the lot of future England players. It was about respect, about being listened to and consulted rather than being patronized. It was about standing up and being regarded as human beings, and not being taken for a ride, as we felt we had been by the RFU for too long.

Crucially, we were all of one mind on this issue, I had no doubt about that. We were all friends, we all believed in one another. Even a plea by Clive for us to change our minds and a warning that the game might not forgive us could not soften our resolve. Yes, there were probably a couple of lads who didn't really want to do it, but they were willing to support the majority decision. It was an action built on firm beliefs but also on trust.

The verdict was relayed to Francis Baron by Johnno at 11.30 p.m., and on the stroke of midnight Clive reappeared, ashen-faced and emotional. For the first time since he'd taken charge he could not support us, he said, making it crystal clear what he thought of us using the England jersey to achieve our ends. Finally, he added, 'I want you all out of the hotel first thing tomorrow morning.'

Given the circumstances, I surprised myself by how calm I was able to remain. I actually didn't feel any different. My stomach didn't churn, I didn't feel physically sick, I didn't lose my appetite. Everyone had expected us to be apologetic, which is why we had to be seen to be really strong. Not arrogant, because we weren't being arrogant. We were desperately disappointed that it had come to this. However, people needed to be aware of exactly why we were taking this radical action and what the RFU were trying to do to us.

I phoned John Steele, director of rugby at Northampton, to tell him the news and to say that we needed all the players to be on board in case the RFU made good their threat to field an alternative England team against Argentina at the weekend. That message was passed to every Premiership club, and the solidarity was total. Keith Barwell, the owner of Northampton, was four square behind our action and my part in it. 'I feel the players get abused by the system and I'm totally amazed that they allow themselves to be so maltreated,' he said. 'They get exploited by the RFU because the RFU are clever and realize the players don't want to be involved in the politics. Respect is a word often used in rugby. I have always had a tremendous respect for Matt and I like to think he has some for me. But I don't think the RFU have ever had respect for the players. I am very proud of the way Matt has handled himself.'

It both was and wasn't a major gamble that we had taken. Of course there were a small minority within the game who were a bit pig-headed about it and didn't try to understand our situation. We expected that. But most people who appreciate professional sport understood where we were coming from. So I was surprised and disappointed to see Bill Beaumont quoted as saying that he would have walked over broken glass to play for England. I have done that, Bill. I, too, played in the amateur era, as did Lawrence and Johnno. We have a foot in each era. We're not three rookies. But the stakes are now completely different. Everything has changed. Of course playing for your country is the ultimate, it always will be. If they turned round tomorrow and said playing for England is now amateur and there is no longer any money in rugby, I'm sure we would all carry on playing. But the reality is that it is our profession, and like any other job you have to do what is right for yourself and your family.

The rest of the squad had left the premises when Martin Johnson, Lawrence Dallaglio and I walked across the courtyard at Pennyhill Park towards the assembled press pack to tell the world what had happened. My overriding thought as I made my way over to the microphones and notepads with only a bottle of Lucozade for support was what a major piece of rugby history we were creating. I hoped we'd got it right. Clive certainly didn't think so. He was unequivocal in his opposition to our stance. 'This is one of the saddest days in the history of the game in England,' he declared. 'The players have let me down and they have let their country down. I think they have made a huge mistake.' Clive has never been one for safe options, but I have to say I was more than a little bit surprised at the way he aligned himself in the dispute. He demanded that we turn up for training at 11 o'clock the following day or we would not see our England shirts again. He then spent much of the day leaving persuasive messages on the answerphones of certain players. His tactic of trying to pick people off in an attempt to get them to break away from the main body upset a lot of the guys and he was playing a dangerous game by resorting to that approach. It appeared then that the damage might be irreparable, but over time he has more than recovered it, which is a testament to his management skills and personality.

Ultimately, it was the diplomatic skills of Peter Wheeler, the former England captain and current chief executive of Leicester Tigers, that rescued English rugby. Wheeler had answered the call from Johnno to drive to Wentworth Golf Club and try to help find a compromise. As a member of the management board he knew how entrenched opinions on both sides were, yet he came up with a scenario whereby nobody lost face. His solution was to take £50,000 from the bonus we would receive if we won the 2001 Six Nations title and divide it among the squad in an immediate one-off payment. That way it would not affect the RFU's accounts as they had already budgeted for it and they could argue they had not improved their 'final offer'. At the same time it gave each of us an extra £380 per game, which raised our guaranteed fee to an acceptable level, within £120 of what we had demanded.

The proposal was put to the squad at a fund-raising dinner for former England full-back Alistair Hignell at the Café Royal in London that evening, and there was unanimous acceptance. The following morning, as the clock fast approached Clive's 11 a.m. deadline, the RFU also gave it the green light. After 34 hours during which the nation had held its breath a four-year deal was agreed and the episode was at an end.

English rugby owes Peter Wheeler a huge debt of gratitude for his role in restoring order. Had it not been for Wheelbrace and the solution he brokered I genuinely believe the boycott would have remained in place for the Argentina game. And then what would have happened? Clive said it would have been out of his control and that it would have been up to the game to decide our fate. My gut feeling is that the supporters would have backed us and that television would have followed suit, because TV doesn't tend to cover games if the stands are empty. But we'll never know for sure.

The team bus pulled out of Pennyhill Park and swept through Bagshot and on to the M3. It was 25 November, Judgement Day, the day we discovered what the Great British public had made of our midweek walkout. Waiting for us at Twickenham were Argentina, who for much of the week had been warned to expect an alternative England team comprising tinkers and tailors. But it was not the reaction of the Pumas that we sweated over, rather the reception we would receive from the 60,000 supporters who had braved a filthy day to be at headquarters. We had been told that England fans had taken a dim view of our action and would tell us all about it before, during and after the game. The *Sun* newspaper even asked them to boo us.

No chance. As we made our way along the motorway even more people than usual were leaning out of their cars, waving flags, sticking their thumbs up, shouting and screaming for us. When we got to Twickenham the car park was buzzing and the stadium was absolutely fantastic, the fans much more vocal than they would ordinarily be against Argentina.

To cap an extraordinary week for me personally, I found myself back in the starting line-up for the first time since Murrayfield. I had seen what had happened before to people who had crossed Clive – in his post-1999 World Cup auto-biography Leicester and England hooker Richard Cockerill

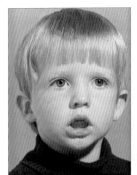

Left: A slightly gormless Daws, aged 2.

Below: Fellow Marlow Minis Paul and Derek look a bit wary of my celebrations.

Below left: My love of football only just lost out to rugby. But I'm still a mad keen Everton fan.

Above: Aged 10. I'm sure my judo exploits set me up to play my aggressive style of rugby.

Left: The Holy Trinity Primary football team after victory over local rivals Danesfield.

Above: Dave Alred would be proud!
Above right: Chiltern Sevens was always a muddy affair but on this occasion success was sweet.

Above left: Thanks for keeping this awful record of an awful haircut, Mum!

Above: My other winter sports included skiing – which will be my first holiday when I retire.

Left: This proficiency award from the Rugby Academy at Taunton School, when I was 14, sealed a week that ultimately drove my passion for first-class rugby.

RUGBY FOOTBALL UNION

RUGBY ACADEMY
TAUNTON SCHOOL
AUGUST 1987

MATTHEW DAWSON

Matthew is a competitive player who has made excellent progress in the basic skills of the game to reach a high standard of play - A really good prospect.

Skill Assessment   Proficiency Award

123 - *Excellent*   Gold = *Excellent.*
Top Mark 124   *Matthew was a splendid*
                                    member of the Academy. Matt. C.

Charlie White
Divisional Technical Administrator

Great School Days. Off the pitch with Princess Diana, Peter Maxmin and rugby master, Colin Tattersall.

With ball in hand and a legendary RGS win against Wellington College in the Daily Mail Cup.

Thanks for all the tips Richard, but I'm off this way!

Above: Marlow Under-17s proudly display their latest Sevens trophy, in the company of two dodgy, hairy coaches.

Left: My pride and joy. All I ever wanted was that shiny purple England tracksuit.

Below: Those youths must have been so scared of that 15-year-old Firm Security Guard.

Above: My pal, Freddie.

Right: Cheer up, Daws! With fellow World Cup Sevens winners Tim Rodber and Nick Beal in 1993.

Below: My first Saints team photo in 1992, and I made the front row.

Above: Harvey Thorneycroft, Paul Grayson, Tim Rodber and Ian Hunter were great company at Aunty Ruth's Bar.

Smashed through the covers for four. Alec Stewart would be so proud.

Mum and Dad are my greatest fans. Thanks a million, guys.

The love of my life, Joanne, has ironically carried *me* through some tough times.

Above: That special day. My first cap for England, against Western Samoa, Twickenham, 1995.

Below: Trying to be flash. Out the side door for the Lions versus Queensland in 2001.

Above: From boy to man. Thrown in to the biggest of Test matches and, yes, I'm trying to boss, lads.

Below: Those forwards love a good huddle, as I dot over in the 3rd Test, Lions v South Africa, Ellis Park, 1997.

criticized Woodward's man-management style and revealed some secrets from inside the camp, and he never played for England again – and I was braced for the possibility that he would pull the plug on my international career. Instead, I was back in the number 9 shirt.

The weather was foul, but it was an experience I would not have missed for the world. The whole team was chomping at the bit from the first whistle, so keen were we to show everybody how united we were. And while the game, which ended 19–0 in our favour, provided an ugly spectacle for the fans, it gave me huge satisfaction. On my last start for England the heavens had opened and we had failed to come to terms with wet-weather rugby; the result had been a win for Scotland and for us another lost Grand Slam. The best part of eight months later and we dealt expertly with the conditions. The lesson of Murrayfield had been learned. What a year it had been.

6
Foot in Mouth

It happened when I was standing on the touchline minding my own business, a pack of ice pressed against the bruise on my backside that had put me out of training. The British and Irish Lions, one up in the best-of-three series, were only days away from potentially killing off the world-champion Wallabies. All minds were focused on the game. Well, all but one.

The night before, the midweek Lions had beaten ACT Brumbies in Canberra with the last kick of the game. It had been my kick, a conversion from wide out. It capped the most emotional evening I have ever spent on a rugby pitch. But Donal Lenihan, manager of the 2001 tour, did not have a herogram in his hand.

'Matt, a word.'

'Sure, Donal.'

I had long known that I would be fined for what I'd written in my diary, which appeared in the *Daily Telegraph* on the day of the first Test, painting an honest but less than flattering picture of the tour. I had prepared myself to lose as much as £3,000, given that at one point it had seemed I would be sent home. But when Donal announced that the figure, decided by coach Graham Henry and himself, amounted to one third of my tour salary, I nearly choked. The basic fee received by each member of the party was £15,000; Donal demanded £5,000. That was bad enough, but his explanation as to how they had arrived at the figure almost pushed me over the edge. He insinuated that the fine was small beer considering that the *Telegraph* had paid me £15,000 for the article.

'What?' I said. 'Say that again? You actually think I'm getting fifteen grand from the *Telegraph*? Are you serious? Donal, I'm being paid five hundred.'

My reply embarrassed him, but he was not for turning. 'Well, that is what we have decided,' he spluttered. 'And that's that.'

To this day I do not accept that I betrayed the Lions in any shape or form. Quite the reverse, in fact: it is my deep affection for the Lions concept which prompted me to speak out. Ask anyone who has worn the shirt. The Lions is supposed to be the pinnacle of your rugby career, the highest high. The 2001 tour, I believe as a result of mismanagement, was everything but.

Let me say right away that I had no axe to grind with either Graham Henry or Donal Lenihan at the start. On the basis of his coaching record in New Zealand and then with Wales, Henry appeared to have the qualifications, while Lenihan had already gone down in Lions folklore for his contribution to the 1989 tour, during which the midweek team he captained was fondly remembered as Donal's Donuts. Nor did I set out to cause trouble. The *Daily Telegraph*, to which I have contributed a column for many years, asked me to keep a diary which they would publish in two parts. I tend to keep one anyway, so it was no hardship. I agreed to write a personal account of a summer with the Lions. Given the success I had enjoyed four years earlier I fully expected it to be a glowing account of a wonderful experience.

It is true that because the 1997 tour to South Africa had been such a success in every way it was always going to be a tough act to follow. That, however, does not excuse the failings in Australia, where there was a total absence of communication, trust and respect. It quickly became apparent that the Lions selectors had got it wrong in appointing Henry. It didn't bother me in the slightest that he was a New Zealander rather than hailing from the British Isles. Wayne Smith, my Kiwi coach at Northampton, could have done the job, no question, because he can coach elite athletes. He doesn't have to start something at the base level. He has this ability to gain respect very quickly because of the way he is. He has an X factor which you can't really describe. Henry, sadly, showed us none of those attributes. I remember the morning after my diary had appeared, when I went to apologize to all the coaches one by one. Henry turned to me and said, 'Daws, I know I'm not being inspirational at the moment. I don't feel I'm inspiring myself at the moment.' We were one up in the series, having just, on the last day of June, trounced the world champions in their own backyard, and he came out with that!

Donal, too, was a big disappointment. Based on what we had all heard of his involvement in 1989, if there was one person who was in a position of real influence to make sure the tour had total direction in every department it was the team manager who had been there and done it. But, as with Henry, it was almost immediately obvious that he wasn't the right person. It was as if he had watched *Living with the Lions*, the video account of the 1997 tour, and decided to replicate it frame by frame. The irony of it was that while he chose the same motivational company his predecessor Fran Cotton had hired, 'Impact' were miles down the line in their development from where they had been at Weybridge four years earlier. They had clearly moved on, but the Lions were still doing the same thing. I remember asking myself the question, 'Are we trying to copy 1997 or are we trying to put 2001 on the map?' It was as if Lenihan and Henry tried to take all the good things out of 1997 but without that core understanding of why they had been done. That doesn't come across in the video.

Take something as seemingly mundane as a pub visit in the week before departure. In 1997 we trained bloody hard, but two days before we left Fran and Ian McGeechan organized a free bar for us at a pub in Weybridge. Everyone just got on it, got drunk and got to know one another. We then piled back to the hotel and mucked about together. It was just a bit of a giggle, but the barriers between nationalities and cultures came crashing down. At the time no one fully understood the magic of that night, but it provided the foundations for a bond that united us throughout the tour. By running around the hotel making fools of ourselves, all of a sudden we had something to build on. I had not known Neil Jenkins, for instance, before that night, but from then on whenever I saw him or sat next to him on the bus we had something to talk about. That was the point of the exercise. Not because we wanted to go out, get bladdered and wreck our bodies.

Geech understood that, Lenihan and Henry patently did not, because four years later when the pub visit was, inevitably, arranged for two days before we flew Down Under, the occasion was an unqualified failure. Initial enthusiasm evaporated when we saw the venue that had been chosen, in the middle of nowhere. And inside there was nothing; no darts, no skittles, nothing like that. Then word reached us that referee Ed Morrison had been asked to come down the next day. 'Why?' we asked. 'Oh, because they've arranged a full contact session, bosh on bosh.' We put our beers down, there was a lot of swearing, and we all reordered . . . pints of Coke. No one wants to be a fool and not perform. We're all professionals. So we drank up, headed back and were tucked up in bed by 11 p.m. There had been a total lack of appreciation as to the point of the exercise, but the management were happy enough. They were able to tick the box beside Pub Visit.

For all that, there was no real bad feeling at the start, even if it did seem like being back at school. Everyone was so professional in their attitude. But then we were split into two groups and it was immediately obvious from the selections what was happening. From minute one, Henry had his Test XV. And he had Rob Howley at scrum-half. I was big enough, old enough and ugly enough to accept that, and to tell myself 'You've been here before, fine. Train hard, play well and enjoy yourself.' But in the back of my mind I thought, 'How can you be so pig-headed? There are bound to be injuries, dips in form. You cannot make hard and fast decisions like that before the tour has even begun.' I had understood in 1997 why Geech put certain pairings together – Rob and Gregor Townsend at half-back, for example. Austin Healey and I were nowhere near Rob at the time, and obviously Gregor was going to play at 10. They needed to build a relationship. But in 2001 Henry put together the whole back line and the whole forward pack. How players reacted depended on their temperament. I, for one, gritted my teeth and vowed to prove him wrong, but some quickly became disillusioned by the treatment they received.

I still get angry when I think of the confident player Ben Cohen was when he left and the shattered figure he cut when he returned home. And why? Because he didn't pull up trees in his first game and was immediately written off and given a starting position in the wilderness XV. Before the tour his dad had died in horrendous circumstances and his home had been burgled. Yet he was made to feel like a spare part in Australia, reduced to the role of sightseer with his family who had come out to support him. I think the final straw came when he unwittingly missed a training session that had been called on a day off on which he'd arranged to visit the Blue Mountains with his mum and fiancée. He had to leave early, before the management had changed their plans and informed the players of the session. Ben was the only absentee. It looked like he had snubbed it, but that was not the case. No one ever asked for his side of the story. It reached the point that he stopped caring.

What upsets me the most is that there were probably 10 or 15 guys on that tour who I still don't know. Contrast that with the sense of camaraderie in 1997, the feeling that we were truly four nations coming together as one, and in so doing were staying true to the Lions' ethos and traditions. 'I've given a lot of things up,' Geech had said on the eve of the second

Test in Durban, 24 hours before we would secure an unassailable 2–0 series lead. 'I love my rugby, I love my family, and when you come to a day like this you know why you do it. It's a privilege because we are something special. You will meet each other in the street in 30 years' time and there will just be a look and you'll know just how special some days in your life are.' Just recalling those words makes me tingle. The hairs on the back of my neck stand to attention. And he was absolutely right. I don't talk to Jenks and Rob Howley very often, but when I do see them we exchange that look and that's all it takes. It gives me a huge buzz to know that a game of rugby can do that to you, and it upsets me that 2001 failed to leave any discernible mark at all. When I see even those guys I know well from that tour I don't think of 2001. We are not bound together by precious memories.

Take one incident in our fifth game, against the New South Wales Waratahs in Sydney on 23 June, when Duncan McRae assaulted a defenceless Ronan O'Gara, hammering him with 11 unanswered punches. As a squad we were incensed, yet it did not bring us as close as it should have done because of the way the tour was managed. The midweek boys were pretty tight with RoG and we were all ready to kick off about it, but because not everyone knew everybody else some only enquired whether he was okay rather than taking him out for a beer. The squad was completely split.

In his book *Henry's Pride: Inside the Lions Tour Down Under*, Henry described my diary as 'an age-old story, a betrayal of confidence and your mates for 30 pieces of silver', and claimed 'it's impossible for players to contribute to the building and bonding process and play the role of critic at the same time.

Scientists will tell you that you're using a completely different set of brainwaves. It has to be either one or the other.' I would agree that you can't build and bond and then criticize, but on this tour we weren't given an opportunity to B and B on our own and therefore people became critical. As I said, I only got to know people superficially. On a tour with a short timespan it is imperative for players to be able to B and B away from rugby. It is a process fundamental to the success of any team. The management patently did not understand that.

Henry further claimed that my diary 'added to the feeling that individuals were inflating the needs of their own egos well beyond any sense of the team and the touring requirements as a whole'. I completely disagree. There were probably more egos in 1997. In fact, I don't think there were any on the 2001 tour at all, other than within the management. Henry also accused me and Austin Healey, who was similarly outspoken in a series of columns which appeared in the *Guardian*, of representing a view 'of what was happening on tour which, at least temporarily, soured their relationships with their mates and couldn't help our chances of achieving what we wanted to achieve as a group with a common aim'. Well, we didn't have a common aim because it was the responsibility of the management to get us all on board, whether it be socially or rugby wise, and they failed to do so. Henry seemed to have absolutely no perception of what it meant to the players to be on the tour. It wasn't a selection issue, as he apparently believed. Of course the ultimate dream was to play in the Test matches, but actually we all just wanted to get the shirt on and play in any game. I've spent the whole of my career being picked and dropped. Ask any scrum-half who has been selected ahead of me or been on the bench and they'll tell you I'll help them to the nth degree, whether it's with preparation or passing. I'll give them ideas to enhance either their performance or the team's performance. That's where I come from.

I thought the players in 2001 were fantastically mature. Just before the first Test we were in Coffs Harbour for a midweek game against the New South Wales Country Cockatoos. In our last training session, Henry used the midweek side to run against the Test side, as though we were Australia. It should have been *our* team run, but we just got on and did it and then went out the next day and performed. There were plenty of examples like this where the players demonstrated maturity, but it just came to a breaking point where we thought, 'Oh come on, you can't keep carrying on like this, you have to treat everyone the same.'

It is not good enough for Henry to bemoan what he terms 'several obstacles built into the framework of the tour which made our aims hard to achieve and splits more likely', i.e. the lack of a social dimension and the late kick-off times. As he said, there was not that 'ideal balance between Being and Winning', but whose fault was that? It wasn't the players who agreed to the itinerary. We needed proaction, not reaction. Before the tour he should have looked at the kick-off times and realized that they would mess around with the social aspect of the tour. Not after we had lost the series 2–1.

Let's get it straight. The number one problem on the tour was communication. The lines of communication didn't have to be 'tweaked', as Henry put it, they needed to be totally relaid. Tweaked? Good grief. The guy's on a different planet.

*   *   *

I actually lost faith from the very first meeting, during which Henry got up and gave this spiel about how he understood the Lions and was immersed in the history and the traditions. I thought, 'Come on, don't try to pretend to be somebody you're not. To us you are a coach. Prove to us you're a really good coach and you'll get everything out of us. We don't need you to be a Lion or a former Lion.' So what was his first selection? Brian O'Driscoll, perhaps the finest centre in world rugby, at full-back. Gobsmacked, I was. What is the point of that? Drico had never ever played at 15. Are you telling me that in a Test match you're seriously going to put Brian O'Driscoll at 15?

My frustrations grew over the coming weeks and I logged it all in my diary as we went from Perth across to the north-eastern tip of Australia, down to Brisbane and Sydney and then back up to Brisbane for the first Test at the Gabba on 30 June. The timing of my article, on the morning of the game, is inexcusable, but what appeared in print wasn't just how I was feeling, it was how the majority of the squad were feeling. We *were* being treated like kids. We had some sensational backs on that tour – O'Driscoll, Jason Robinson, Dafydd James, Mike Catt, Rob Henderson and Jonny Wilkinson to name but six – but we must have spent the first two or three weeks being taught how to scissor and mis-pass. I'm talking here about basics. When Smithy first came to Northampton I remember him teaching us how to scissor, but that was fine because there was a technical reason for it: he wanted to change the way we did it and he kept it to two minutes each session. With Henry we did it session after session. It was so unneccessary.

I would never say that coaching the Lions is easy, but Geech certainly made it look easier than Henry, and he didn't have anything like as much talent at his disposal. He just pointed us in the right direction and guided us. I was a raw arse in South Africa, but by the end of the tour I felt I had total control of what I was doing. That was as much down to Geech as it was to me. He made us believe we were the best players in the British Isles, and out of that belief came increased confidence. Four years later why did Henry not go to O'Driscoll and Wilkinson and work with them on attacking strategy? How are we going to do this? How do you want to work this? Why did he not feed off them, because those two are incredible talents and were in the sort of form that could have ripped the Wallabies apart. And they were not alone. Look at the first Test, which the Lions won 29–13. People put it down to great coaching, but Jason Robinson, man on man, skinned his opposite number alive for the first try. You don't coach that. You don't spend six weeks teaching Jason how to do 'fast feet'. Then Drico ran in from 50, breaking through a tackle, stepping past two men and finishing off. You don't coach that either. That's natural talent. The win was not down to any coaching masterstroke. The guys just went out and played.

But by then the damage had been done. My diary, published that day under the headline 'Harsh regime tears us apart', detailed how I was shattered three days before we even left the UK. It then went on to describe wall-to-wall training sessions, with no time for anything else but sleep. I had been consumed by frustration to the point that I hadn't been able to see the dangers in going public with some fairly heavy thoughts. At the time I genuinely hadn't foreseen any serious consequences. In fact I hadn't given it a second thought until Austin, with whom I was sharing a room, came up to me just before we left for the Gabba.

'You're in deep shit, mate,' he said.

'Yeah, right, Oz.'

I picked up my diary and skimmed through it again.

'What's wrong with that? I said that Henry didn't inspire me. Well, he doesn't.'

I can now look back and admit that this was symptomatic of how I was as a person at that time. I was a little bit blasé. My brain didn't say to me, 'Okay, Daws, that might be how it is, but people don't necessarily need to know that right now.' If I'd put it across in a better way, not used emotive phrases like 'treating us like kids', it probably wouldn't have created such a stir, because the actual text was not too bad. It was just certain words that sensationalized it. And because Donal didn't give the press anything all tour long they were baying for something to get their teeth into and make a meal out of.

But I was insensitive to such matters of detail so during the Brisbane Test match I was oblivious to the storm brewing. I couldn't understand why a television camera kept following me around. I was just doing what I normally do when I'm on the bench, encouraging and loving every minute of it. So why wouldn't that camera leave me alone? I kept thinking it must be because I was about to come on. But it wasn't that at all.

I remember thinking it was strange I hadn't been brought on because I thought I'd been playing well in the games in which I'd been involved. It had been a close call, they went with Rob. Been there before, I thought. No worries. But Rob was tired, he'd worked really hard, and I thought I must get on. It wasn't until I got back into the changing rooms at the end, after falling out with some jobsworth for taking a match ball to give to Martin Johnson, that I began to realize the trouble I was in. As I handed the ball to Johnno, our media liaison officer Alex Broun tapped me on the shoulder.

'Daws, I need to talk to you.'

'Okay, Alex, in a minute.'

'No, Daws, now. It's Donal. You've got to speak to him.'

Life with the Lions – part one of my account of the 2001 Tour

Saturday, 26 May
Drove down to Tylney Hall with Ben Cohen. Beautiful old manor house with great surroundings and facilities. See a lot of familiar faces, but also many who are known to me only by reputation. Rooming with Neil Jenkins, an old mate from the Lions tour to South Africa in 1997. Has some unique habits, particularly when parading before bedtime. Great to catch up with him and other old friends over food before Impact, the management team-building group, set us our first test. Lots of puzzles to solve. A solid third place out of five sees us win early respect. Bit restless in evening as real rugby starts tomorrow. Really looking forward to training. Two weeks' rest has done me world of good.

Sunday, 27 May
8 a.m. wake-up call. Teams listed by Graham Henry [GH] for first two matches on tour. I am down to play in second game. Morning training sees us run through some loose patterns before two sessions with Impact: a chat about qualities that make a Lion followed by dragon boat racing. Get wet, but good

for team building. Still time for continuity training with [assistant coach] Andy Robinson [AR], two kicking sessions with Dave Alred [DA], plus tests on my shoulders and legs for insurance purposes. So knackered by end that I'm fit for nothing.

Monday, 28 May
Meet to discuss lineout moves and core techniques and structure with GH and AR. Then more kicking, followed by midday date with Impact, who bring in musical group specializing in samba. Idea is that we each have a role (instrument) to play in team situation (band). I play bass drum which seems boring but when we come together the place is jumping. Wicked activity – thoroughly enjoy it. Lunch offers a chance to mock tone deaf among us before we go to Aldershot for open session. Feeling tired but like defence, and it's our turn with Phil Larder [PL]. Sense we are moving along as a squad very quickly. Not running before we can walk, just travelling with engines firing on all cylinders. See Impact again after dinner for open-your-heart session. Had to outline personal qualities – at best, at worst, at most irritable. Learn a lot about each other and most importantly about myself.

Tuesday, 29 May
No rugby – just as well, as feeling shattered. Morning session with Impact, who divide us into teams of four and challenge us to climb a 33ft telegraph pole onto a 4ft by 4ft platform. Some find it easy, some struggle, but all make it. Support and trust very evident among squad. Most encouraging. Media afternoon at Tylney Hall. Absolute frenzy. Photos, interviews, you name it. Hate the way people keep bringing up 1997 and

Rob Howley's injury. Let me just get on with it. If I make it, great. If not, Rob or Austin Healey get my full support. Simple. Blazer and slacks arrive just in time for farewell dinner in London. Bit of a trek, but suppose it has to be done. Great trip back with Woody [Keith Wood] and Hendo [Rob Henderson]. Find a level of banter. Had heard a lot about Hendo without knowing him. Top man. Great wit. Very sharp.

Wednesday, 30 May

Wake at 8.15, absolutely shattered. Legs and mind have been worked hard. No rest or unwind time, therefore not sleeping very well. Train at Aldershot where reinforce line-out and scrum moves. Defence with Larder scheduled for 75 minutes. Turns into nearly three hours. Final session with Impact after lunch in which we discuss code of conduct. Divide into five groups to discuss dos and don'ts and come up with tour slogan: To Be The Best Ever. Supper, then off to pub on organized trip. Boys initially up for it but lose enthusiasm when learn referee Ed Morrison is in town to oversee contact session tomorrow.

Thursday, 31 May

Deemed to be most important day so far. Long meeting with GH regarding vision and selection policy, followed by contact session. Lot of running, but at least have afternoon off. Play few holes of golf with Brian O'Driscoll [Drico] and Ronan O'Gara [RoG]. Six-over for 11 holes. Quite pleased with that. Back to room to sort out kit. So much it's ridiculous. Leave loads behind. Chill out with food in room and then early night.

Friday, 1 June

Fall for old school trick of agreeing to radio interview without checking time. 7.10 a.m. get call from Radio Five Live. Just get packed in time for 8.15 departure to Heathrow. Singapore Airlines flight takes off at midday. Business class? That will do nicely. Sleep for three hours out of 14, so watch four movies. Austin in seat next to me sleeps whole way. Boring bastard. Quick stop in Singapore. Balsh [Iain Balshaw] and I spend it in gamezone trying to tire each other out so that we will sleep on onwards flight. No chance. I'm given seat next to gaffer who I've never really spoken to before. Plenty of time to break ice, plenty of brown-nose banter from boys. GH seems very knowledgeable and a genuine enthusiast. Very analytical of teams and individuals, yet likes to see flair and imagination.

Saturday, 2 June

Arrive in Perth at 2.30 p.m. and try to go for jog and stretch, but feel dizzy and tired. Doc sends me to bed for an hour or so. Feel much better, but wide awake by 10 p.m. Join Mike Catt, Jason Leonard [Jase], Hendo, Balsh and Oz [Austin Healey] for beer in Fremantle. Excellent time to unwind. Creep in about 1 a.m. and sleep well.

Sunday, 3 June

Up at 7 a.m. to train. Coaches thought boys would all be up wide awake. How wrong they were! We need a few more hours, especially with two sessions, full contact. AR growls a lot at us. Few knocks. Jenks clashes heads with Jeremy Davidson and needs 10 stitches. Buzz needs none.

Monday, 4 June

Team formally announced for Friday night against Western Australia: Rob playing, Oz on bench. Very disappointed not to be on bench, but will be fully focused for Tuesday's game. More contact sessions. Boys starting to tire quickly. 75-minute session becomes two hours. By time we have lunch and 45 minutes' sleep it's time to go again. Light session, but still on legs and mentally switched on. Jason Robinson has ankle knock in which management take great interest. He must be vital to their plans.

Tuesday, 5 June

At last a lie-in as Friday team trains first. Then it's our turn. [Fitness and conditioning coach] Steve Black [Blackie] warms us up with shuttle runs. Bit excessive as it turns into a short fitness session. As if we haven't run enough! Next it's catching drills with DA, followed by defence with PL at ruck and maul, then structure off lineout with GH and AR. Too structured – all we need is three or four calls and to execute them well. In a match have to play what's in front of you. Lawrence Dallaglio [Lol] runs into my jaw and fear for moment that my tour is over . . . then I start talking again, much to others' disappointment. Stay behind after session to kick and feel legs stiffening up. Thankfully we have a day off tomorrow.

Wednesday, 6 June

Relaxing day's golf with Drico, Mark Davies [Carcass], Jase and Rob. Message from Northampton team-mate Paul Grayson that he might be on bench for England in North America.

Blimey, must be desperate (only joking). Card school pleasant until Oz came in and skinned us.

Thursday, 7 June
Train hard. Warm-ups like full session. Friday team have short run. We do full monty. Think there is too much full contact and my suspicion is confirmed when Phil Greening twists his knee.

Friday, 8 June
Matchday. Beat Western Australia 116–10. Game is a nightmare. WA are awful, an amateur side playing the best in Europe. Spend game as waterboy, ferrying messages onto field between coaches and players. Prompt Robbo three times into making calls for the team. Rob and Oz play well so pressure is on for Tuesday. Grab bite to eat out as hotel food is appalling.

Saturday, 9 June
7 a.m. training so out of way in time for long journey across Australia to Townsville, but 5½-hour flight takes 14 hours – nightmare. Nightmare too for Simon Taylor. Took a bang on knee in last minute of game against Western Australia and has grade two anterior cruciate ligament tear – a shocker. All feel for him as we say goodbye at Perth. No time to dwell on injuries or you'll get dragged down.

Sunday, 10 June
Spotters [walking-pace manoeuvres drill] with AR. Not on same wavelength at moment. Out of England context things are not the same. Instead of feeding from my strengths, which

is understanding game, AR constantly credits himself with my ideas. Of course he's a coach and should be seen to coach, but he and PL seem to be on ego trip. Players getting a bit cheesed off with them. GH, on other hand, is impressing me more and more. Seems to listen to senior players and then adapt his ideas. Good tips on running lines and support lines. Teaches me not to ignore any kind of advice: it may be the one tip to complete the jigsaw.

Monday, 11 June

Go to Dairy Farmers Stadium, where tomorrow's match is to be played. Very humid still. Long session. AR and PL want to say and do their bit. Too long. Out in sun for two hours. Mindless preparation for game. Others have had two full contact sessions. Accidents waiting to happen. Lunch and sleep in afternoon. Haven't seen other part of squad for days. Meet over dinner and that's it. Already there is a sense of Test team being drafted. Rob, I feel, is in box seat, but I've been there before so I'll keep training hard and playing well tomorrow night will put pressure on selection.

Tuesday, 12 June

Matchday. Beat Queensland President's XV 83–6. Decide to shave head way it was on '97 tour. Feels good to have crop again. Just before boarding bus for ground get pep talk from GH. Bit over the top. Too fiery for second match on tour. Get a vibe that there are too many voices saying stuff that they don't know anything about. Keep quiet until half-time but then lose plot. Blackie in warm-up too panicky, AR and PL shouting and screaming. Players worrying about decisions that don't really concern them. Air views after GH addresses us at half-time, score 10–6 to us. Second half goes well as we win 83–6. Pleased with my physical and mental performance. Hope GH sees the bigger picture. Why no recovery fluids and food on bus? Shoddy. We are expected to train like maniacs and recover for the next day, but there are no recovery supplements or specific nutrition to help.

Wednesday, 13 June
Named in 22 for Queensland game. Disappointed not to play but at least in squad. Means I have to train *again* this morning. Warm up, but still sore from cramp in calves. Can't train. Have to watch. Good flight to Brisbane.

Thursday, 14 June
More mindless training. Coaching staff taking it too far. Boys are not enjoying themselves at all. No energy for bonding. What's the point of all that work and expense at Tylney Hall if boys never have time or energy to get to know each other when it counts? Lot of unhappy people, which is a shame because I think there's a better bunch of individuals than '97. People are scared of going out in case they are too tired to train. Midweek team (Stiffs) will depend on team spirit. Go out for team Chinese. Poor meal, poor service. Hendo and Oz nip out to McDonald's and sneak it in under table.

Friday, 15 June
Train for too long in morning then two hours of kicking at Ballymore with Jonny (Wilkinson), who can't get enough. Meetings in evening. More talk. Too much talk. Need more

enjoyment. Good chat with one of Welsh lads, who also feels quite strongly about how poor the tour is. He feels we are not being trusted. If it all goes wrong then players will get the blame because coaches have done all they can. They don't seem to realize that by flogging the boys they are not getting the best out of them. Should I calm down a bit? Perhaps.

Saturday, 16 June
Matchday. Beat Queensland Reds 42–8. Spotters and walk-through in Botanical Gardens bring back painful memories of day after 76–0 thrashing in '98 when John Mitchell beasted us as a deserved punishment. Martin Johnson [Johnno] at helm for first game on tour which lifts everyone. Get off to cracking start. Very physical, plenty of fights and shoe. Rob takes bang in ribs. Game won after 50 minutes (39–3 up) so I go on. Find it difficult to get into. Defend well, but have kick charged down for Queensland's only try. Gutted to have fucked up my chance to impress. Great win, but can't really join in cele-brations. Go for drink with Oz and Balsh, who says how he's hating tour so far. Symptomatic of how it's been for new boys, who expected best tour of their lives. Things need to change.

Sunday, 17 June
Travel to Sydney. Have chat with AR, who asks me if I am pissed off. Simple answer is yes, but have no time to explain. Fix meeting with him in Sydney tomorrow. Mood is better in camp because of win.

Monday, 18 June
Met with AR. Tell him how I feel about way management are treating players. I understand that there's a lot to get through, but there is too much wasting energy. We are spending too much time on the set-piece and not enough reacting to what's in front of us. Also tell him training needs more variety. The boys need it. We are simple souls, easily pleased. AR says he's finding it hard because he's not the boss. Has to support GH. No wonder Wales are so poor!

Tuesday, 19 June
Matchday. Lost to Australia A 28–25. Spotters at 11 a.m. Did far too much running, especially the forwards. Seems like coaches have forgotten what a long season the boys have had. Yes, we're up for a Lions tour, but there's only so much that is good for you. Drive to hotel in Gosford where doze, before being woken by DL telling us to change in hotel as dressing rooms at ground are too small (they aren't). GH does pre-match but doesn't inspire me at all. Too much shouting and screaming. Picks out individuals to wind them up but all very childish. We then play like dicks. No territory, no initiative, no energy. Look tired mentally and physically whereas Aussies play basic football. Come off bench and, with Oz, change pace of game. GH told me to make a difference and I think I do. But miss two kicks that could have won us the match. Really pisses me off. I have to kick my goals. DL hacks me off with post-match comments. Treats us like kids. As if we wanted to lose. Having flogged us for three weeks, defeat was waiting to happen. Senior players had warned management, but they didn't listen.

Wednesday, 20 June

Rob not fit for Saturday so I'm in against New South Wales. Coaches give us a bollocking about defence and decision-making in Australia A game. Twenty tackles missed. Highest I've ever been involved with in all rugby. Training put back to afternoon. Boys would have rather trained in morning to give longer period of time off, but management plainly don't know how we tick. Train for 2½ hours. Lots of defence. Neil Back and Dan Luger clash heads. Luges fractures eye socket. Big blow to Test team as he was on fire.

Thursday, 21 June

It's official – some of the boys have decided to 'leave the tour'. We said at Tylney that if this should happen we would implement peer pressure, but to be frank with so many young players it is hard to avoid. Oz had drunken chat with DL late last night, telling him, 'This is the shittiest tour I've ever been on. I'm the best player on the tour, why am I on the bench? If I'm on the bench any more I'm going home.' Probably had a little too much beer, but at least management now get picture. Balsh and I go shopping and then meet at Doyle's for official team dinner, only to find that everyone has gone their own way. Sums up feeling in camp at moment. Tell myself that from now on I'm going to be positive and focus all my energy on Lions and playing to my full potential. Saturday is big day for me. No one thinks I can get selected. I'm going to prove them wrong.

Friday, 22 June

Meet Mum and Dad, who have flown in to follow rest of tour. Are very upbeat and encouraging when I mention under-currents in camp. Surprisingly tired so have early night. Feel a little edgy, but want to get this shit show back on the road. I have nothing to lose. I will give it everything. If it works, great. If not, so be it.

Saturday, 23 June

Matchday. Beat NSW Waratahs 41–24. Game a 40,000 sell-out with arrogant Aussies everywhere. How the English can be accused of arrogance is beyond me compared to this. Jason Robinson stopped in street by one guy who asked what the ntl logo on shirt meant. JR, being a polite type, starts to explain. Bloke interrupts and says, 'And I thought it meant "no talent, lads".' One funny guy, eh? Evening kick-offs are such a drag. Too much time to think about what may or may not happen. Up and down game. Get off to good start but end up letting them score four tries. PL won't be happy. No doubt he'll piss us all off even more. Fairly happy with my game, but get done completely in last minute, stepping aside from high kick for a shout of 'my ball' from behind. One of their guys!

Sunday, 24 June

Travel up to Coffs Harbour. Arrive just in time for more line-out, more scrums. Team for Tuesday is announced. Balsh at full-back, to give him confidence. He doesn't need confidence, he needs the ball in space. So much structure, not enough heads-up rugby. Boys genuinely hate playing the way we are. How can a team be successful when none of the players agrees with gameplan? It's inflexible and one-dimensional. Gut feeling is that we'll lose series 2–1. Terrible thing to predict, but it's how I feel. Obviously a low day for me. Get some sleep and have another look tomorrow.

Monday, 25 June

Difficult day. Our Aussie liaison guy, Anton Toia, dies in a freak swimming accident. Terrible, terrible thing. Reminds me that life has to be lived to the full. Have a surprisingly good feeling about tomorrow's game. Boys feel abandoned by coaching staff but have personnel to play their own way. Please just play what you see – and get Balsh in that outside channel.

Tuesday, 26 June

Matchday. Beat NSW Country Cockatoos 46–3. Game reflects how the boys feel – frustrated and disjointed. We feel like driftwood following the Lions. Big scoreline, but not good game at all. Have a few beers in team room – the first time we have celebrated victory as a team. Says something. Have a great moan to Mum and Dad and let off a lot of steam, which I think upsets them because it's a big tour for them as well. They want to look after their little son and don't like to see him so upset at such a huge moment in his life. Am trying to stay positive but I can't get away from how poor management have been towards the preparation.

Wednesday, 27 June

Test team announced. Disappointed to find I am on bench. Train for 2½ hours in pouring rain. Full contact, set-piece, the usual. Back to Brisbane. Day off tomorrow. What's this? Announcement from DL. 'Enjoy the day off, lads. Free day. Except for the meeting at 3.30 for lineouts and restarts. But that's it.' When will they learn that rest is better than training? Everyone, even Johnno, has a furrowed brow.

Thursday, 28 June
Spend morning in bed, then spotters in park followed by walk-through of moves we already know. Thanks, Donal. Go through diary column with Mick Cleary, ahead of its publication in *Daily Telegraph* on Saturday. So many mood swings. Realize how schizophrenic I have been. Strange how one's view can totally change from day to day. To think I said GH impressed me. He is absolutely useless. No management skills other than dropping hints of how good southern-hemisphere rugby is. PL and AR have got their arms tied because GH doesn't take any advice, on or off pitch.

Friday, 29 June
Kick at Gabba with DA and Jonny at 9 a.m. Return from 'walk-through' at 12.45. Hope we have enough in tank tomorrow. Boys train really well. Look sharp, but session just a bit too long. Rumour has it that there are 15,000 supporters here. Fantastic atmosphere.

Saturday, 30 June
Matchday. 1st Test: beat Australia 29–13. What a weird day. Spotters at 2 p.m. then back to room to chill. Oz has been talking to journalists and ribs me about a storm brewing over my diary that has been published today back in the UK. Little do I

know he is telling the truth. Game is sensational. Realized it would be a special day from moment we left hotel. Willie John McBride had made a surprise pre-match address in team room at hotel. Stirring words. Even though game is professional, he said, nothing has changed. The Lions shirt is everything. Great match. Encourage boys from bench. Gutted that I don't get on but Rob Howley looks sharp throughout. No sooner does final whistle sound than I realize that shit is going to hit fan over my article. Donal is quizzed on television about the piece but knows nothing of it and seeks me out. He is, naturally enough, angry with me. Brief Johnno about situation. Go back to hotel with Dave Williams, my agent, to address what to do. Frustrated by interpretation back home of my comments about players 'leaving the tour' – they weren't physically going absent, just mentally. Can't sleep because I know I'm in deep trouble. How deep will be up to management. I might be on my way home because of my selfish attitude.

WE SAT in a small room inside the Gabba, Donal Lenihan and I. Donal said he had just been interviewed by Sky who had told him that I'd said all the players were unhappy and that 12 people were leaving the tour. I replied that I hadn't said that, only that people were unhappy. I *had* said some boys had gone 'off tour' but it was just an expression; they hadn't literally left the tour. But Donal wasn't interested in my explanation. He simply asked me if the words in the article were mine. I told him that they were.

Then I got on the bus where all the boys were doing their newspaper columns. 'What have you done?' was the general comment. There were two viewpoints: either, 'Fair play, Daws, that's exactly how I feel,' or 'Not really bothered.' Not one player gave me a hard time. Not one. When we got back to the hotel I went straight to the internet room to download the *Telegraph* and check that my words were as I had filed them. They were.

My head was spinning by now, and it didn't help things when Dave Williams, my agent, phoned me in my room from reception to say that Mum had fainted outside the hotel at the shock of hearing the trouble I was in. (I would later find out that Mum and Dad were sympathetic with my position. They knew, because they were out there, that other players felt the same. They had caught the vibes from talking to parents, wives and girlfriends.) I had that same feeling in the pit of my stomach I used to have when waiting outside the head-master's office as a kid. Johnno popped in to see how I was. The answer he got was very tearful.

That night I couldn't get to sleep. Dave stayed in the next bed because Austin was spending the night away with his wife, Louise, in a nearby hotel, and we chatted until I eventually nodded off. But I woke early and the churning feeling returned to the pit of my stomach. I got up, dressed, and went to say sorry to all the coaches, one by one. I went into Graham Henry's room and said, 'I'm coming to apologise for the timing of that article, but not the content, because it's how I feel.' That was when he admitted to me that he felt unable to inspire himself let alone the rest of the squad. In other words, he was basically agreeing with what I had written in the paper. He gave me the impression that he was finding it really tough.

We had a team meeting before we travelled up to Canberra

for the game with ACT Brumbies. I had asked Johnno, Welsh prop Dai Young and Jason Leonard whether or not they thought I needed to speak to the squad, because in the state I was I didn't know. Their advice was that it wasn't vital because it was basically how everyone felt. I told them that the management felt I should formally apologize to the group, and that I would quite like to do it to clear the air.

It was awful walking into the players' room because the whole thing had been building and building, making me look like a whingeing idiot. In the room there was a circle of chairs. Austin, bless him, put one in the middle, and when I got up to go to it he started shouting, 'Stone him, stone him!' To my right, Jase, Lawrence and Austin sat next to each other ready to wet themselves while I spoke. I had to turn my back to them because had I caught sight of them I would have gone. They were all, apparently, bent double at the sight of me getting all emotional as I apologized and told the players that I felt I had let the squad down. But you have to be responsible for your own actions. You can't run away from them. That's part and parcel of life. I've done a lot of great things in my life I'm proud of, but there have been just a few that have dismayed me. I acknowledged that I should have kept my thoughts to myself but said that I wasn't going to retract what I'd written because that was how I felt.

I don't know how I would have coped with the tour had Austin not been around. Without his presence people would have been slitting their wrists. You need characters like him to lighten the mood. Seeing him getting a bollocking from Henry for talking or whatever provided light relief for everybody else. He knew that. He knew the mood needed to be changed and he took it upon himself to do it. He was brilliant. When the storm had first blown up around my diary I'd gone back to the room we were sharing only to find Oz packing my bag for me. 'I thought I'd do this for you because you'll be off tomorrow,' he said. There I was, in a world of bother, and Oz was ripping the piss out of me. Most other people would have made themselves scarce and left me to fester in my misery. Not him. It was exactly what I needed.

The other reaction which meant the world to me was that of Johnno, who threatened to quit the tour if I was sent home. That said to me that he knew exactly where I was coming from, that he knew the players were unsettled. I asked him what he thought was going to happen to me; were they going to send me home? He assured me that the players were sticking by me. He said he knew the tour had not been perfect and there was no way in the world I would be going home early unless he was sitting next to me on the flight. Knowing Johnno as I do, he would have done all he possibly could behind the scenes to rectify things because he's a player's player. As a person, a rugby player and a captain he is a top man. He has to be up there as one of the greatest captains ever because he is there for the players. Full stop. On the pitch he doesn't say an awful lot, he just leads by example. He does what he wants to say. He has this ability to think very quickly on his feet and be very calm. It's quite sickening really. He has not been taught how to be a captain, it's just the way he is as a person, and to this day I am very, very grateful to him for speaking up for me. Once he'd done so, I was never going to be sent home. It was a crucial intervention, akin to the Queen getting the late Princess Diana's butler Paul Burrell off the hook during his trial, because until then me getting my marching orders was, apparently, a very real possibility.

More than two years later, in a television programme entitled *The Henry Files* on ITV1 Wales, Henry said the following: 'Maybe, in hindsight, it would have been better to send him home.' Ah hindsight, the perfect science. If that was the way he felt at the time he should have done it. And I would have put my hand up and said, 'Well, all right, no problem.' Of course I would. What other options would I have had? As I said to him at the time, 'Do what you've got to do. I'm not going to retract what I said. If you feel you need to take that action I will have to deal with it.'

Following that players' meeting we tried to draw a line under the episode, although I realized it was not the end of the matter when Donal pulled me aside and told me I was to be fined. For public consumption, at least, the matter needed to end there, because if it was seen that there was continuing animosity within the England camp it would only fuel the fire and play into Australia's hands. We were, remember, one up in the series at the time with only a few days until the second Test.

Had things been different from a personal perspective, my attitude on and reaction to the tour might well have been very different. I had split up with Natalie, my long-term girlfriend, before coming away. It had been brewing for a while and I'd made the decision before leaving because I didn't want to go away with it unresolved. It was an opportunity to make a clean break, but it wasn't easy. Inevitably we ended up talking to each other on the phone, and we both got upset.

At the same time, of course, the tour wasn't going well. Austin was a great friend but I needed a few mates to chew the fat and chill out with, and then really focus on my rugby. I didn't want to go out and do anything stupid, sow my wild oats or whatever. I just wanted to draw a line. But that didn't happen, and subconsciously I'm sure it affected my mood. It was a very difficult time, and it reached a point where I just wanted to be somewhere else. But there was nowhere I could go, nothing I could do, except yet more training. There was always training. No other release or outlet for my pent-up emotions. Rugby players, like all other human beings, need emotional recovery time, and we just weren't getting it.

I knew Natalie would be upset at home and I thought it was only right that I phoned her to check she was okay. I couldn't just never speak to her again. She was finding it tough living in London and I was anxious for her because she sounded very low. I called her a couple of times, but there was nothing I could do really. I couldn't just jump in the car, go and see her and have a chat or take her out for a drink or for dinner. The situation became more and more stressful.

I had been through a period in my life where people around me weren't bringing me into line. Natalie might have told me every now and then not to be so rude, but I'd always have an excuse. There was no one to grab me by the scruff of the neck and say, 'Oi, Daws, fucking remember who you are, sunshine.' Not until that night in Brisbane when I was suddenly called to account, and it was like, 'Shit, what have I been doing?' It was my fault; there was no one else to blame. I had become a product of the international rugby environment I was and am in, where everyone always wants to talk to you because of your position rather than because of who you are. I had started to believe my own press. It was only when I got home and put it to Mum and Dad that they agreed I could be bloody unapproachable and that there had been times when they'd wanted to give me a good clip around the ear.

With the series still to be won there was no time for any deeper introspection, and I was fortunate to have a chance straight away to put things right against the Brumbies on 3 July. The emotion going through my body that day was indescribable. And the photos of me after the game sitting in that cubicle with my head in my hands, crying, said it all. I don't tend to show my emotions. But it was such a release of feelings which had been pent-up for the best part of four days. For that 80 minutes I was just my own person. I had a chance to redeem myself, and I took it.

Even in that game Henry didn't want me to kick. I missed two or three from long distance before the message came on to let Ronan O'Gara take over. Fair play, RoG turned round and said, 'Daws, no way, mate. You carry on.' I was so grateful to him for that because I could have sat there until I was blue in the face and said, 'I love the Lions and I love playing for them and I'm sorry.' But to actually have an opportunity as an individual to say something in a team game by landing a touchline conversion to win the game was something else. To have that one chance to decide a really big physical and mental battle, after all the cheap shots and verbals that had come our way, was a dream come true.

When Austin crossed the try line after the hooter to make it 28–28, I sank to my knees. I was so tired – physically, but more so mentally. Then I realized I had to take the conversion. It was a big moment for the squad that we won that game, in order that we kept the momentum going into the second Test. A deep breath, and over it went. Then came the tears. The majority of the team saw I was upset and came over to give me a hug – or to take the mick, depending on who they were. It was a really special moment. It was probably the first time I had cried in public since losing the final of the minis tournament for Marlow under-9s, and I like to think that was the start of the new me. I'm no longer afraid of showing my emotions. Maybe I was before.

Twelve hours later, I was brought crashing back down to earth when Donal told me I was to be fined a third of my tour fee. It was a totally arbitrary sum and I had no say in it. Simon Cohen, my contracts lawyer, was adamant I should appeal, but I couldn't be bothered with the process that would entail, not least because I knew I would be appealing to the people who had fined me. When Austin was called to a disciplinary hearing after the tour his judges were Lenihan and Henry. He was found guilty of bringing the game into disrepute and fined £2,000. So I chose to regard it as an expensive lesson. At that stage I was starting to see the light a little bit and had come to the conclusion that it was time everything about me moved on. I didn't want any stigma attached to me for the next few months, so I let it go.

The tour moved on to Melbourne and we were within 40 minutes of clinching the series when Henry delivered his half-time team talk under the roof of the Colonial Stadium. We were leading 11–6, and so good had we been that the Aussies would have gone in thinking they were 20 points down. They were getting absolutely battered. Scotty Quinnell was booming it up, smashing everyone. He was like a man possessed. Nothing new, just doing what he was good at, and they couldn't handle it. We were feeding off him and it felt awesome. So Henry pipes up, 'Fellas, what's going on? We're using Scott Quinnell far too much. He's getting smashed all the time. Let's play it wider, play it through the thirteen channel.'

I was dumbstruck. Did he just say that? Why did he just say that? I walked out of the changing room for the second half totally baffled as to why Henry had said those things, because we had such a good gameplan. They would have been shitting themselves. Scotty is a confidence man, and he just shrivelled. In the second half he wasn't in the game; he did nothing. We started to play from our own 22, trying to fling balls out wide, and all of a sudden it was us who were getting smashed. And then Jonny goes round the short side, tries to play the ball wide, gets intercepted by Joe Roff and the tide turns. From a position of dominance midway through the game we crashed to the heaviest ever Lions defeat to Australia, by 35 points to 14. Everyone was just so disappointed because they had been there for the taking.

What followed was just a shambles. Shocking, really. Austin and I, aka the Terrible Twins, were drafted in for the deciding Test in Sydney on 14 July, but the good news ended there. Our injury list was a mile long, and the training for those still standing was just crap. We were preparing for the biggest match in years and we were training in open parks with people surrounding the pitch pointing video cameras at us. What the hell were we doing? It was a complete nightmare. I could feel a series we'd so nearly won in Melbourne slipping away through our hands. Every day it was becoming more and more difficult to win this bloody series.

Austin took it upon himself to alert the coaches. 'Fellas, for fuck's sake, look at those people there under brollies with cameras stuck down their coats. Donal, who are those guys?'

Donal went over and talked to them before coming back wearing a self-satisfied grin. 'Oh, don't worry, they're just supporters,' he said.

'Are you serious, Donal?' I replied. 'If you were a fan videoing a training session you'd be doing it properly, not producing the lens from down your trousers, looking as though you're doing something you shouldn't be.'

It was so ironic that the Terrible Twins, who had supposedly wrecked the tour, were the only guys with the common sense to question what was going on. And our fears were realized come matchday. 'They seemed to be in position for the throw before we were,' said Keith Wood, our hooker and thrower-in. That's because the Wallabies knew all our lineout calls; they had indeed been spying. I know that for a fact because a member of Australia's 1999 World Cup-winning squad later confirmed it to me. They had someone at every single one of our training sessions in some way, shape or form. They knew everything. And is it any surprise? Our last session before the first Test in Brisbane, for instance, when we walked through our lineout moves, was staged in the Botanical Gardens, right across from their team hotel. Then, on the morning of the game, we went into Brisbane city centre and found a bit of grass in a pedestrian precinct where there were hundreds of people watching us.

So it was no coincidence that Justin Harrison took that ball off us at the last lineout of the deciding Test, when we were in a position to win the series with a late try. They'd been doing it all bloody game. I don't blame the Aussies because that is what we should have been doing. So there it was. Despite matching the world champions try for try courtesy of scores by Jason Robinson and Jonny Wilkinson, we had come up agonizingly short. The Wallabies ran out 29–23 winners. All that huff and puff, pain and heartache, and we had lost the series. I came home utterly disillusioned.

This was the second professional Lions tour, yet it was so unprofessional in so many ways. I would go so far as to say it was the least professional tour I've been on since the game went open. You name it – food, training, socializing, supplements – it was inadequate. They were flogging us to death in training yet there were no recovery drinks or sandwiches straight after the game. Everyone knows you need food straight afterwards. But there was none of that. No power bars or protein shakes. Nothing. Instead, we went into a tea room and got chicken and chips. What did they expect from us? We could only give so much; our bodies weren't able to do any more.

I went from quite tired to knackered to totally shattered. But despite that, I don't think that in 2005 the season has to be tailored around the Lions tour to New Zealand. Both the 1997 and 2001 tours came on the back of very busy seasons. We were just as tired in 1997 as we were in 2001. It is simply a question of how you manage the situation. Fran Cotton, team manager in 1997, took loads of stick, but my God, did he get things done and for the good of the whole travelling squad. My personal opinion is that that was not a priority for Donal

Lenihan and Graham Henry. Success, for them, was all that mattered. But the little things add up. The way they treated the media, for example, affected the players. The media felt shortchanged, so they tried to get hold of the players on their phones or tried to call them in their rooms. It was a distraction which could have been avoided had things been managed better.

The second of my two tours of duty has not, however, ended my love affair because it was a couple of individuals my gripes were with, not the Lions. The brand of the Lions is still immense, and the shirt should still be something every rugby player aspires to wear. That red shirt is worn by the best of the best, as was proved in that first Test in Brisbane. That performance was just phenomenal. We took the world's best team to the cleaners. The Wallabies subsequently proved their class by doing their homework, changing a few things and bouncing back to win the series. Fair play to them for that. But the team that took to the field at the Gabba – Matt Perry, Jason Robinson, Brian O'Driscoll, Rob Henderson, Jonny Wilkinson, Rob Howley, Tom Smith, Keith Wood, Phil Vickery, Martin Johnson, Danny Grewcock, Martin Corry, Richard Hill and Scott Quinnell – was by far the best Lions team I've been involved with. And that's one memory I will never forget.

Life with the Lions – part two of my account of the 2001 Tour

Sunday, 1 July
Feel like a schoolboy going to see headmaster. Quite appropriate in that what I did was a schoolboy error. Go to see Donal,

GH, AR and PL in turn to apologize for timing and breach of trust and confidence. I'm not making excuses or reneging on what I wrote, but I fully understand that it has harmed their reputation and taken the gloss off the squad's victory the night before. They all respond differently and in fact give me the kick up the backside I needed. Realize I have many bridges to build so it's head down and work for me. Team meeting before we head to Canberra. Ask Donal if I can address party. He agrees, so I put my apologies across and tell the boys how bad I feel at having let squad down. Some players feel I have nothing to say sorry for, but there might be one or two who think I have so it is a worthwhile exercise. Unbelievable support from lads. Donal pulls me aside and tells me I am going to be fined. No complaints.

Monday, 2 July

Train early at Bruce Stadium. Very light team run and kicking. Dave Alred [DA] tells me I'm kicking tomorrow. Looking forward to responsibility. Car runs out of petrol on way back to hotel and we spend 1½ hours waiting to be picked up. Straight into team meeting for Test 22. Feel tired so sit at back. Phil Larder [PL] senses I am a little low and offers me a protein bar. Appreciate gesture. Sleep until captain's meeting for tomorrow's game against Brumbies. Dai [Young] and Gibbsy [Scott Gibbs] motivate us by telling us a few home truths. See Mum and Dad and have a good chat about life here and at home. Mum had passed out on Saturday night due to a combination of no food and shock at trouble I had got myself in. Seems okay, but a little upset she had to be put in a wheelchair in front of her friends.

Tuesday, 3 July

Matchday. Beat ACT Brumbies 30–28. Feel nervous because I want to prove critics wrong about why I wrote what I did by having a big game. Want to show that it wasn't sour grapes or petulance on my part. Austin Healey ties scores by scoring try with last move of match, after hooter has sounded. Comes down to my conversion. That kick has more pressure on it than I can describe, but I nail it. Get a little emotional afterwards. No doubt I'll get some shit from boys but I've got used to that this week. Have held my head up high. Each of management shake my hand and praise me for having balls to land kick. It is a small way to repay damage of Saturday. Now hope I can make second and third Tests to further bridge build.

Wednesday, 4 July

Can't train for dead arse so Donal Lenihan [DL] takes opportunity to pull me to one side and break my run of 12 hours feeling human. Knew I was going to get fined, maybe as much as two or three grand, but when he says damage will be a third of my tour fee I nearly choke. To make matters worse he insinuates that fine is small fry considering what I have been paid by *Daily Telegraph* for article. Embarrass him by revealing I am getting £500 and not £15,000 as he thought. Miserable for rest of day. Speak to Johnno who, according to terms of our contract, should have been consulted about fine. Says he wasn't. Decide to drop topic to concentrate on second Test. Will appeal after tour. Travel to Melbourne and end day in casino.

Thursday, 5 July

Day off, except that required to do spotters with forwards. Take part in BBC Online forum. No surprise that majority of questions concern my *Telegraph* diary. Encouraged by mixture of reactions.

Friday, 6 July

Kicking practice under roof at Colonial Stadium with Jonny and DA. First time in enclosed arena. Very impressive. Session started well but kept thinking of Tuesday night's dramas, which distracted me. Team meeting in changing rooms with Graham Henry [GH]. Gets quite intense about tomorrow's game, warning against complacency. Think he's trying to get talk out of way so boys can get on with it tomorrow. Andy Robinson [AR] later gives forwards great chat before Johnno tells the whole squad we are on threshold of joining Lions legends. Only hope lads realize what we are heading for. Aussies don't often lose two games in a row. It's gloves off time.

Saturday, 7 July

Matchday. 2nd Test: lost to Australia 35–14. Matt Perry and I do not get up until 1300. Down for lunch and sample atmosphere in reception. Hundreds of people milling about singing and chanting. Their energy is to be applauded. It's relentless. 1700: meet with DL and GH. Donal speaks very well about the history and tradition of Lions. Good stuff. All the sort of motivating factors you need to tip balance your way. GH speaks about rugby and defence and smashing them in scrum and lineout. Blah, blah, blah. We've thought about that all week.

He just shows a nervous panic in his voice. Leave it out, will you? Should be a time to have hairs on neck standing up, not thinking about structure. He hasn't a clue. Have a great warm-up and boys get stuck into Aussies in first half. We make two or three breaks but don't finish them off. Scott Quinnell [Q] is immense. 11–6 up at half-time and go in for chat from GH. I stay for five minutes before having to go and kick. In that five minutes he decides to change the way we are playing. 'Stop using Q so much, let the midfield set targets,' he says. I have never heard so much shit in all my life. Q is destroying Aussies single-handedly. Why stop doing that? We just need to finish chances. Needless to say, Q stops taking ball up and midfield gets smashed trying to run from deep. Lose direction and shape. Aussies start getting ball in our 22, where they are deadly, and give us a good kicking. I can't believe what GH said at half-time. Get on for last three minutes – just in time to get a mouthful of sledging. 'Ready for Sydney, eh?' From high of Brisbane to low of awful performance in Melbourne. Rob has damaged ribs so I may get my chance in decider. Austin gives me one of his knowing looks, as he predicted at start of trip that we would play one Test together at 9 and 10. Get back to hotel where fans still give us royal welcome. They are magnificent. I've never been a believer in doing for anyone else other than the team, but might have to make exception for these fans.

Sunday, 8 July
Get up for recovery session in pool before going to casino to spend my winnings from Wednesday. Lose it in about 30 minutes. Sums up weekend in Melbourne. Drift back to hotel

where I see Rob Howley. Told he has broken a rib and is definitely out of third Test. Fly to Sydney. End up in cool yet fairly dodgy bar in clubland Sydney. Come back and spot the lads not in 22 getting hosed in bar. Good for them.

Monday, 9 July

Gym in morning. Good to get a decent weights session in early in week. Sleep all afternoon. Westy [Dorian West], my room-mate, kept me up all night with his snoring so it's time to catch up. A team dinner has finally been arranged, at Rib and Rumps restaurant. Can hardly walk back to hotel. Body doing overtime to digest about 4kg of meat. Play some abusive games around table. Taking the piss out of anybody, anything. Good night, good banter. Should have done this weeks before.

Tuesday, 10 July

Today and tomorrow are going to be the main rugby days so that we can get some rest on Thursday and Friday. Go over new strategy relating to territory during video session. Field position is going to be key as we got it so wrong in second half in Melbourne. PL and GH make it fairly clear how they want to go about it. Sounds very simple. Certainly not rocket science. Hopefully boys can get their heads round it pretty quickly. Looks like I'll be playing as coaches ask my opinion about team strategy. Afternoon training is a little flat. No wonder, having sat around all morning. At this stage of tour I think we should train in mornings. Energy levels are so fragile. They need to be monitored.

Wednesday, 11 July

Stark contrast in session this morning. Even though everyone is soaked the team run goes really well. Think conditions focus the mind. Go through kicking strategies which will be vital for Saturday. Coaches very conscious of clock and not spending too much time out on pitch. Maybe earlier complaints have not been totally ignored. GH has quiet word about how we should make sure we are on same wavelength this week. Don't know what to say. Food at hotel has not been that good so order a sandwich and go to bed to chill. Later check on Ben Cohen who missed training as he was visiting Blue Mountains with his family. Was told yesterday that training was only for Test 22 so he and RoG thought they were not needed for week. RoG got taxi to ground but no one knew where Ben was. Bless him. Met with Mick Cleary to discuss second diary article for *Telegraph*. Shall I continue where I left off or leave further controversy for a later date?

Thursday, 12 July

Now used to the fact there is no such thing as a free day. Today is one of those free days. Leave my room just after 10 a.m. for a trip to Stadium Australia and do not get back in until 3.30 p.m. It is a long ride from Manly up to Homebush where the Olympic Stadium is. That is the reason for the trip – to get the boys used to having to spend the best part of an hour in a bus before running out. I'd been there before, playing for England against Australia two years ago. The whole site is now done up, which it wasn't then. However, the athletics track has disappeared as they have reconfigured the stadium. Shame. The lads were looking forward to seeing where Cathy

Freeman and Denise Lewis had done their stuff. Have a long kicking session. Am back-up to Jonny. Have my own press conference to try and satisfy hounding hacks that me and GH are cool. Manage not to give much away. Worry for Oz, who has got a pain across his body like a stitch.

Friday, 13 July
No rest for the wicked. 11 a.m. team run at Manly Oval. Stay for more kicking. It has to be a walk-through as so many people not able to train properly – Oz, Q, Neil Back, Hendo and Drico not at full throttle either. Supposed to be a closed session. Impossible at Manly, which is ringed by open spaces. Must be 200-plus people watching us do our spotters. Lunch with Mum and Dad. Have to wear civvies and shades because place is heaving with supporters and I need a couple of hours with them to chill. Starting to get a little edgy about tomorrow. Really want to perform but just hope we've enough in our bodies to cope with the adrenalin of all day Saturday. Friday night before big game is not ideal time for a major signing session. But sponsors ntl bring at least 50 shirts into team room for us to autograph. Hotel food is again awful. This is getting ridiculous. So unprofessional. Have to order pizzas as not enough carbo-food. Try to stay up late but very tired. Nervous energy had started kicking in during earlier meeting when AR and Johnno spoke and I was asked to say a few words. Mood is well set for tomorrow.

Saturday, 14 July
Matchday. 3rd Test: lost to Australia 29–23. Bit edgy. Can't sleep so get up and go down to breakfast. Not like me. Usually

sleep to midday when there is an evening kick-off. Hear first rumours that Oz is out. Go back to room and sleep. Get up for spotters. There is Andy Nicol, Scotland scrum-half and emergency cover for Oz. Andy Nic was on holiday leading a tour group. He has a pile of papers with him with all moves and calls on. Let him stand in during spotters. He has a lot to catch up on. Still edgy. Finding it hard to kill time. Twiddle thumbs. That doesn't last long. See copy of Austin's controversial *Guardian* column in local paper. See Alex Broun [media liaison] look at me. Give ironic smile. Leave hotel at 4 p.m. Boys are in good order. Forwards are feisty and aggressive. Much different from Melbourne. The game is hard. I get a fierce rucking after five minutes. I wonder why they've targeted me. Ploy has worked. My hamstring is throbbing. Have to keep icing it through the game. Have a decent half. Great start to second half when Jonny scores. But we're not on top of it. Give away too many positions and penalties. We're not quite there. The game is lost – so too the series. Changing room is silent. Donal speaks and gets emotional. Don't really feel for him. No good getting emotional when we've lost. He could have been a big influence on getting things done but missed a few tricks. Feel it's all his fault as in 1997 the strength of team manager Fran Cotton was that he got what he wanted. Boys shake hands with one another but, to be brutally honest, we weren't good enough as a team to win. Individually the talent was tremendous, but we were undermined as a unit by all the injuries and by the public show of disinterest GH gave the midweek boys. That cost him the respect of some of the boys. Post-match reception is fine. Aussie boys are good lads despite Austin's obvious hatred of all men born in Australia. Suppose it is good that someone else is in shit instead of just me.

Sunday, 15 July
All over, then. Minimal sleep. The Stiffs have convened a 12.30 meet in the bar. Can't shake off sense of disappointment. Know what it's like to have won a Lions series and realize what a monumental achievement it is. All need to reflect on how Lions tours should work. Our build-up was crazy. Some boys were playing their fiftieth game of the season. Not due to leave until Tuesday. A bit of a holiday. Rugby is going right to the back of my mind.

2001 Lions tour to Australia: squad and results

Forwards: Jason Leonard (England), Phil Vickery (England), Dai Young (Wales), Darren Morris (Wales), Tom Smith (Scotland), Keith Wood (Ireland), Robin McBryde (Wales), Phil Greening (England), Danny Grewcock (England), Martin Johnson (E, capt.), Scott Murray (Scotland), Jeremy Davidson (Ireland), Malcolm O'Kelly (Ireland), Neil Back (England), Richard Hill (England), Martyn Williams (Wales), Colin Charvis (Wales), Scott Quinnell (Wales), Lawrence Dallaglio (England), Simon Taylor (Scotland); replacements: Gordon Bulloch (Scotland), Dorian West (England), David Wallace (Ireland), Martin Corry (England)

  Backs: Iain Balshaw (England), Matt Perry (England), Dan Luger (England), Dafydd James (Wales), Ben Cohen (England), Jason Robinson (England), Mike Catt (England), Will Greenwood (England), Mark Taylor (Wales), Brian O'Driscoll (Ireland), Rob Henderson (Ireland), Jonny Wilkinson (England), Neil Jenkins

(Wales), Ronan O'Gara (Ireland), Matt Dawson (England), Robert Howley (Wales), Austin Healey (England); replacements: Scott Gibbs (Wales), Tyrone Howe (Ireland)

(P10, W7, D0, L3, F449, A184)

Western Australia 10 Lions 116 (Perth, 8 June)
Queensland President's XV 6 Lions 83 (Townsville, 12 June)
Queensland Reds 8 Lions 42 (Brisbane, 16 June)
Australia A 28 Lions 25 (Gosford, 19 June)
New South Wales Waratahs 24 Lions 41 (Sydney, 23 June)
NSW Country Cockatoos 3 Lions 46 (Coffs Harbour, 26 June)
1st Test: Australia 13 British Isles 29 (Brisbane, 30 June)
ACT Brumbies 28 Lions 30 (Canberra, 3 July)
2nd Test: Australia 35 British Isles 14 (Melbourne, 7 July)
3rd Test: Australia 29 British Isles 23 (Sydney, 14 July)

7
Going Off the Rails

I had hit rock bottom. My personal life was a mess, the Lions experience had been a nightmare and I was out of the England squad, dropped after our latest Grand Slam misadventure. What promised to be the sweetest of years had turned horribly sour.

Six months earlier I'd been surfing the crest of a wave. England, playing their best rugby of the professional era, had been on the rampage in the Six Nations Championship, breaking more records than a bull in an HMV shop. I was a Lion again, dreaming of emulating the glory days of 1997, and I was still in a relationship. Then came foot and mouth, the epidemic in the countryside which put the Six Nations on hold and stopped our momentum in its tracks; then my candid account of life with the Lions which caused such a rumpus. Sandwiched in between, Natalie and I split after six years together. And then, in October 2001, just when I thought things couldn't get any worse, we went to Dublin.

For half a year we had anticipated this postponed match against Ireland, knowing that victory over an opponent England had beaten in her last six meetings would bring with

it the Triple Crown, the championship title and, most importantly of all, a first Grand Slam since 1995. How could we not
feel good about the prospect, having already rewritten the
record book with 215 points and 28 tries in beating Italy,
Scotland and France by unprecedented scores; and registered
England's biggest ever win in Wales? And when I was then
reappointed as captain, after Martin Johnson broke his hand in
a club match, life seemed to be taking a turn for the better. But
it was a trick of the light. Fate had got plans for me and they
didn't include a champagne weekend in the Irish capital. The
alarm bells should have rung in my head long before a 20–14
defeat that required me, for the second year running, to pose
with the Six Nations trophy while appearing to chew broken
glass. During the abortive summer in Australia I had become
reactionary and over-emotional. I was a timebomb waiting
to explode.

It had probably begun on the first day of June with a phone
call from John Steele as I'd stood in the departure lounge at
Heathrow, waiting to fly to Perth in my Lions blazer. Steeley
and Pat Lam, coach and captain respectively at Northampton,
had spent all season saying they wanted me to captain Saints
for the 2001–02 campaign. We'd discussed it at length,
debated which players we were going to bring in, the whole
thing. I was really excited about it. It felt like the perfect time
in my career to become club captain.

'Daws, best of luck on the tour, hope it goes well for
you . . . Oh, and by the way, we've decided to make Budge
captain.'

Bang. Just like that. Totally out of left field.

'What? . . . Why?'

'I just think he's going to be under less pressure than you,' came the reply.

Sorry? Come again? Correct me if I'm wrong, but are we not talking about Budge Pountney, captain of Scotland?

That started the demise of my relationship with John Steele. It also set me on a downward spiral that would take an entire year to turn around.

Five weeks later I took another call. I was in Canberra, standing in the clubhouse at Bruce Stadium at the tail end of the most emotional evening of my career. My Lions diary was the talk of the rugby world and I had just shown what the Lions really meant to me by landing the match-winning conversion with the final kick of our game against ACT Brumbies. The tears were still wet and I was still pumped up as I had heard via another player that Clive Woodward had said on Sky that I should have been sent home for my *Telegraph* article. I took my mobile out of my blazer pocket and saw Clive's number come up.

'So, Clive, you want me on the plane, do you?' I said, wading straight in.

'Pardon?'

'You want me on the plane, do you?'

'Sorry? Why are you saying that?' Clive asked, the irritation obvious in his tone. 'I didn't say that at all. What I said is that had it been my regime you would have been on the plane home.'

'Oh . . .'

Well, that was just typical of what I was like. A loose cannon, not thinking about what I was saying before the words boomed out of my mouth.

And when England lost to Ireland almost four months later, I still hadn't learned to apply the safety catch. I fired off an email to Clive in which I gave a brutally honest assessment of where I thought we had gone wrong. 'We are very quick to, say, do 100 things 1 per cent better rather than one thing 100 per cent better,' I noted. 'Yet when we're being critical we always say, "Oh, that doesn't make any difference." But it does.' As in Australia with the publication of my *Telegraph* diary on the day of the first Lions Test, my timing was all wrong. I probably made four or five little points that might not have made a difference to that game in Dublin but which I considered important to maintain player harmony and team bonding. Clive, I suspect, took them as excuses for the team rather than as constructive criticism.

I had been injured during the game at Lansdowne Road, leaving the field just before half-time with a hamstring strain, but I would have been fit for the autumn series against Australia, Romania and South Africa. Clive left me out of the squad. From captain to non-runner at a stroke. Only later did he sit me down at Pennyhill and explain himself. 'Look, Daws,' he said, staring me straight in the eye. 'You're off the mark. I think you've got an attitude in the way that you're talking.' He then proceeded to give me both barrels about how I had lost my focus on rugby because I was too busy satisfying my personal sponsors and doing media work for the BBC. He spoke in a measured way. He was not angry and he did not raise his voice, but it was nonetheless one of the first occasions in my life that someone had actually given me a bollocking to my face. Clive had collared me after receiving an email from my agent, Dave Williams, who, in the course of seeking to reassure him that I would never speak out of turn in an England environment as I had during the Lions tour, had remarked that 'a lot of people see Matt as a good voice of rugby', and I don't think Clive liked that at all.

Clive's reaction was exactly what I needed to hear at precisely the right time, even though I was hurt by the suggestion that I was being unprofessional by putting commercial gain ahead of my responsibilities as a professional rugby player. It was not the first time that claim had been made against me. Earlier in the year former England lock Paul Ackford, writing in the *Sunday Telegraph*, had levelled similar charges and I had resented it deeply. I'd thought, 'Who the hell do you think you are? You don't know anything about what I practise and when I do it.' So angry was I, in fact, that in the next game I'd played, for Northampton against Saracens at Franklin's Gardens, I'd run to the main stand after scoring a try clutching the club badge and shouting out loud in a very overt show of what it meant to me to play for Saints. There'd been emotion, frustration and anger within me that I'd needed to get out of the system. 'I wanted to remind the crowd how much playing for Northampton means to me,' I explained to the *Daily Mirror*. 'My whole rugby career has been committed to the club. I have just finished my tenth year at Northampton. Yes, I kicked like an absolute drain the other week, but sometimes you have days like that. It does not mean I'm less committed. Tiger Woods has the odd bad game of golf, but that does not mean he is not committed, and he's doing media here, there and everywhere.'

At the time Saints played Sarries, England were three games into a Six Nations campaign I will never forget, even if history will not mark the 2001 season down as anything particularly special because the Grand Slam eluded us and the foot-and-mouth outbreak stretched the tournament over two seasons. That is harsh, because a comparison of recent England championship years shows what a special effort it was.

Year	Games	Tries for	Tries against	Total points	Position	Avg points (tries)
1999	4	8	7	103	2nd	26 (2)
2000	5	20	5	183	1st	37 (4)
2001	**5**	**29***	**6**	**229***	**1st**	**46 (5.8)**
2002	5	23	4	184	2nd	37 (4.6)
2003	5	18	4	173	1st	35 (3.6)

* championship record

We started in Cardiff on 3 February with a fixture which never fails to raise the pulse. Anglo-Welsh rivalry is intense at the quietest of times, but this game was set against a backdrop of death threats sent to my Saints and England team-mate Ben Cohen. His crime? To have been sort of stitched up in a television interview cut mid-sentence when Ben was asked how he rated Shane. 'Shane who?' Ben replied. 'Shane Williams or Shane Howarth?' Only they cut it after 'Shane who?'

I know a thing or two about hate mail, following the Murrayfield prize-giving episode the previous year, and it's not very nice. Abuse is one thing, though, death threats are another. Unfortunately there were people in Wales who took great exception to what they heard Ben say in that TV interview. You have to be a fairly sad person, I think, to actually put pen to paper to threaten someone's life, family and house, especially after what Ben had just been through, losing his father as he had. It was so unbelievably insensitive. The guy must have had a mental problem. Even if Ben *had* just said 'Shane who?', okay, write a letter of disapproval. We've all had those. But to threaten someone's life is just appalling, beyond the pale. Ben dealt with it very well, probably because there were so many more important things going on in his life at that time, like looking after his family and playing his rugby. He had to get the police involved as a precaution, but to his credit he didn't dignify the act by reacting to it. That was the right way to handle it. He took a lot of stick from the crowd that day, and again when Northampton played Llanelli in the semi-final of the Heineken Cup, but he stayed calm and cool-headed.

The nonsense didn't end there. When we visited the Millennium Stadium the day before the game, we discovered life-size cardboard cut-outs of all the Wales players in our changing room (they are used on stadium tours to show who changes where). But Wales never change in the visitors' room, and anyway, stadium officials knew we were coming along. I was wound up for the game and we were in no mood to be messed around. It was a bit like the red carpet row in Dublin two years later. They were just trying to do something to mess us around. So I walked up to the figure of Scotty Quinnell, who is a mate so I knew he wouldn't mind, flew at his head with a big karate kick and then screamed at the jobsworth to 'get these bloody things out of here'.

England and Ben had the last laugh. The team won 44–15, and Ben bagged one of the six England tries. It had been one of our goals to silence the Millennium Stadium, and we managed it that day. We quietly got on with the job. Nobody was smiling or screaming in the papers. We kept the powder dry until matchday, when we lit the fuse. The first five minutes was absolute carnage, as if they had 20 men, but we held firm and then we scored on our first attack. Wales double-teamed Jonny Wilkinson, which freed up Will Greenwood, and he helped himself to a hat-trick of tries. You just can't give Will that type of room.

The biggest fright after those opening five minutes probably came on the team bus after the game when we were confronted by two blokes sticking the Vs up at us. We were waving at them and winding them up a little bit. Then they decided to run at the side of the bus. One of them charged, butted it and split his head open. His mate then came round to the front of the bus, stood in the way and accused us of running his mate over. We told the bus driver to keep going, and he proceeded slowly. As the guy stepped out of the way of the bus the wing mirror knocked him clean out. Our doc, Terry Crystal, had to get off the bus and look after him. The mood was nasty by the time the police turned up.

Next up, we stuck 80 points on Italy in what was Mike Catt's fiftieth cap and Jason Robinson's first. Catty led England out that day, but it was Jason who stole the headlines without even touching the ball. In the 35 minutes he was on the field as a second-half substitute, England scored 40 unanswered points and Jason didn't receive a single pass. Looking back it doesn't surprise me too much as he is not one of those characters who demands to be given the ball. He is a very humble guy who will do what he feels is best for the team. He would not have wanted to play the big shot and be the centre of attention in his first game, demanding the ball and boasting that he would win us the game. He first wanted to understand the game, to know where to stand and what lines to hit.

We had not seriously considered that the championship could be disrupted before the game between Wales and Ireland was suddenly postponed due to the escalating foot-and-mouth epidemic. It remained business as usual for us, however, as Scotland's visit to Twickenham on 3 March was given the go-ahead and we took the opportunity to avenge the horror of Murrayfield a year earlier. Our 43–3 victory contained two tries and a man-of-the-match performance from Iain 'Brave-heart' Balshaw, who had come in for some bizarre pre-match criticism from the former Scotland and Lions captain Finlay Calder. Writing in the *Scotland on Sunday* newspaper, Calder had said, 'If Balshaw is an international full-back then I'm Mel Gibson.' The England squad doesn't tend to use such pieces to get us going anymore as our motivation comes from within. Unless it's particularly offensive or extremely contro-versial, it's not really something we worry about. Finlay's article was more funny than inspiring. But I do think a lot of other countries pray for England to say something so that they can turn round and call us, as All Blacks fly-half Andrew Mehrtens once did, 'arrogant pricks'. On this occasion, how-ever, the post-match comments emanating from the Scotland camp were unfailingly complimentary. 'England are as good a team as I've ever played against,' declared their captain Andy Nicol. 'It was similar to playing New Zealand in the summer. I'm just glad we don't have to play them every week.'

The summer and autumn before we had won four matches in a row against southern-hemisphere opposition for the first time. There was real good momentum. We were a really solid team, mentally as well as physically. For the first time people were genuinely rating us as a world-class outfit and speaking of us in the same breath as the All Blacks and Australia. Before we had always been damned with faint praise. A good team, but too inconsistent. Now we were absolutely flying. We were a tight squad, too; we really enjoyed one another's company. We were having a real good giggle away from the training park, but in training we were enjoying the lines we were running and the forwards were giving us a great platform. There was so much excitement around the squad. We wanted to work harder. We felt fresh and enthusiastic and were loving playing for our country . . . and everything was going our way. It was almost too good to be true.

France at Twickenham on 7 April was England's final fixture that spring, but before then Northampton had to play Leicester, our great East Midlands rivals as well as the champions of England. There was a full house at Franklin's Gardens for the biggest club day of the season and a massive buzz about the place. It was the sort of day I play rugby for. Except that it didn't go according to plan. Leicester won the game, largely because I missed two late penalty kicks at goal. Worse still, I let myself down with my conduct. There is nothing I hate more in rugby than cheap-shot merchants, but on that day, in the heat of a pretty fiery derby encounter, I was guilty of gross hypocrisy as well as dangerous play.

Tigers full-back Geordan Murphy was tackled in front of me, I tried to nick the ball, went in hard and boomed him in the back with my knee. The referee missed it, but a couple of players saw what happened. I played it down in the press but I was really angry with myself for being such an absolute nob. I got hold of Geordan's phone number and apologized to him, then spoke to Dean Richards, Leicester's Director of Rugby, and said sorry to him too. I felt I needed to do that because I had been out of order. I had done something that was wrong and totally against the spirit of the game. Northampton fined me £200. No complaint from me. Dean then phoned and said he would need to talk to his players before deciding how Leicester would react. I replied that if anything came of it, if they saw it as a dangerous act, I would take any punishment on the chin. I kept repeating that there had been no malice, but it was at the very least reckless.

A week after the offence Leicester decided to take no action out of loathing for a system which, Dean argued, is unjust as 'the higher the profile of the player the more chance of his being cited'. I felt no great sense of relief, just an overwhelming disappointment in myself. Whatever had possessed me to do something like that? Looking back, I presume that was the first indication of the weakness in me that would get me into trouble with the Lions and then with Clive Woodward after Dublin in October. It was a tell-tale sign and I didn't pick it up.

A fortnight later I was again seething, this time over Ackford's article accusing me of shortchanging the club. I am very aware of what goes on in the commercial world, I admit that. I have a tie-up with Lucozade, and if I can drink out of a Lucozade bottle then I will. But I didn't see a problem with that, only with a person whom I don't know and who doesn't know me trying to interpret what I think. Ackford doesn't have a clue what my feelings for Northampton are. He may have his own opinion, but for him to present that as fact in his newspaper made me livid. How could he possibly write something like that? It offended me.

Instead of lashing out, I should have looked at myself and what I was becoming. The truth is that away from rugby I lacked discipline in my life; I needed someone to give me a kick up the backside or a slap on the wrists. I had spent most of my rugby career wrapped up in a world of back-slappers and autograph hunters with nobody close to me, in terms of family or a girlfriend, who was willing to tell me I was doing wrong. Therefore I carried on believing I was always right. My mum would pick up the phone and say, 'You know it's your grandma's birthday today,' and I would reply, 'Oh yeah, right, I'll give her a ring,' and then I would forget all about it. I would phone her the next day instead. Mum would then find out and accept my explanation. But that is not what I needed to hear. I needed a dressing down. I needed to be told, 'What the bloody hell do you think you're doing? It's your grandmother's birthday. Don't be so bloody selfish. Phone her. I shouldn't have to keep reminding you.' Or, if I phoned her late, 'How can you be so rude and forgetful?' But there wasn't any of that, and I was becoming very slack about little things that meant quite a lot. By their own admission Mum and Dad allowed my standards to slip. They didn't see me a lot, and when they did, perhaps only in a 20-minute slot in the tea room after a match, they did not want to use the time to sit there and get stuck into me. They wanted to know I was healthy and happy in my life.

In that spring of 2001 I was certainly content with the way things were going with England, particularly after we thumped France 48–19 at headquarters. We won by six tries to one, after which France coach Bernard Laporte admitted that French rugby had to change its habits and become more professional. That was a huge compliment to us, and you can only tip your hat to Bernard for saying that. It takes a big personality to realize and acknowledge that your old enemy has got one up on you and you've got some catching up to do. England felt like that for a couple of years when we were constantly chasing the southern-hemisphere teams. Where Laporte was smart was that France took on board what we were doing but not at the expense of their identity. You can't just copy, you have to have your own characteristics. The French have now become more professional, but they have not lost their flair and classic Gallic attitude which have been essential ingredients of their great teams in the past.

It was a real blow, after scoring 28 tries in four games, to have our momentum checked by foot and mouth. There was a real sense of disappointment we couldn't complete the job after our experiences in previous years at Wembley and Murrayfield. This was the first year since 1998 that we were scheduled to play our last game at home and we'd been looking forward to taking on France with the Grand Slam on the line. Instead, *le crunch* had come and gone with a tangible sense of anti-climax. Excitement over a Lions summer soon drove the disappointment out of my system, however. Immediately that became a huge focus, and I was satisfied to leave the Six Nations until the autumn and deal with it then. We were on a good roll and were confident things would go well. But you forget that time changes things. A winning formula in March and April does not necessarily translate into a winning formula in October.

Not that we were ever arrogant or complacent enough to think that we only had to turn up at Lansdowne Road to win, based on our form in the spring. The mistake we made was to think we could play the way we did in the spring in a one-off game, when Ireland had two games already under their belts and had ironed out the creases in their game, and we'd not had even one. It is enormously difficult to play one-off games and challenge for silverware away from home. You can't just expect to click into gear and play like you did half a year earlier. We know that now. We were two totally different sides in the way that we played. We had no choice but to put it down as a huge lesson learned, players and coaches alike, in terms of selection, training and everything else. It was un-believably disappointing, and not just because it was another Grand Slam loss to hang around our neck and be reminded of ad infinitum. It was also a missed opportunity to complete a very special campaign. I would like to think that people will remember the 2001 Six Nations for the four games we played during the meat of the campaign rather than the one we lost in the rump of the autumn. Sadly, I suspect they won't.

It would certainly be a long time until I would be forgiven for my part in the episode – five months, to be precise. Five of the longest months of my life.

The envelope lay on the floor beneath the letter box through which it had fallen. I was in my flat in Northampton and there were only a few days until Christmas. A week after that and 2001 would finally be over. Good riddance to it.

It was a Christmas card from Clive Woodward, who had dropped me from the England team two months earlier and from whom I had heard nothing since. His greeting was seasonal, but only up to a point. 'At the moment you are struggling to be third choice,' he'd added. 'Your mind is away on TV, this, that and the other. If you get yourself right I know you are going to be back in it, but it's down to you. Prove to me that you really want this.'

My first reaction was to think, 'What the hell . . .?' Then I thought, 'Hold on, he's taken the time to put pen to paper to tell me what he thinks he sees in me,' and it really struck a chord with me. I phoned him and asked if he would meet me in the New Year. He agreed.

So there we were, back at the Compleat Angler in Marlow, sitting at the same table at which he had offered me the England captaincy in 1998, across the Thames from the church of All Saints where as a boy I sang in the choir wearing my rugby kit under my cassock so I could go straight to training afterwards. Clive had not come bearing gifts this time, only advice. His message, quite simply, was that I had to sort myself out if I wanted to play for England again. I appreciated his honesty but also his concern, because he didn't have to take a personal interest in me. We talked everything through: what I needed to do, where he saw me in the pecking order, what he wanted from me as a rugby player, what he wanted from me as a person. It was just a listening session for me. There have been occasions when I have maybe not agreed with the way Clive has done things, but I can never say he hasn't given me time. It would be fair to say that we have a complex relationship. We have been through some very close times, some emotional and argumentative times. But he has made a hell of a lot of effort with me and I'll always be grateful for that.

We ordered another coffee, changed the subject to golf and agreed to get together for a game when the ground dried out a bit. Then we shook hands and I left him, pledging to refocus and to get my head down.

Had I returned there and then to the England environment things might have improved sooner. But with Kyran having gone well in my absence, wearing the number 9 shirt with distinction in fine victories over Australia (21–15) and South Africa (29–9) in November 2001, Clive was in no hurry to rush me back. Anyway, there was still much he wanted me to prove. So it was back to Northampton, where I was less than content. The hurt I had felt over being snubbed for the captaincy never went away. As a result I was putting more and more distance between myself and my team-mates and growing ever more disenchanted with life. Ben Cohen and Steve Thompson, speaking to *Rugby World* magazine some months later, called it correctly. 'He was a lost soul, both in rugby and in his personal life,' said Ben. 'He didn't strive for anything. He just went with the flow.' Thommo was equally candid. 'We could all see that Daws wasn't content because he wasn't ribbing people all the time. He seemed happier away from people. He just wasn't right in himself. He wasn't the chirpy Daws we all know.'

My explanation is this. I had come into a big boy's environment as a 20-year-old scrum-half whose job was to chirp away at the forwards. In hindsight, no wonder I developed into an arrogant prat. I thought I was the bee's knees, but in truth I was a young upstart who continued to be so for the best part of a decade.

Help (as far as I was concerned) arrived at Northampton just before Christmas 2001 in the form of Wayne Smith, formerly coach to the All Blacks. He had come to the club as part of Keith Barwell's move to arrest our dismal early-season form. Smithy is very, very switched on, not only to rugby but to life. People's personalities and characteristics are close to his heart. He sat me down and washed through my values. What was important to me, and what was not. I took to him from the start because he is a straight talker. I accepted his judgement as fair, open and honest because of the huge amount of respect I already had for him, based on his playing and coaching pedigree. He had no axe to grind with me, he just wanted what was best for Northampton. And at the end of the day, I am no different.

At our first meeting he told me I had been resting on my laurels for too long. He said, 'There's no question about your rugby ability, but to get the best out of you we need the players around you to not just think of you as an international scrum-half who plays at the club now and again and is on a whistlestop tour of rugby; they need to be able to feel that they can treat you as one of the lads and have you as one of the lads.' That's all I ever wanted to be. As a person, I like to be liked. I like making friends, I like having friends around, I like people phoning me to have a chat, and I do tend to keep my distance from people I don't trust. I'm not out there making false friendships. But it was clear from what Smithy said that I had let things slip.

It was a very lonely time in my life. The rugby wasn't going well, I was getting injured, I was getting dropped, and I didn't really have anyone to share those low times with. I was living in Spratton on my own in a five-bedroom house. It was like being in solitary, and that's just not for me. I need to be around people. Without Grays, and in particular at that time Nick Beal, I would have lost it. I spent a lot of time round at Bealer's house with him, his wife Jo and their son Thomas. Their second child, Joshua, was on the way, but they let me into their lives and gave me the company and friendship I needed while I worked out what I was going to do with myself. I cannot thank them enough for that.

I had to work at rebuilding certain relationships at the club, but I knew it couldn't happen overnight. At the start I had to make a lot of effort, but hopefully now my new attitude just comes out naturally. In a rugby environment you have to have, and to give out, a lot of trust to people with whom you don't necessarily socialize off the pitch. I'd been missing the point there. Previously I would never have phoned up Thommo to see what he was doing, or just to check he was all right. I just wouldn't have bothered. I'd be a little bit cheeky and take the piss a little bit, but because I didn't have any other social interaction with him he resented it. He would say, 'Get off my case, will you? I don't know you and all you do is take the piss out of me.' I had forgotten that you need to get to know someone before you can enjoy the sort of mickey-taking banter you do with established mates. Because I'd grown up with the likes of Nick Beal, Paul Grayson, Tim Rodber, Ian Hunter, Martin Bayfield and Gary Pearce, that was already inbuilt in our relationships. When the new breed came in, I just hadn't spent the time getting to know them.

On the second weekend in March 2002 I finally got my season back on track. After two hamstring strains, a concussion, a dislocated ankle, a blown Grand Slam and the loss of my England shirt, I at last gave myself something to get excited about. In the semi-finals of the Powergen Cup, Northampton wiped the floor with Newcastle, playing our best rugby of the campaign to beat them 38–7. I had a decent game, and three days later I was recalled to the England squad.

There was no shouting from the rooftops when I saw my name in the squad to face Wales at Twickenham. Nor when I came off the bench to replace Kyran for the last quarter of what turned into a 50–10 victory, England's biggest ever over the Welsh. Nor, indeed, when I retained my place in the squad for Rome and was one of four former captains brought off the bench together in the 56th minute of a comfortable 45–9 triumph. As Clive had requested and Smithy had advised, I was keeping my head down and letting my rugby do my talking. And when I did speak, the smart-arse remarks of the Old Daws were conspicuous by their absence. My tone was sober; no more would I get ahead of myself. There was just one more score I wanted to settle, and I would have to come back to Twickenham to do it.

In the world of rugby, there is not one person I genuinely dislike other than Brendan Venter. To my mind, he is one of the most hypocritical, cynical, dirty and underhand players I have ever played against. I can't stand anything about him. He is a bad loser and a bad winner, an all-round horrible person. He was also the focal point of the London Irish side awaiting us in the Powergen Cup final on 20 April.

Venter is a man of strong religious beliefs, which I obviously have no problem with, but he regularly goes beyond the bounds of acceptability, which I have an almighty problem with. I have got to know him through playing against him, watching him and watching videos of him. The public perception is that he was the heartbeat of London Irish, and that makes my teeth itch. The game is about the players. Conor O'Shea was the man who made London Irish tick, yet Venter took all the credit. I thought it was awful. Irish had got a great set-up, great support and great players, but a hypocritical, self-centred guy at the top of the tree. It was purely about Brendan Venter and what sort of reputation he could build.

I know I take a lot of flak from other coaches for the way I communicate with referees. A lot of people think I'm talking back to referees when I'm just talking to them, but that's fine. There is probably one person in every team who does that. Rob Andrew at Newcastle, Martin Johnson at Leicester, Lawrence Dallaglio at Wasps – and Brendan Venter at London Irish. He slaughters me for doing it, but he is far more guilty than me. If there is one thing I do not do it is curse at the referee. I would never swear at an official or call him any kind of name. I might question a call or ask for his views on it, but I wouldn't abuse him. But I have been on the pitch when Venter has verbally abused the official. After we beat London Irish at our place in December 2001 he went off on one about me in the media. It was real sour grapes stuff. I didn't react to it, I just left it, because he looked a fool.

In my view, Venter is an out-and-out thug. I reckon every single person who has played the game has done something he regrets at some point in his career. Made a cheap shot and got away with it. I know I have. Geordan Murphy knows I have. I've done things that have really disappointed me and I've apologized personally to the player afterwards. But Venter seems to constantly go around the pitch high-tackling, or running in from 10 to 15 yards with a swinging arm. It genuinely baffles me how the public could not see what he was doing, and how the media built him up to be this London Irish icon. We all play against very physical, very hard people who take a lot of knocks and have got very high pain thresholds, because that's all part and parcel of the game we love. I've played with and against some of the hardest rugby players in the world, taken tackles, been hit, been rucked and smashed and all the rest of it. I accept that. What I will not accept, however, is someone going out there blatantly looking to punch my lights out and put my livelihood at risk.

You could not pay me enough money to go and have a sociable conversation with Venter because there is nothing about him I like. Even Corne Krige would get a Christmas card from me ahead of him. And that is saying something. There is no doubt in my mind that my issue with Venter contributed to the way I handled myself in that Powergen Cup final, and to the frustration which led to me tangling with Budge Pountney. My Northampton team captain had gone into print on the eve of the game, basically repeating what he had said after Saints had beaten Irish in the league at the turn of the year; namely that I 'manipulate' and that he didn't know how I found time to play for all the talking I do. He then challenged his team to match my decibel level, because while 'it's not easy talking and playing, Matt has mastered it and has proved it works'.

The longer the game wore on, the more wound up I was allowing myself to become with Venter's antics. I turned to referee Steve Lander and implored him 'please just to watch Brendan Venter go into a tackle next time and see what he does. Just watch him, watch his technique, and you'll see he's coming in from miles away just to boom someone and try to take their head off. Normally mine.' But Lander seemed more concerned that I hold the ball at its absolute tips when I fed it into the scrum.

I have spoken out time and again against foul play, but at the end of the day whether it's foul play or persistent professional fouls, players will continue to offend for as long as they can get away with it. I fear that we do not have the necessary strength of character in officials in this country to handle it. They don't seem to understand that we would be hugely respectful (as we are) to refs who are strong and consistent with both sides. They might have a bad day at the office, but if they are consistently bad to both sides you know where you stand.

At Twickenham, with Saints 24–0 behind in a cup final to a side with Venter playing in it, my frustration got the better of me. After a lot of hard work pulling my chin off the floor, it was back down there again.

I was ready to jack it all in. To turn my back on Northampton and walk out on a rugby club and a town that had been my home since my schooldays. I knew I wouldn't want to play for another team in England. Fine. I'll give it all up. How dare they put me through this after all I have done for them?

My mind was spinning as I stood before a disciplinary hearing under the new stand. The anger inside me was battling to get out, and the look on my face made no secret of the fact.

It was just a week ago that Northampton had lost the 2002 Powergen Cup final. Actually, correct that. We had been thrashed 38–7 by a London Irish side that had come into the game as underdogs. On the stroke of half-time I had been involved in an incident with Budge. And here I was, called to account to explain myself.

First, the incident. We were getting beat fair and square, London Irish as a team were playing a lot better than we were, and I was growing increasingly agitated. With only minutes left in the first half we seemed finally to get our game going. We had loads of possession, and as we pressed against the Irish line I felt they killed the ball. The whistle duly blew. But as I turned to Steve Lander, I saw him signalling for half-time. I was completely incensed. I walked towards him to tell him that I thought he was being one-eyed and had made a bullshit call. 'What do we have to do here, Steve, to persuade you we want to try to play some rugby and be positive?' Lander just turned away and walked off.

Budge, quite rightly as captain, intervened. 'Daws, leave him alone, I'll deal with it.'

As he spoke he put his arm across my chest, as if to hold me back. I told him to get off me and pushed his hand away, snapping, 'Budge, just sort that effing ref out.' That was it. The problem for me was that from a distance it looked like I was telling my skipper where to go, and as it happened, as the whistle went for half-time the Sky cameras were on the ref and caught me pushing Budge's arm away. That was when Sky's former England fly-half Stuart Barnes got on his high horse and started going on about dissent in the Northampton ranks. He concluded that Budge and I 'arguing' was symptomatic of

Northampton's plight. Most decent commentators would have dismissed what happened as a moment of frustration and moved on, but Sky made it into a big issue and to my mind were wholly responsible for Northampton's subsequent reaction.

John Steele had been replaced by Wayne Smith as head coach midway through the season and been moved into the newly created role of director of operations. I had got on with him for years and years, though his appointment of Budge instead of me as club captain had soured things, and now here he was all of a sudden turning on me. I kept asking myself 'Why has Steeley done this?' and not coming up with a plausible answer, other than that he was wanting to make a point that he still had some clout. It seemed to me he'd become very officious and unnecessary in his new role, and as far as I was concerned he was totally out of order. He seemed to try to make an example of me, and I couldn't understand why. It was a real 'blazer' thing to do, and I've not been the same with him since. He used to be a very good friend, someone I thought I could trust. He may well still be, but I would no longer choose to trust him because he's now shown a chink or two in the loyalty the club should be showing towards me. And these things are two-way, aren't they?

Budge was also involved in the hearing, and I was pretty disappointed in him as well. He could have quite easily turned round and defused the situation by saying 'Come on, don't be so stupid, fellas, it was just something that happened in the heat of the moment.' He chose not to, even after I went to his house and said I was sorry, that 'you know very well it wasn't directed at you. I was angry with the referee and I shrugged you off.' It happens in pretty much every game we play. If a forward is in the middle of a fight and I pull the back of his shirt to get him away, he turns round and tells me to fuck off. I don't then go to the club and say he should be summoned to a disciplinary hearing. It's a physical game. But Budge took it to heart. I don't know if he thought I was undermining his captaincy. I can't believe for a minute he would be like that.

My punishment was to be dropped for one match. They could not fine me because they had no evidence against me. Had they tried I would have got my lawyers on the case. So to this day I don't understand why the club called that hearing. All it achieved was to diminish my affection for Northampton.

It had been an horrendous season for me on and off the pitch, and I was utterly fed up. My immediate feeling was that I had had enough of being in Northampton and of playing for Northampton. The only reason I was in Northampton was for my rugby. I have no family there, no ties there other than the rugby club. And yet my reward for that commitment was to be treated like a criminal. I felt let down that the club were treating me unreasonably and that Budge was not prepared to stand up for me, to tell the hierarchy not to be so stupid and to play it down as the moment of frustration that it was. Did nobody really know me?

There were only two people I felt I could confide in, and one of them was Dad. I poured my heart out to him over the telephone one evening. I talked, he listened. 'What am I going to do?' I said. 'I've had it up to here with Northampton, with the place and with all that is going on. There is no reason to be here other than rugby, and now they're having a pop at me when all I want to do is play my rugby here, play passionately and give everything I can. That's the return I get. I don't want to be involved in it any more.' We agreed that there were two ways I could go: either I could get a strop on, say bollocks to the lot of them and leave the club, or I could ask myself why Budge had felt that way about me. Why had he felt unable to stick up for me? The more I pondered the question, the more it dawned on me that there was still an issue to deal with.

Fortunately for me, Wayne Smith could also see my angle. I could see in his eyes that he understood why I was getting upset. I went to him and opened up to him too; I really got emotional. He sat me down and did what I thought the club should have done after Twickenham. 'Right, come on,' he said, 'let's sort this out. What's making you upset, what's making you frustrated?' For the first time in a while I was very teary because it was something I felt very passionately about. I just let the emotion out. I told Smithy how much the club genuinely meant to me. I don't think anyone at Northampton fully understood that before. He got it out of me by being honest with me. He was honest about what the players thought of me, off the pitch as well as on it. He explained that the incident with Budge was not so much about pushing Budge, more another example of me not being aware of how I should be conducting myself.

Sometimes you do have to take some pretty hard criticism in order to bounce back a better person. I am forever thankful to Smithy for coming to the club, not just for the rugby but because he opened my eyes to what I hope I am being now and will continue to be, both on and off the rugby pitch.

8(i)
Headstrong to Humble

BASHED BY THE BOKS

'You may never play again.'

Five words that will stay with me for the rest of my life. Along with the body language of the specialist delivering them, the tone in which he uttered them, even the smell of that December day in Northampton when my career appeared to be at an end.

Life had taken a significant turn for the better in the months since the end of the 2001–02 season. In fact, it was so good I had to keep pinching myself to be sure I was not living a dream. I had fallen head over heels in love with Joanne Salley, a teacher from Harrow School, I had played myself back into the England team, and I had contributed fully to an historic autumn series. On three successive weekends in November we had beaten New Zealand, Australia and South Africa. It doesn't get any better than that.

There was, predictably enough, a price to be paid for my new-found state of happiness. I started experiencing neck pains in the days following our 53–3 win over the Springboks on 23 November, comfortably the most brutal game of rugby I have ever been involved in. Whenever I turned my head I would get pins and needles all the way down into my hands, and my index finger was numb. I simply could not feel it.

Undergoing MRI scans has been a routine part of my career, and of most other scrum-halves I would imagine. So I was not unduly concerned when I went along to get the results of the scan on my neck. It was then that I heard those five words, and a few more besides which I did not take in as the initial shock washed over me. There was something about me being just one tackle away from becoming a paraplegic. I had a load of swelling around a disc in my neck and it was impinging on my spinal cord. Everything depended on the swelling going down. If it didn't . . .

I left the hospital, sat in my car and cried. I was on my own, and I suddenly felt very alone. I drove round to Paul Grayson's house, sat down and repeated to him what I had been told. I then started to cry in front of him. As far as I was concerned I was never going to play again. My career was in the past. What the hell was I going to do? There was nothing Grays could say, but he was there for me, as he always has been. I needed to unload on someone, and I have no better mate than him. I then went to see Wayne Smith, who knew I had been for an MRI. His reaction was one of shock. 'Shit,' he exclaimed. 'Right. Go away somewhere and rest.'

I got back in my car and called Jasper Burnham, a good friend who lives in London. Jasper works in the record business and is a great lad to be around. He told me to come straight down, that he'd think of something to take my mind off things. Hours later we were on the sauce, big style. We went mental for three days, virtually lived in Langham's, had lunch and dinner there and generally went la-di-da. 'Finish in style,' I thought to myself.

When I returned to reality I called home. Dad answered the phone and I broke the news to him. Again I became very emotional, but I made him promise he wouldn't tell Mum. That was really tough on him because they are the closest of couples. They keep no secrets from each other. But I just couldn't put Mum through it, at least not until it was definite one way or the other. I knew she would have gone mental. The poor guy texted me every day, saying, 'Can I tell her, can I tell her? This is killing me.' It was the right thing to do, because had I told her and then carried on playing it would have done her in. Mum knew I had something wrong with my neck, but she had no idea it was as serious as it was. They were talking about removing a disc and putting a rod in, and all sorts of major operations. Had they done that, I wouldn't have been able to play again.

Only seven people knew the full extent of the problem: Dad, Jasper, Grays, Smithy, Nick Beal, Dan Luger and Joanne, who was absolutely brilliant about it. She shut it out, assured me everything would be fine and did her best to help me get on with a normal life. But there was one other person I knew I needed to tell. Clive Woodward.

We were at the BBC Sports Review of the Year after-show party when I finally broke the news to him. There was a heck of a din and I think he thought he had misheard me. He dragged me outside.

'What do you mean, you might not be able to play again? What the fuck are you talking about?'

He was livid. Not with me, but with South Africa.

The Boks had been last up on what for me was the Payback Tour. Four and a half years earlier England had been creamed down in the southern hemisphere by Australia, New Zealand and South Africa on the Tour from Hell. Now it was our turn to deliver a few home truths.

First into bat for the opposition, on 9 November, were the All Blacks, understrength due to a conscious decision they had taken to leave a number of senior players at home. (Sound familiar?) John Mitchell, England forwards coach when our makeshift team went to Hell in 1998, was now in charge of New Zealand. England scored three tries in an eight-minute period to run up a 31–14 lead, yet by the final whistle we had come perilously close to blowing our 15-game winning streak at Twickenham. Two tries by Jonah Lomu made it eight in seven Tests against England for the big man. But it was another meaty winger, my Northampton club-mate Ben Cohen, who won the day. It was his try, complete with extravagant scoring dive, which put England in the box seat. And it was his last-gasp tackle, on New Zealand full-back Ben Blair inches from the England line, which made sure we stayed there to the end. But it was too close for comfort.

Seven days later the boot was on the other foot. It was the Aussies who were sitting on a 12-point lead after scoring three tries in 10 minutes to turn around a 16–6 deficit and take a 28–16 advantage into the last quarter. But we refused to buckle. We regained our shape and our composure and dug deep. Jonny kicked eight out of eight, Ben scored another two tries, and we nicked it 32–31. Did I say New Zealand had been too close for comfort?

South Africa was perceived as the easiest of the three challenges, not least because they came into the fixture on the back of defeats by France and Scotland. No touring Springbok side had ever before returned home winless. England had also won the last three meetings. But nothing comes easy against the Springboks, except bloodshed. For they are the most physical opponents of them all. When we met in December 2000 the treatment room at Twickenham resembled a *M*A*S*H* field hospital. Neil Back, Richard Hill and Japie Mulder between them needed more than 50 stitches. There was blood everywhere. None of us seriously expected the 2002 version to be any different – which was just as well.

History and the record books will remember the game in different ways. In black and white terms England won 53–3, far and away the biggest win in a series which dates back to 1906. But this was no monochrome occasion. It was shrouded in red mist from first whistle to last. Afterwards, none of the England players wanted to mix with any of the Springboks because we felt they had turned in a fairly disgraceful international performance. It was nothing short of dangerous. And as fellow international rugby players, we felt it just wasn't good enough. We can all accept being boomed by Jonny Wilkinson or run over by Jonah Lomu or rucked out of the back by the French pack for being on the wrong side. That's all part of the game. But the Boks went way beyond that. So when their players walked past us saying, 'All right, guys?' as one we indicated that, no, we were not all right. Don't give us the 'how you doing?' bit. Have a look at yourselves. Backy suffered a fractured cheekbone, Lewis Moody sustained a shoulder injury that would require surgery, Jonny also did his shoulder and would not play again until the New Year, and Jason Robinson perforated an eardrum. Oh, yeah, and I hurt my neck.

If there is one player in the England squad not given to exaggeration, it's Jason Robinson. He is one of the most gifted yet humble sportsmen I have ever met. Therefore his version of events, quoted in the newspapers two days later, can be relied upon for accuracy:

> They were really going in to hurt us on purpose. This game is tough enough as it is, yet every time we got the ball a hit came after contact. It was dirty from the start. The boys had bloody noses inside minutes. I was clattered very late and I may need an operation as a result. I can hear, but only in a muffled way. I don't have a clue about eardrums so I don't know what damage has been done. What I do know is that what happened out there is totally unacceptable. It had nothing to do with football. There's a difference between physicality and cheap shots and their game was full of cheap shots. If they concentrated more on playing the game than trying to maim everyone they would go a lot further.

Jannes Labuschagne, the South African lock, was sent off by referee Paddy O'Brien for a late charge on Jonny, and Werner Greef, their full-back, caught Phil Christophers with a dangerous high tackle which brought us a penalty try and Greef a foul-play charge. Yet he was subsequently cleared, and

Labuschagne got a 23-day ban which meant he would spend less time out of the game than his 'victim', Jonny. Justice – don't you just love it?

South Africa, laughably, claimed that it always takes two to tango. 'We have two players concussed and one with a dislocated shoulder,' their coach, Rudi Straeuli, pointed out. 'Do you think we concussed ourselves?' It was meant as a rhetorical question, but Sky Sports, who had broadcast the game, came up with an answer, and a damning one, later that week on *Rugby Club*. The evidence they unearthed, from going through all their footage with a fine-tooth comb, was deeply shocking. And to nobody more than me and my family.

Clive Woodward had been angry enough after watching the game unfold from his usual perch in the West Stand, but when he saw Sky's video nasty and then learned of my injury fear, he flipped. The tape showed the full extent of South Africa's brutality that day and revealed it to be far, far worse than it had appeared at the time. It exposed Corne Krige, the Boks' captain, as thug-in-chief and yours truly as the most sinned against. Krige was caught on film launching into my head with a flying butt. He also caught me in the face with a blatant forearm smash which after thudding against me put his own team-mate, Andre Pretorius, out of the game. Two to tango? Actually, no. Krige was also seen punching Jason and Jonny and attempting to do the same to Lawrence Dallaglio. Luckily, for his sake, he didn't make contact there. Before he was finished he stamped on Phil Vickery and planted a shoulder into Mike Tindall. It was inexcusable behaviour.

When I saw the footage I became incredibly angry. And I did not keep it to myself. There I was, waiting to hear whether my career was at an end as a result of the rough-house treatment meted out by those idiots, and here was evidence which said to me that the whole thing had been pre-planned. Mum and Dad were also beside themselves with rage. Mum was particularly distressed. Dad couldn't understand why Krige had not been dealt with in a harsher manner. In any manner, for that matter. He was not best pleased when Krige was subsequently named as South Africa's captain for the 2003 World Cup. Dad is convinced to this day that the Boks came to Twickenham to do a particular job on two or three people: the half-backs and Jason Robinson.

It was no wonder that my parents were so angry because they still had fresh in their minds a shocking incident that had taken place a year earlier at Franklin's Gardens in a club game between Saints and Harlequins, when I was knocked sparko by a forearm punch from Quins lock Bill Davison. By the time the medics were on I had regained my senses. I was able to tell them what month it was and to correctly recount the months of the year in reverse order. But all was not well. I played on for another 15 minutes before being forced from the field with a tweaked hamstring. I was so angry. I had been dropped by England following the loss in Dublin three weeks earlier and I had been desperate to make a statement. Now I was injured.

I walked into the home dressing room and through into the toilets where I proceeded to kick the shit out of the door while shouting and screaming in frustration. At that very moment there was a dead hush outside as Ali Hepher prepared to take a penalty kick at goal. From down below, inside the stand, my yelled expletives floated up.

Dad looked at Mum. 'I bet that's Matthew,' he said.

A moment later and the Tannoy announcer turned on the microphone. 'Would Mr [Ron] Dawson please go down to the home changing room.'

Dad managed to calm me down, but it was clear I was not right in the head following Davison's punch. The doctor was called and he put me through some medical checks before sending me off to hospital in an ambulance.

The next thing I remember is coming round and seeing Mum's face. I was lying in bed and she was sitting beside me, but I didn't know where I was. I just kept asking Mum the same question. 'What was the score?' She'd say 13–13, and literally five minutes later I'd ask, 'Did we win?' Mum disguised her deep concern for me, only later admitting that it was one of the most frightening experiences of her life as the nurses repeatedly came over to check my vitals.

Dad is always going on about how rugby players need more protection from the referee. But when you think that that video of the England–South Africa game had to be slowed down to show what had really happened, you can't blame the referee at all. In fact, I thought Paddy O'Brien did a hell of a job in the circumstances. You can blame the authorities, however, for not taking more appropriate action afterwards. How pathetic, said Dad, that the only player called to account by French citing commissioner Paul Mauriac was Greef. Monsieur Mauriac should have had the freedom to act after seeing the tape. There should be no time limit on the pursuit of justice.

Hard rugby I have got no problem with. But those pictures of Krige whacking into me with a flying head-butt made me think, 'Jesus Christ, what am I doing?' Mum had never felt at ease watching me play rugby at the best of times; what on earth was she going to think now? No wonder she worries about me every second of every game. Had that head-butt caught me flush I dread to think what might have happened. As it was I was in enough trouble.

For almost three weeks after the game I lived with the fear that I would never play again. Everywhere I turned I was confronted with scary thoughts.

'Right, you're not playing rugby any more. What are you going to do?'

'I don't know, what *am* I going to do? Where am I going to get money from? How am I going to pay my mortgage?'

I panicked. I don't have any personal insurance. I'm covered by policies taken out by the club and the Rugby Football Union, but I haven't got anything on top of that because after all the injuries I have had the annual premiums are ridiculously expensive – between £8,000 and £10,000. I hope it doesn't sound flippant, but I always took the view that I would rather spend ten grand on something else. If my career ended because of a wrecked knee, then so be it. As long as I could still walk I'd be all right. All of which was easily said when I was as fit as a flea.

I did not want to go to Oxford to see the second specialist. I wanted to hide away from the truth and live a lie, if that meant not having to confront my worst fears. But I wasn't a kid any more. Northampton needed to know, England needed to know, I needed to know.

As I headed for my appointment, my thoughts turned to Andy Blyth, who was paralysed while playing for Sale in 1999. His is a remarkable story, but one which those who play try not to dwell on, as there go we all but for the grace of God. I visited him in hospital at Stanmore the day after his accident and found him lying in bed with a sensor in his mouth which he was to bite on if he required assistance. I didn't know what to say to him. It was shocking to see a guy I had known so fit and active reduced to that state. What I didn't think as I sat there with him was that I play the same game; it could happen to me. That thought was very much swirling around my head as I shook hands with my specialist, though. He was brilliant. He did a CAT scan and then eased my worst fears a little by telling me that there are 'probably a few rugby players in the UK at the moment who have this and don't even know about it'. Which was all well and good, but what if I took another knock on my neck? Where would that leave me? I started thinking about Blythy again. Had he been in this same position just before his injury? Because he always used to go flying in, making big hits. I thought, 'Shit, it *could* happen to me.' Well it could have, couldn't it?

A second opinion was required, so I went to see another specialist in London who confirmed that he had seen the condition a lot. I must adopt a wait-and-see approach, he explained. Nothing more scientific than that. The tell-tale sign, he said, would be if I got a 'stinger' and it went down my arm to my hand again. That would mean I was verging on a bit of trouble, the disc was swollen and I had to stop playing.

I returned to rugby on 11 January 2003, restored to the Northampton side for a vital home tie against Biarritz in the Heineken Cup. I did so after Smithy levelled with me.

'Daws,' he said, 'I cannot play you unless you're full bore.'

'Smithy,' I replied. 'You know what you'll get out of me. I am a hundred per cent right physically and mentally.'

And I meant it. Since then, touch wood, things have been fine, but the memory of that time will stay with me for ever. As will my admiration for Blythy, for making such an inspiring recovery. Looking back to that day when I visited him, it is no bloody wonder he got through it because even at that horrific time he was cracking jokes about not being able to get a hard-on. He was completely positive. Initial optimism is one thing, however; the months and years of fighting after that are quite another. When I think of the amount of times he must have fallen over on his crutches, he has to be one tough cookie. And I never had him down for that sort of mentality. In terms of his recovery, for effort and commitment he put even Jonny Wilkinson to shame.

8(ii)
Headstrong to Humble

GRAND SLAM AT LAST

Breakfast time in Dublin, and the countdown was well and truly under way. It was the morning of the Grand Slam decider, unbeaten Ireland against unbeaten England, and Neil Back was in an unexpectedly animated mood. I was sitting with Paul Grayson, Will Greenwood, Lawrence Dallaglio and Jonny Wilkinson, pushing bits of All Bran around my cereal bowl, mentally rehearsing the day to come, when Backy pulled up a chair.

'Do you know something,' he announced. 'We're going to beat these boys by forty points today.'

It was one of those double-take situations. Backy is not quite to England what 'Whispering' Tom Smith is to Northampton, but he's not a million miles off. He doesn't waste words, shall we say. He certainly doesn't go in for outrageous statements.

'What did you say?'

'All right,' he came back, 'I'll give them six points. We're going to beat Ireland by forty points to six today.'

England know all about going into Grand Slam games with high hopes only to finish with egg on face. I should certainly know; I'm one of the few who played in 1999, 2000 and 2001.

But so had Backy. Played three, lost three. Now here he was, predicting a rout.

Eight hours later, Dan Luger scampered over for the last of England's five tries in stoppage time to round off what by any standards was an impressive performance. I looked up at the Lansdowne Road scoreboard, then I looked around at the other lads. Will and Lawrence wore the same expression of disbelief as I did, so too Grays, standing by the dug-out. England led Ireland 40–6. Never before had we willed Jonny to miss a conversion.

Of course, he didn't.

The 2003 Six Nations Championship had begun with all the usual high expectations as to what England would achieve. Title favourites and odds-on for the Grand Slam despite our propensity to do a Devon Loch in the final furlong, and despite France having slammed the Six Nations a year earlier. The theory this time was that because France had to come to Twickenham, where England had not lost in 18 Tests, in the opening round of matches on 15 February, we would have the title won then and there. None of the England squad sub-scribed to that. Ireland had beaten Australia, Fiji and Argentina in the autumn, and we all thought they were easily good enough to go to the end of the competition undefeated. Their home record was solid, and none of us thought Scotland and Wales were ever going to trouble them, even with home advantage.

Fit again after my neck scare and happy in my private life, I could not wait to get going. The spring was back in my step. I felt rejuvenated. I had moved in with Joanne, who has a flat in Harrow, and my emotional scars were healing fast. Not only did I feel my rugby had improved as a result of my contentment off the field, I felt I was becoming a better person, too.

Joanne and I got on from the start. You don't usually talk about certain topics when you first meet someone, yet we were straight into fairly deep and meaningful conversation. Because we'd both come out of long-term relationships there was an element of 'let's get on with it, then'. There was very little 'false' time, and that was fine by me. I didn't want any of the bullshit. We both agreed that either we got on, and got on as mates, or we'd go our separate ways. She immediately made me feel good about myself again, and within a week or two of meeting her I felt the need to go and have a sit-down with Mum and Dad.

From the day I'd first left home and gone to Northampton, I think Mum and Dad had felt a little bit left out, what with Keith Barwell sorting out so much of my life for me in the early days. If I ever needed words of advice or help in any way I had my parents on the end of the phone, but I became lazy, selfish even. I was caught up in the whirlwind of rugby and all that goes with it. I thought I was seeing loads of my parents because I saw them each weekend at the game. In fact, I never properly saw them. We would meet for, maybe, 20 minutes over a cup of tea after a game, but we would be constantly interrupted by people wanting a signature. I never sat down and shared quality time with them. Mum and Dad understandably became very frustrated with this routine, but they're such lovely people that they didn't want to upset me. They didn't want to be seen to be butting in. They saw that I was enjoying what I was doing, and enjoying living in

Northampton, and I think they were a little bit wary of upsetting the applecart.

It was not until I met Joanne that I saw the error of my ways. She reminded me how important family is and how imperative it is that you hang on to what's precious. That day in Marlow I said sorry for years of neglect, and I told my parents that from now on things would change. Not just with them, but with my sister Emma and my grandparents too. 'I know I haven't been the ideal family member over the years,' I started. 'I know I've been a bit lazy and have taken you all for granted, your love and your support, but Joanne has straightened me out.' At the same time I asked of them that they speak their mind to me, rather than bottle up thoughts. I told them I needed their criticism as well as their approval. At the age of 30 I wasn't asking them to put me over their knee and slap me, but a tone change in their voice when they disapproved would help me keep firmly in touch with reality.

That is a huge part of what Joanne does for me. If I'm behaving like a prat, she will tell me. If I need an emotional lift, she will give it to me. If something needs to be done, she will ensure I get it done. If I speak improperly to someone, she will admonish me. One of the first things she ever commented on was the speed at which I ate my food.

'God, you eat quickly, Matt.'

'Pardon?'

We were out for dinner with our good friends Tony and Di Stratton at the time, and I thought she was joking. She wasn't.

'I'm actually quite happy with the way I eat, thank you very much,' I said.

She said nothing more until we got home, when she re-opened the discussion to explain that she thought it impolite for me to finish my food 10 minutes before everyone else. I had never thought of that. I exist in an environment where you get half an hour to eat your food at lunchtime, you get it down, then you go out and train again. I'd just got into a bad habit. Little things like that convinced me that I'd been missing out on a trick. The great thing was that I didn't take offence at what she said. She made me very much aware of what was right about having a rest, putting your knife and fork down, having a chat, being sociable, and she made it apparent that it was quite a nice thing to do to take your time over your food and enjoy it. At last there was someone treating me as a human being rather than as an international rugby player. Before, people would say, 'Oh, it's Matt Dawson, I won't say anything.' With Joanne, if I carried on doing the wrong thing she wouldn't want to go out with me.

When I first met her, in a bar in London during the summer of 2002, she had not heard of Matt Dawson the rugby player. She didn't have a clue who I was. On our first date she asked me what I did. I told her I played a bit of rugby in Northampton. She asked if I had ambitions to play for England. I told her that actually I already had. 'What, for the third team?' she said. It was brilliant, a huge attraction. I was with someone who wanted to go out for dinner with me as a person, not as a rugby player.

Meeting Joanne capped the best off-season I had ever had. I had told Smithy at the end of the 2001–02 season that I wanted to move down to London, basically because I had nothing at Northampton other than my rugby and most of my single friends were down that way. Smithy agreed. He's a great believer that if a player is happy off the pitch then he'll produce on it. So I moved in with Dan Luger in Chiswick.

The two of us spent a week off the Adriatic coast in Croatia chilling out on a 70-foot speedboat. Then I spent another week in the British Virgin Islands with Martin Corry, before returning to west London to train and party with Luges. We would often be out until five or six o'clock in the morning. Not drinking, just partying with loads of mates. Then we would crash, get up at nine, go and train, sleep at lunchtime, train again, then more sleep. It was the greatest time. By the time I returned to rugby I was a new man. Happy, content, secure.

'I despise them as much as they despise everybody else. They are chauvinistic and arrogant, they look down on everybody. As long as we beat England I wouldn't mind if we lost every other game in the Six Nations.'

So said France number eight Imanol Harinordoquy as the Six Nations Championship began on a predictable note. It is a schoolboy error to go bad-mouthing your opposition, and though, as I have said, England don't use that sort of rant as motivation any more, the man Dewi Morris famously called 'Hairy Donkey' on Sky had revealed a weakness in the French camp which we duly noted. Come matchday, we had enough in our armoury to avenge our defeat in Paris a year earlier, but the memory of our 25–17 victory will forever be tinged with sadness. What should have been a day of national celebration to mark Jason Leonard's hundredth England cap became an occasion for mourning following the tragic news that Nick Duncombe had died suddenly while at a training camp in Lanzarote.

Nick had followed my career path into the England side during the 2002 championship when coming on as a substitute against Scotland and Ireland. A fellow scrum-half and former pupil of RGS High Wycombe, he was destined for many more caps. He was very quick and very elusive, always a threat to the opposition. Obviously I had an affiliation with him because of our school. But fundamentally he was a rugby friend that everybody had lost. We will all look back with fond memories on the way he played rugby.

Mark Evans, his boss at Harlequins, visited the England camp the night before the game to inform us of what had happened. Mark pulled the Quins boys to one side and told them first. Word quickly spread along the corridors of Pennyhill Park, numbing the senses of us all. It had been a turbulent 24 hours for me, a calf injury forcing me to withdraw from the team on Thursday, but my problems immediately paled into insignificance.

My first reaction was to see how the Quins boys were, especially Dan Luger. Nick and he were very close friends, almost like brothers, and he took the loss harder than anyone. I can only imagine how horrendous it must have been for him to be told his best friend had died and then to have to run out at Twickenham and take on France. In the same circumstances, I don't know that I could have gone out onto the pitch, I really don't. Certainly no one would have blamed any of them had they turned round and said, 'Look, I can't do this.'

It was a very odd time. One of the biggest games England had played at Twickenham for many years, and nobody had any appetite to take part. I felt particularly sorry for Jason, who led the team out but was in no mood to make anything of his big day. It was such a shame. I hope he can look back on his career and still fondly remember his hundredth cap, but sadly I think it will go down in his mind as the day his mate passed away. You don't often see Jase as anything other than his smiley, cheeky self, but that day it was evident how much he was hurting.

As a team, England failed to fire and were outscored three tries to one by the French. We looked jaded. There had been a lot of training and mental preparation for this game, and it had perhaps showed. Fortunately, Jonny's boot totally eclipsed that of French fly-half Gérard Merceron and we were content to take the win and move on. It was a W, but that was about it.

There was little more to be said for the victory in Wales the following weekend, a game I again missed with my calf injury. The principality was braced for the worst after going down to Italy in Rome in the opening round, but they got off lightly. I watched the game in a bar in Puerto Banus with Joanne. I was on the Costa del Sol for three days of warm-weather calf resting (it rained for two of them). Everyone in the bar expected England to absolutely stuff them. I was sitting with a Welsh supporter who owned a box at the Millennium Stadium but had come down to the south of Spain for a week's fishing because he knew England were going to dick them. I couldn't believe that attitude. There are always upsets in the Six Nations, as Italy's win over Wales had shown. I can't remember a season when there wasn't one, and as a player you have to keep reminding yourself of that.

That awareness brings with it a fear factor which when you play in Wales, in the Millennium Stadium, is heightened. It's a particularly daunting arena when there are 75,000 Welshmen raising the roof. This time they were given plenty to shout about as England clung on to a narrow 9–6 lead just before half-time and were reduced to 14 men with the sin-binning of Phil Christophers. Had Wales scored a try then they would have been all over us. Momentum would have been with them. They did get away with a lot, though. They were slowing ball down through cheating, but they did it very well. It seemed we were just trying to fling it around everywhere and score tries off first phase. The breakdown was loose and scrappy, and it makes a huge difference when you haven't got solid ball and you're getting scragged at the base. It's no way to launch the back line when you're giving the scrum-half that type of ball.

I imagine England were quite pleased to get in at half-time and reassess. Thankfully, Jonny had been chipping away with drop goals and penalties before we played our Cardiff joker, and Will Greenwood, a hat-trick scorer on his last visit, came up trumps again. Joe Worsley added a second try but the game remained scrappy, and with mixed emotions I headed off for a plate of paella. Delighted that we'd won but desperate to be fit again. Looking at things from outside the group, I sensed I could make some valid points and help tighten up on a few issues.

Andy Gomarsall had worn the number 9 shirt against France, then Kyran had taken over against Wales. I would have preferred Gomars to have kept it because I always get a bit nervous when Kyran gets in that shirt. He's such a great player. With all due respect to Gomars, I have always considered Kyran the better scrum-half. As soon as he pulled on the shirt I knew I'd have a fight on my hands to get it back.

Fortunately, the Powergen Cup semi-final was wedged between England's games against Wales and Italy so I had a shop window in which to parade both my fitness and my form. The fact that it was a repeat of the 2002 final between Northampton and London Irish made it all the more appealing to me. The memory of that day at Twickenham might have been 11 months old, but it was still red raw. There was a lot of pressure on me personally, given the need to prove my fitness, and also because of what had happened between Budge and me last time round, but I enjoy pressure. I enjoy people doubting me and questioning me, and I like answering those questions. I am a fairly confident person anyway, but I have also developed a positive attitude by working at it.

Rarely in sport does your performance exceed your own expectations. You may surprise other people occasionally, but every competitor knows they are capable of excellence, that there is always potential for improvement. It is the eternal optimism of playing sport. Confidence comes from belief. The ability to turn 'Can I?' into 'I can!' Belief is about preparing mentally and physically so there is no doubt left in your mind that you are equal to a challenge. Confidence will take you everywhere.

In the 1950s, scientists concluded that a sub four-minute mile was impossible. Roger Bannister knew he was capable of it, and with the right preparation, in the right conditions with a pace-making team who knew him well, he succeeded. In the 18 months after he had broken the record a dozen men ran under the 'impossible' barrier; it was as if a dam had burst. Bannister had broken through a psychological barrier and set a new platform of belief. On the British Lions tour to South Africa in 1997 it felt like the only people who believed we could win the series was the 47-strong touring party. We used our underdog's position to boost our confidence and propel our team morale into the stratosphere. The preparation was great, the conditions were right, and we believed we could do it. And we did.

Fear can prevent success. The challenge is to persuade yourself that your nervousness is illogical. Your mind holds the only key to conquer your fear. Playing away from home is a great example of how lack of belief can hinder your performance. If a slight doubt slips into your psyche about an away disadvantage, your own mind has given the opposition a head start.

That March day at the Kassam Stadium in Oxford, we left London Irish in the blocks. The forwards were awesome and there were a few gaps for me. Our whole team had been doubted because of what happened the year before. Everyone remembered our thrashing in the 2002 final, but that game had been just a massive blip in an otherwise great end to our season. We'd played some fantastic rugby before then and some brilliant rugby afterwards.

Increasingly these days motivation comes from within. I used to look outwardly for motivation and sit there and think, 'We're owed this. We've been to two cup finals so we're owed this one.' But you're never ever owed anything. Nobody owes an individual or a club anything. Regardless of what has happened in the past, you have to earn the right to win in the present. It's only recently that I and other players at the club have actually come to terms with that. Smithy, however, had long known it, and he showed his class as a coach by playing down the revenge aspect of the fixture and insisting that our motivation must come from within ourselves. 'It's not about revenge,' he said. 'It's not about righting that wrong. It was just a bad day at the office. Put it behind you.'

I don't know what London Irish were focused on, but we were obviously way ahead of them on the day. We didn't need any other motivating factors, or to see pictures of them parading the trophy. All we needed was an opportunity to go out and play some rugby. Fortunately the weather was great, the surface was excellent, the support was second to none (as usual) and the boys played really well. Almost a year earlier we had lost by five tries to one. This time we won by that margin, the final score 38–9.

After that I thought I would be involved against Italy. Even though I had been injured for a couple of weeks I thought I'd played well enough in that semi to come straight back into the side. And so I did, in what was a much-changed line-up. Martin Johnson, Neil Back, Ben Cohen, Jason Robinson, Kyran Bracken and Charlie Hodgson stood down for one reason or another and Jonny Wilkinson was handed the captaincy for the first time. With so many regulars missing I was one of the senior figures in the squad and was excited by the challenge. I really enjoy playing with new players, certainly with England these days. As recently as two or three years ago I would have been a little bit wary playing in a side with that much inexperience, but everyone slotted in so well. Probably the biggest difference that week was that due to the lack of senior players we tended to do too much. The coaches, quite rightly, had to go through everything for the benefit of the new guys, but the upshot was that we spent an awful lot of time on our feet. I remember looking around after the Thursday session, and while we weren't exactly blowing, there weren't many people staying behind to practise their own skills. They had all shot off to get their feet up and get rested.

I think that was probably reflected in the way we played the Italians. Five of our six tries came in the first 20 minutes, during which time we were on fire. The contact situation was good, the breakdowns were quick, turnovers were efficient. We were playing at a pace Italy couldn't live with. And not just Italy, I suspect. We would have caught a lot of people out that day.

I was pleased for two guys in particular: Josh Lewsey and Mike Tindall. With Jason Robinson around you might say that the full-back slot was fairly well taken. You might; Josh wouldn't. His two-try display on his championship debut provided a perfect example for anyone who wants to play for England about taking your opportunity. With Jason injured, Josh got one chance and took it very impressively with both hands. Mike also crossed the try line, which was satisfying for him after being told by his boyhood idol, Will Carling, in a column in the *London Standard* that England are a better team without him. Clive Woodward disagreed vehemently (as do I) but said he was concerned that if such negativity continued Mike might start believing it and go backwards. I can't believe someone of Tinds's quality would allow criticism like that to get to him, to be honest. What surprised me about the article was that I have Carling and Tindall down as fairly similar players. As a former captain, Will should know not to slag off his own countrymen, however strong your personal thoughts are. Will is still within the rugby community so he should be careful about that.

At half-time, everyone thought we had just had a dodgy ten-minute spell and that normal service would be resumed when we got back out. I've only got one theory as to why we didn't get it back. The boys were knackered, certainly in the last 30 minutes. There was lethargy in what they were doing. The calls, the moves – there just wasn't that spark about us. Italy, to be fair, changed their defensive pattern, which made it a little bit more difficult, and we probably weren't as sharp or as cute as we could have been. But I think the amount of work we had done in the build-up was the biggest factor. The coaches recognized that, and we went into our last two games, against Scotland and Ireland, on the back of very light weeks. I believe it is no coincidence that we went on to produce our two most impressive performances of the campaign.

Jonny made no fuss about being captain. He was no different than he would be in a normal week. But it wouldn't really have mattered who had captained that side that particular day. The message from any of us, on a one-off occasion in the middle of the championship, would have been much the same: 'Get on with your own jobs and I'll toss the coin.' Obviously it was a great honour for Jonny, and I have been very honoured to do the job myself, but Clive could have appointed anybody. You're never going to fill the boots of someone like Martin Johnson. You've got to try to be your own person. Jonny didn't put any more pressure on himself. He didn't take it upon himself to go and cajole the players, or even to boost them up. There was no shouting or screaming from him. He knew everyone was happy, so he was happy. His label had changed from vice-captain to captain, and that was pretty much it.

Clive actually withdrew Jonny soon after half-time in order to give Charlie Hodgson a run-out at fly-half. Charlie had played the previous two games at inside-centre because the management wanted him to get more game-time in the bank in case injury to Jonny required him to take over as play-maker. This time, though, the plan backfired. Charlie wrecked knee ligaments after catching a boot in the turf and was later told it would require reconstruction. It was very sad for him as I'm sure he would have started the Scotland game. Indeed, Clive had said as much. But he is young and his chance will come again.

Charlie's misfortune meant that my mate Paul Grayson came in from the cold, four years after winning what most people thought would be his last cap in Paris. England had lost a World Cup quarter-final against South Africa, and it was the signal for a changing of the guard. Out went Grays, in came Jonny. Except that Grays never saw it that way. He never accepted that his international days were over. He has always had so much to offer but has maybe not always been guided in a way he responds to. The caps he won prior to his second coming were achieved on natural talent alone. He never had the individual coaching or analysis of the rest of his game. All he had was a kicking coach, and all he was told to do was to 'go out and win us the game', which he usually did.

When Wayne Smith arrived at Saints, Grays had slipped to probably third-choice fly-half. He certainly wasn't playing anywhere near his potential, but it just seemed to be accepted.

The attitude seemed to be 'he's not playing well; never mind, we'll get someone else in'. Grays became an occasional full-back and started to think about jacking in playing and becoming a coach, so disappointed was he with the club. He did in fact go on the England tour of North America as kicking coach in 2001, while Dave Alred was away with the Lions. But just when he was ready to hang up his boots, Smithy arrived to transform his game and revive his international playing career.

Seeing Grays return to England colours has given me great pleasure because he has had some genuinely horrible years through no fault of his own. His dip in form coincided with some domestic difficulties. Neither he nor his wife Emma were to blame, it was just one of those unfortunate things that happen, yet they were mature enough to take time out and work at it, and later they got back together. For that I'm eternally grateful, because they make the most fantastic family and are just a brilliant couple. There is no question in my mind that getting back with Emma and having the twins has inspired Grays to be the person he now is, not just on the field but off it, too.

When, on 22 March, he came off the bench against Scotland shortly past the hour mark I was absolutely thrilled for him. I can picture now the smile on the faces of his parents, and especially Emma and his eldest son James, who must have been so proud of him. He has taken a hell of a lot of flak, and it was a big two fingers to a lot of people. As he might have put it, 'I never said I was going to retire. You all retired me.'

Jonny had kicked seven goals out of seven by the time he made way for Grays, and I was pretty pleased with my contribution too. I was very clear on my job description, my roles and my key tasks. I knew exactly what I had to do. I had them all visually practised in my mind and on the training park and that took nerves out of the equation. I had a hand in most of the tries, which was satisfying, but the game we were trying to play was always going to be squeezed in around me. What I did to deserve a stray boot in the face right at the end I really don't know, but it ripped my nose open and I needed 13 stitches to close it up. Head wounds tend to bleed worse than anywhere else (not that there's too much blood running around my brain), and this one was no different. I got hit, went onto my haunches, and within a second it was dripping. The final whistle had gone, everyone was walking off the pitch, and I couldn't believe it had happened. I got it seen to, then went upstairs and saw Mum and Dad. They started fussing. I couldn't blame them. They were only concerned.

Anyway, if I couldn't wear a smile now, when could I? With our 40–9 win over the Scots we'd earned ourselves another shot at redemption. A Grand Slam day out in Dublin beckoned.

'Look . . . if you had . . . one shot . . . one opportunity to seize every-thing you ever wanted . . . one moment . . . would you capture it . . . or just let it slip?'

It was the video tape of our dreams, played to a backdrop of booming bass and the lyrics of Eminem's 'Lose Yourself'. Johnno and Ben Kay towering over lineouts; Wiggy (Graham Rowntree) and Jase Leonard powering forward in the tight; Lawrence exploding off the base of a scrum; Richard Hill, Steve Thompson and Backy marauding in the loose.

'His palms are sweaty . . . knees weak, arms are heavy . . . there's vomit on his sweater already . . . Mom's spaghetti . . . he's nervous, but on the surface he looks calm and ready . . .'

Time and again the ball was spun wide. Time and again Will and Tinds danced through gaps. Time and again Benny Cohen, Josh and Jason dashed, powered, scorched away from defenders to score. Time and again Jonny kicked his goals and nailed opponents in the tackle.

It was 29 March 2003, the night before the Grand Slam decider, the night before Backy would come down to breakfast and read us our fortune, the night before Judgement Day. We could do it because here was the evidence of what we were capable, glorious extracts of our unbeaten season strung together.

But we had been here before. Several times.

The mood in the camp was unfailingly positive. We had one shot, one opportunity, and this time we were damn well going to take it. It didn't matter that the Irish side facing us was better than the Welsh, Scottish and Irish sides that had denied us in our previous Grand Slam bids. This time would be different. We'd had a chat at the beginning of the week and agreed not to hide from the challenge, not to wrap it up in any other story or to play it down in any way. 'This is a huge, must-win game for England,' Clive told us. 'There is no hiding place, no one to blame.' We agreed to cut out all bullshit for the whole week. We knew what we had to say to the media. We needed to just get on with it. We all knew how big the game was, and because we got that out of the way early there was no one individual thinking, 'God, this is a big game!' Nobody was thinking about winning or losing; it was purely focusing on the process. We didn't consider the height we had to scale or how far the fall was.

A lot of people have learned through the experiences of others, or indeed their own, about what should and should not be said to the media. It's all based around what the opposition will read. Everyone already thinks we're the most arrogant nation in the world, so let's not give them any ammunition. Often, in fact most of the time, we'll find it's the opposition who are mouthing off about how they are going to beat England. It doesn't come from us. We are very humble and always have a huge amount of respect for the team we are playing against. And that is not preached to us, it is genuinely the way the players are: very confident but in no way the arrogant bunch we are so regularly made out to be.

A further sign that we were on the ball before the Ireland match was Clive's decision that all our work must be done before we left England. Smart move, I thought, as it showed he had learned from the bad experiences of others. Remember the 2001 Lions and all those Wallabies with video cameras under their coats? Remember Gloucester's Heineken Cup tie in Munster during the 2002–03 season when their gameplan mysteriously turned up in the back of a taxi? It has also been suggested to me that before our Grand Slam game in Ireland in October 2001 one of the waiters was instructed to copy down all the notes from our team room.

But that was not the only reason that come matchday we played a game Ireland had not expected. At the beginning of the week we'd had a strategic meeting where we'd reviewed the Scotland game and gone through plans about what we were going to do in Dublin. I was concerned that it was too predictable and that we would be playing into Irish hands. My theory was based on the experience of Northampton's two most recent Powergen Cup ties against London Irish. Saints had been playing brilliant rugby in all the games leading into the 2002 Twickenham final and were favourites to beat London Irish easily, but Irish had done their homework. They set out to spoil us from the outside and to prevent us getting the ball wide. They absolutely battered us. So before our 2003 semi-final we decided to totally change the gameplan, to play a really forward-orientated game and really go strong up front. The change totally threw them. I was able to make breaks through the guts and set up simple targets for the forwards, and Irish didn't know what had hit them. I thought the Ireland game could potentially be a mirror image of that. I put it to Grays and Ben Cohen. Ben said, 'You won't say anything, you'll just talk to me about it.' I thought, 'We'll see about that.' Jonny Wilkinson's room was opposite mine, and I went and put my concerns to him. Then I went to Will Greenwood, the man in charge of attack.

It wasn't a case of going behind anybody's back. We weren't trying to take any credit, we just wanted what was best for the team. Looking back, I'm pretty sure that meeting won us the game. Consider Mike Tindall's try, the second-half score that finally broke Irish resistance. Nine times out of ten from that scrummage we would have gone wide, looking to flood round the outside channel, but this time Grays called a short move off Will. All the dummy runners came round as it was going wide and then Tinds shot up the guts where Ireland weren't defending. Ireland didn't have a clue where we were going. The midfield is a very strong area of the Irish team, there's no question about that, but they were expecting us to play the way we had in the previous two games and were caught out. Clive enjoyed this end product too. I think he was pleased we had sorted ourselves out. It was a sign of the growing maturity he wants from his players.

The atmosphere inside Lansdowne Road was, of course, extraordinary, and the England team, staying true to their pledge not to hide from anything, were immersed in it early. Warming up on the pitch beforehand we were getting a lot of banter from a very confident home crowd. If one of us dropped the ball we really got it. If anything, it made us focus even more as we quietly got on with our drills. It is amazing what you hear coming out of the crowd before kick-off; once the game starts, of course, nothing gets through. Joanne told me afterwards about the crowd's fantastic rendition of 'Fields of Athenry'. I have no recollection of it whatsoever. The ground could have been silent for all I knew. My mind was focused on where the ball was, where my position was . . . detail, detail, detail.

But I do remember the red carpet row before kick-off, when we were lined up to meet the Irish president, Mary McAleese, only to be told that Ireland wanted to stand where we were. Apparently it was their lucky end. Martin Johnson was approached and asked to lead us along the carpet to the other side of the halfway line. He politely declined. And quite right too. Though it would have been easy for us to cave in and move in order to keep everyone happy, in that environment it would have been wrong. It would have sent totally the wrong message to our opponents – that we could be pushed around. And on that day, of all days, we were not going to be pushed around. With Johnno back at the helm that was never going to happen. There are certain games where the force of personality in the captain is very significant, and this was definitely one of them. In that type of environment there isn't a player in the world to get even close to Johnno. He's in a different league. You could not pick a better guy to deal with all the shenanigans that were going on before, during and after that game. He knew that in such a hostile environment we had to stamp our authority on proceedings. Before we'd left the changing room he'd called us all together and said, 'Right, we're not going to take any shit here. Go out and win.' Typical Johnno. Straight to the point. No wasted words. The mood was set before they started messing us around on the carpet. I just knew that not one England player was going to move. Not one. Johnno stood there and told the official, 'You can whinge all you like. Get on with it.' All I could think about was what the BBC would be making of it. The clock was ticking and the game hadn't started. There would be someone going absolutely spastic in Mission Control. 'We're running eight minutes late. What the hell is going on? Come on, get on with it! We've got Final Score at 4.45!' It was like being back in the school playground. It was so pathetic.

When I first heard that RFU president Derek Morgan had sent a letter of apology to the Irish president, I must admit I was pretty annoyed, especially after I was told of a comment made by Donal Lenihan in relation to the episode. 'England,' said Donal, 'are a fantastic side, but they do let themselves down. They do make it easy for people not to like them.' For your information, Donal, this was not an incident of England's making. Hence, Derek's letter was not an admission of guilt, rather an apology should any upset have been caused or offence taken. Personally speaking, far greater offence was taken at the way my parents were treated at the after-match function. Did I get a letter of apology from the president of the IRFU for my father being denied entry into the environs of the dinner so that he could take a photo of me picking up my fiftieth cap? Did I hell. I implored two security guys to let him through and then some little old duffer backed them up. They were just adamant: no ticket, no entry. These jobsworths were never going to get that power again; this was their one chance. Sadly, my dad will never again get the opportunity to take that photo. Mum and Dad had made great efforts to get out there, only to be told that after watching each of my 49 appearances all over the world they could not see me receive the silver cap to mark my fiftieth. Well, thanks very much indeed.

I hadn't wanted to make anything of my fiftieth cap earlier in the day for fear that I might get emotional and lose focus. So I'd turned down the chance to lead the side out, as tradition dictates, and told Johnno to do the honours. I wanted the Irish crowd to see him first: his size, his stature, his body language. 'No regrets,' we had said beforehand. And I had none.

Lawrence had been first across the try line, just as he'd been at Murrayfield in 2000. This time it wasn't a precursor to disappointment. From Ireland's first scrummage put-in, England called a little wheel, we got a good hit, they were under pressure. It was a walk-in, really. Hilly was all over scrum-half Peter Stringer and popped the ball up to me. I saw off David Humphreys and Geordan Murphy before giving the scoring pass to Lawrence. Other than that, we spent most of the first half defending as they threw the kitchen sink at us. It was pretty fierce stuff. Hilly, Wiggy and I had to go off for running repairs (my nose had split open, despite assurances from the doc that it wouldn't when he'd taken the stitches out the day before), and when I returned the battle was at its height. Jonny, in particular, was booming everyone. Crucially, though, we kept Ireland out while managing to score on each of the few occasions we got near their 22. At half-time, leading 13–6, we walked off thinking we had done bloody well.

The mood in the changing room was one of great excitement, but I felt there was too much noise, too many people saying what we should and should not do. Too many times you go in after a good first half and get this sort of talk. So I took it upon myself to calm the place down. 'Hold on . . . *quiet*!' I said. 'We've won the first half because of our preparation in the week. Let's not change it now.' Half the problem was that the boys couldn't wait to get out and finish the job.

I had my nose reassessed while I slugged down as much Lucozade as I could, in readiness for a lung-busting final 40 and the possibility of a drugs test afterwards. I didn't want to be hanging around trying to produce enough to fill a bottle, regardless of the result, so I polished off a litre and a half. Some of the other boys had a nibble, but I eat three hours before the game and then I won't touch anything.

As it turned out, this was one of those occasions when I could have run all day. I found myself haring across the pitch from side to side during the second half and I never seemed to get tired. At one point I went ballistic when we tried to run the ball out of defence once too often. 'What the hell are we doing?' I screamed. 'We've got the breeze, let's use it. Get the ball down there. Stop messing about with it. We don't need to be playing any rugby down here.' The message hit home, Jonny started pinging it everywhere, and the forwards really began driving the lineouts. It was proper armchair stuff, almost to the point of being boring. The only way Ireland were going to score was to run 80 metres – and they weren't going to do that.

With 25 minutes remaining, Jonny went off to be patched up and Grays entered the fray. Once again the debate was reignited as to how dependent England are on Jonny. My thoughts are this. Jonny is a great player, one of the world's best. Were we to start a Test series or a World Cup campaign without him, I'd be thinking, 'Gee, that's a major, major weapon we haven't got.' But in the middle of a game there isn't any player who I think would leave us in the shit if he went off. Not even Jonny. Here was a case in point. There had not been a bigger game for this group of England players than this one, and when the heat was on and the game needed to be won, Grays came on and won it. There he was, as bold as brass, doing the business. A fantastic crossfield kick which nearly put Ben in, then he called the move that put Mike Tindall in. In addition to Grays, Charlie Hodgson is also right there in the frame. The pair of them would probably walk into most international sides.

Tinds's try was followed five minutes later by Will Greenwood's first. For the first time in the game I looked at the scoreboard; we were 27–6 up. I knew we had won it. I think we all felt the same. There was no way, I reckoned, that the Irish were going to score three converted tries without reply to level the scores, and that thought enabled us to relax a bit and play some more rugby . . . and score another 15 points. To the death we were focused. 'Give them fuck all,' was the constant cry. 'No tries. Let's nil them.'

I'm sure that at that moment the minds of England fans scanned all those near misses: Wembley 1999, Murrayfield 2000, Lansdowne Road 2001. But I didn't give them a second thought. I was in the here and now and loving it. If my try in Cape Town for the Lions was my greatest moment in rugby, this was to date my greatest day, without question. It was time to soak up the atmosphere, to look around at the players you were playing with and load up the memory bank. It was as if I was watching the video. I was enjoying watching the people I was playing around.

And then, as the moment of glory approached, I had a bizarre falling-out with a fellow member of the squad. It was similar to my Powergen Cup final incident with Budge Pountney in that everyone has his own interpretation of what had gone on.

Ireland had been targeting my nose throughout, and it was constantly bleeding. That didn't bother me as it meant they weren't concentrating on something else, and we had 14 others to exploit their lapse. With 10 minutes left, referee Jonathan Kaplan told me to go off and get it sorted. Simon Kemp, the England team doctor, took issue with him. 'Hold on a minute, I'll just wipe it off,' he said. The ref had given us a penalty, but then reached for his whistle as if he was going to reverse it for dissent. I bawled, 'Doc, for fuck's sake, man, I'll get off the pitch. Just leave the ref alone.' The game still had time to run and I was conscious we needed to keep the ref sweet and not give away any silly penalties. The last thing I wanted was for Jonathan to give a penalty against the doctor. He didn't, and Jonny kicked the goal.

In injury time Will and Dan crossed for further tries, and then the whistle sounded. My emotion was not relief, as you might think, but an overwhelming sense of pride. I have won the championship on numerous occasions, but there is an edge when you go undefeated. Being a Grand Slam winner really does make you feel you are part of history. It's quite humbling, I have to say.

After that, we could confidently say that this England side was a good one, but not that we were a great side. Before the advent of the World Cup, had England enjoyed the results this group of players had, home and away, we would probably have been labelled a great side. But now there is something by which every good side can be measured every four years, so the accolade of greatness must be reserved for the team that wins the World Cup. Look at all the southern hemisphere sides that have won World Cups. They were genuinely great sides. In the spring of 2003, we were a good side with the potential one day to be great.

England's 2003 Grand Slam players and results

Forwards: Jason Leonard, Graham Rowntree, Steve Thompson, Robbie Morris, Julian White, Trevor Woodman, Mike Worsley, Mark Regan, Ben Kay, Danny Grewcock, Simon Shaw, Martin Johnson (capt.), Richard Hill, Neil Back, Lewis Moody, Joe Worsley, Lawrence Dallaglio

Backs: Matt Dawson, Kyran Bracken, Andy Gomarsall, Jonny Wilkinson, Paul Grayson, Charlie Hodgson, Alex Sanderson, Dan

Luger, Will Greenwood, Mike Tindall, Ollie Smith, James Simpson-Daniel, Ben Cohen, Josh Lewsey, Jason Robinson, Phil Christophers

(P5, W5, D0, L0, F173, A46)

England 25 France 17 (Twickenham, 15 February)
Wales 9 England 26 (Millennium Stadium, 22 February)
England 40 Italy 5 (Twickenham, 9 March)
England 40 Scotland 9 (Twickenham, 22 March)
Ireland 6 England 42 (Lansdowne Road, 30 March)

9(i)
Shooting for the Pot

HISTORY LESSON DOWN UNDER

'Keep practising, you useless bastard!'

The voice came from a complete stranger, and a school kid at that, from the other side of the car park of the Inter-Continental Hotel in the New Zealand capital, Wellington. It wasn't directed at one of his mates, either, but at Dorian West, the Leicester and England hooker, who was minding his own business, rehearsing his lineout throws with coach Simon Hardy. If I'd doubted the Kiwis respected us before we arrived, I now knew for sure.

England had only ever won once in New Zealand, and that was 30 years ago. The record in Australia, our second stop on this summer 2003 tour of rugby's toughest destinations, was even worse. Played ten, lost ten. We had ground to make up to gain the respect of the locals, but none of us could possibly have imagined how much.

Touring New Zealand and Australia so close to the World Cup was always going to be a gamble. The potential for damage to our self-belief was clear if we got it wrong. But Clive Woodward thinks in positives, not negatives. He saw it as a chance to lay down a marker before the World Cup, to make the people of Australasia aware that being Grand Slam champions of the northern hemisphere means something, while convincing ourselves before the tournament that we could beat the All Blacks and the Wallabies. To a man we bought into his vision. Unlike in 1998 when England had travelled short-handed to this part of the world and paid a humiliating price, everybody was up for this one. We all felt in our water that this would not be another Tour from Hell. We just had to go out and prove it to the people of New Plymouth, Wellington and Melbourne.

The jibes began long before the jet lag had cleared the system. In a nutshell, England were a team of forwards and no backs, we were boring, bad for the game and too old. Oh yes, and we were about to get our arses kicked. Sure enough, three weeks and three games later the ledger read played three, lost three. But it wasn't England who had drawn a blank, it was the southern hemisphere. Another slice of humble pie, Mr Campese?

I just don't understand why it is that wherever we go England are always perceived to be the princes of arrogance. Does nobody in New Zealand listen to themselves speak? That, my friends, is arrogance, and it's coming from your lips. I have always had fantastic memories of being in New Zealand, from the time I toured with Marlow to my stint playing for Te Awamutu shortly after joining Northampton. Even the Tour from Hell, when I captained England for the first time and we lost every game, is a positive memory. I have met loads of Kiwis who have been great, from Buck Shelford through to Wayne Smith, and there is no rugby country I respect more. Yet this time, for the first time, I could not believe the reaction we encountered in New Zealand. I couldn't believe the arrogance of the people, talking up the All Blacks and rubbishing anything and everything English. I had always associated respect and humility with New Zealand rugby, but this time what came our way was downright disrespectful. We were crap, we were past it, and we were going to get beaten.

On 13 June, the night before England played New Zealand in Wellington, I went out with some of the midweek lads. Injury had ruled me out of the match so we had a few beers. Word got round that a few of the England lads were in the bar, and when I went to the toilet I overheard a couple of locals talking about us.

'Arrogant bunch of pricks these Pommies. I couldn't stand it if they won,' said one.

'No worries, these Pommies are going to get their arses kicked,' replied his mate.

Later on, they tried to be all matey with me to my face. I wasn't interested in the slightest.

There has long been a perception that Super 12 rugby is the real deal and that club and provincial rugby in the northern hemisphere pales by comparison. Personally, I always thought it was one-eyed nonsense. There are qualities to admire in both styles of rugby. But it was crystal clear to us all that our opening game against the New Zealand Maori would set the tone for the tour and go some way towards settling the debate. The Maori had been unbeaten in 24 games until losing to a full Wallabies side in 2001, and during that run had beaten 12 international teams. Those wins included a 62–14 pummelling of England in Rotorua in 1998. They picked Christian Cullen, the All Blacks' record try scorer, and former national captain

Taine Randell, and they pretty obviously expected to win, especially as their opponents had just flown across the world and were not yet acclimatized.

A column appeared in the *Sunday Star*Times* on the day before the match under the heading 'Time to bring Poms down a peg or two', written by a journalist called Phil Gifford. In it he admitted that English rugby had always 'copped a bagging' in New Zealand. He then proceeded to portray a stereotype of our game which belonged in the amateur era and refused to give England any credit for their one and only win in the Land of the Long White Cloud, back in 1973. 'The English tactics varied from kicking the ball in the air to kicking the ball to touch,' he scoffed. It was unbelievable stuff, but quite revealing in that an element, at least, of New Zealand had clearly not kept up with the times. They had focused so hard on Super 12 and their beloved men in black that they had not noticed the strides made by European rugby in general and English rugby in particular. To my mind it was complacency born of arrogance. Put simply, they never thought the northern hemisphere game could or would trump theirs.

And so to Yarrow Park for the Maori game, where it struck me that the monsoon rain conditions might not be ideal for the Super 12 brand of rugby. The Maori didn't see it that way, however, as they started chucking the ball around from the start . . . and dropping it. England kept it tight, drove up the middle, and kept control of the ball. Paul Grayson kicked three penalties and converted second-half tries by Simon Shaw and Andy Gomarsall. I was delighted for Grays, who came in for a lot of well-deserved praise from Clive for the way he steered the side home. A lot of people will probably knock him and say it was the 'same old Grayson', but because of the awful conditions we needed a pinpoint kicking performance early on to get our forwards in the game. On occasions when we needed to hit the short side, run the ball and bring Jamie Noon into the attack, he did that as well. Grays wasn't particularly happy with his performance because he would have preferred to show more of the running game he had exhibited at Northampton during the year, but it showed the quality and the experience Grays has that in a real pressure environment he was able to boss the show. England not only won, they stopped the Maori playing any type of rugby.

The Kiwi reaction was predictable. 'No-frills Poms shut out Maori' read the headline in the *Daily News*, whose correspondent Murray Hills pointed out that 'If you were English, and happy with a no-frills approach to the game, it would have been damn good viewing.' The inference was that non-Poms had been short-changed, especially when he added, 'It would have been almost good to watch if England had managed to do something with all the possession. But they didn't.'

For the record, England won by two tries to nil.

The locals went on about 'boring' England, but you cannot expect to win a game of rugby if you're going to throw the ball around no matter what and turn it over so many times. England played to the conditions, yet New Zealanders assumed it to be the English style of rugby. 'On a dry ground, it's unlikely England will have the skill or the pace to match the All Blacks,' the *Daily News* concluded. That theme was taken up Ali Williams, the All Blacks lock, who was quoted in the *Dominion Post* as saying, 'You have to throw it around regardless of the conditions at this level. I don't think New Zealand rugby needs to change its style. Throwing the ball around and all that jazz is part of who we are and part of the way we play the game.'

The Maori win gave the Test team back in Wellington a massive lift. New Zealand was a step into the unknown, but our defensive pattern had worked brilliantly against what was effectively an All Blacks second string. We totally closed them off and they had nowhere to go. The boys put them under enormous pressure, pressure they'd not experienced before. The Kiwis are used to having a little bit of room to throw it around and for their big fellas to get a bit of momentum. Very rarely did the Maori get that freedom. Kyran Bracken played the first hour at scrum-half before being replaced by Andy Gomarsall, who did well and deserved his late try. The game was crying out for the scrum-half to attack as the Maori defence was so fanned out. Gomars did that effectively, mixing his game very well. He ran down the short side, picked and went round the corner. He might have made only two or three yards a time, but you do that and the opposition starts to get worried about you, about leaving a gap. Then all of a sudden you start shipping the ball out, and bingo. The one thing I said to Kyran afterwards was that he should have a go more. He is such a dangerous player, but in that game I felt the opposition didn't see him as a threat.

Kyran and I have always offered each other advice, and it is always done sincerely. On this occasion, however, there was another reason for trying to bolster him. I had strained my thigh in training two days earlier and was doubtful for the Test match. By Wednesday, a decision had been taken: Kyran would wear the number 9 shirt against New Zealand, just as he had done on his England debut 10 years earlier.

People don't understand what it means not to be in the shirt because of injury rather than selection. It is a sickening feeling. You haven't lost it, you've given it away. I was more gutted giving up the shirt than I was at missing the match itself. I had worked so hard over the previous 18 months to make it my own, so just to hand it away because of injury was unbelievably frustrating. At the end of the day, though, it's a game of rugby. I'm not going to let something like that faze me now. In the past I would have become moody and really irritable about it, and looked to blame someone. I probably would have gone off on one about not having had an MRI in the five weeks since I originally did the injury in a club match against Leeds. I would have found someone else to blame, rather than just deal with what was in front of me.

On this occasion, Dan Luger put me right before any such thoughts could take a hold on my mind. 'Daws, it's only a game of rugby,' he said. He looked at me, and I knew he was thinking of Nicky Duncombe. And I thought, 'Shit, Luges, you're totally right.' As much as it does mean a lot to me to play rugby, it is not a matter of life and death. Recent experiences have given me a perspective on life and rugby which maybe I didn't have before. Whatever the reason, I took a decision which was in the best interests of the team. Maybe I could have got through the game. If I was selfish and I wanted to keep Kyran away and take the money, I might have been able to fool the medics. But had I broken down inside five minutes because I needed to sprint, Kyran would have had to come on, leaving no scrum-half on the bench for the rest of the game. I would have let down my team-mates and I would not have done myself any favours either. Being 80 per cent fit is no good at this level. So I took the decision away from the medics.

Pre-match talk centred around the pace of the New Zealand back division and what the likes of Joe Rokocoko and Doug Howlett would do to us if they got the ball. And they would because they had flamboyant playmaker Carlos Spencer calling the shots. Once again it was arrogance at work. They had picked nobody who could kick the ball. Not one player. They thought that in the most massive of Test matches they were going to have loads of ball and would run us off the park. We thought, 'Hold on a minute.' If England went into a game with that approach we'd get absolutely pasted by our critics.

We knew it would be a fairly hefty battle up front, and that gave us encouragement. If we could dominate in that area we knew it would take a lot out of the New Zealanders. We targeted certain players, Spencer among them. We have all always rated Carlos, but we felt that if he was put under pressure he would drop back deeper and deeper. And that was proved in the first few seconds of the game when Steve Thompson and Ben Kay jumped all over him and charged his kick down. Of course we were also wound up by what had been written and said about us in the build-up, to the point where the day before the game Clive had finally snapped. 'They [the NZ media] have this impression of English rugby that we all play in wellington boots and we play in grass two feet long. There are one or two balanced reporters, but mainly they are just totally one-eyed. Nothing is based on facts. I see the game as very evenly matched but the [New Zealand] public think England are going to get smashed. The media is just so behind their own team, but we will do our talking on the pitch. This team is way beyond being wound up by things in the press.'

The match will be remembered for the fact that England won, by 15 points to 13; for Williams, the New Zealand second row, trampling on the head of Josh Lewsey and getting away with it; and for the period during the second half when six England forwards packed down against the All Blacks eight and stood firm. We played poorly, let's make no bones about it. When we had the ball we were fairly shocking. We didn't seem to have a passion and desire to entertain when we had the ball. What won us the game was our defence. We reserved our best work for when we didn't have the ball. It was one of the best rearguard displays ever seen from an England team. We were shown examples after the game of intensity levels. The levels of workrate of certain players when England had the ball was low, but then when the ball was turned over the intensity increased tenfold. That pretty much said it all. Maybe we were too worried about what the opposition could do given the chance, so our mindset was probably defend first and then we'll see what happens when we get the ball.

Across in Australia, David Campese accused us of not knowing where the try line was and of driving fans away from the game through negative tactics. His exact words, in his column in the Sydney-based *Daily Telegraph*, were as follows:

There was a time when rugby was exciting. Remember that? I know it is a professional sport, but England are happy to win no matter what. I'm not sure they know what scoring a try is any more. And it's very bad for the game. The reason why a try is worth five points was because the International Rugby Board were hoping that teams would score them. That's not the case with England. And it's a real worry. The way England play just sends people away in droves. It's clear that English rugby hasn't moved on a jot over the past ten years. They are completely reliant on the boot of Jonny Wilkinson – even when they get into the opposition 22.

There's always going to be people like Campese who think they are still better than everyone else in the world at playing the game. They've got them in all sports. He's one of those players who just tries to get some sort of reaction out of people by being very controversial. At the time it was very difficult to answer that kind of argument because on that wind-blown evening in Wellington we *were* fairly poor with the ball. We didn't score any tries, and to be perfectly honest we didn't look like doing so. In fact, in the changing room afterwards there were wry smiles on the faces of pretty much everyone, as if to say, 'How the hell did we win that game?' But we had, and, as the southern hemisphere used to delight in telling us, it is all about the winning.

We knew we were going to get slated in the local press. But we took it because we knew against Australia the track was going to be quick whatever the conditions because we were playing indoors, so we would have ample opportunity to answer and silence our critics. We hadn't felt that in either the Maori monsoon or the Wellington wind there was any point in trying to toss it about as the likelihood was that we would only have succeeded in falling into the trap laid by the likes of

Campese. The time to entertain and play champagne rugby was in Melbourne.

How extraordinary that our playing style should have been the topic of debate following the game rather than the footwork of Ali Williams. First of all, how did the officials miss it? I was up in the stand and I could see it from 150 yards away. It was a disgraceful assault on Josh Lewsey's head which could have ended his career, or worse. For me it was a *déjà vu* moment: it took me back to the 1998 tour when Ian Jones stamped on Graham Rowntree during the first Test in Dunedin. Insufficient evidence, they said then. Insufficient evidence, they said this time.

What absolute bollocks. When Williams was cited my reaction was, 'I should bloody hope so too.' The video was shocking, and we all wanted to see a little bit of justice. We didn't expect it, mind, not after what had happened with Wiggy on the Tour from Hell. And sure enough, when there was none for Josh we shrugged our shoulders and just got on with it. It had happened before and it had happened again. Clive said that had an England player committed such an act he would probably have been locked up.

Fortunately, nobody was seriously harmed, but what is it going to take for an All Black to be punished? What if Josh had been concussed and a doctor had turned round to him and said you'd be stupid ever to play rugby again? What then? Williams being let off not only did no justice to the England player in question, but rugby as a whole was let down. Josh was angry, and he had every right to be. He had two big gashes in his face and one on the side of his head. To his immense credit he bit his lip and we gained revenge on the scoreboard. That is the best way to do it.

And England have become masters of self-restraint. The following week in Melbourne, for example, Richard Hill absolutely annihilated Nathan Grey in the first 10 minutes of the game. He just battered him, and Grey didn't want to know. Two years earlier Grey had put Hilda out of the Lions series with a high elbow in the very same stadium. Later in the evening Mat Rogers swung at Josh. Had it been a boxing match Josh would have left him in a pile because he's as hard as nails. But he bided his time, then stepped off his wing and, wham! Rogers was left squealing like a pig after the best and hardest tackle of the whole summer.

I want rugby league's 'on report' system introduced into union. At the moment offenders either get 10 minutes in the bin (while the victim is perhaps concussed or out with a long-term injury) or he gets away with it altogether. I've played in games where I've been whacked. The referee knows something has gone on but rather than admit he hasn't seen the incident he has busked it. Far better to be able to refer it to an 'on report' committee and allow the facts to be examined and a suitable punishment imposed in the cold light of day. Now, even the 'on report' system isn't perfect. Look at the fact that Werner Greef was the only Springbok to be cited after the game between England and South Africa at Twickenham in November 2002. The citing commissioner had time to study the tapes but failed to spot the catalogue of misdemeanours subsequently picked up by Sky. Generally speaking, though, it has to be the way forward. And make no mistake, something has to be done. I'm convinced incidents of foul play will

Getting smashed in training while in Rotorua on the 1998 Tour of Hell.

Clive Woodward and I have a complex relationship. He's made a hell of a lot of effort with me, and I'll always be grateful for that.

A proud season of captaincy in 2000, even though the final result was a chilly cock-up in Edinburgh and the end of yet another Grand Slam dream.

Am I jinxed at Twickenham? I missed out on European glory in 2000 through injury as Saints beat Munster to win the Heineken Cup...

...lost out to Lawrence Dallaglio and Wasps in the Tetley Bitter Cup Final...

...and ended up on the losing side again against Gloucester in the 2003 Powergen Cup Final.

Lions tour to Australia 2001. It's all too much for me, after my last-seconds conversion clinches victory over ACT Brumbies.

My chance to make amends as I take over from an injured Rob Howley in the 2nd Test in Melbourne. But we were already on the way to a 14–35 defeat.

All work and no play...well, maybe the odd loss at Cribbage when Iain Balshaw was around.

Above: Painful but pleasing. My first try of the 1999 World Cup, against Italy at Twickenham.

Right: Plenty to celebrate. Dublin 2003 and Grand Slam hugs with Wilko.

Below: Battered and bruised, I couldn't believe the trophy was finally in my hands.

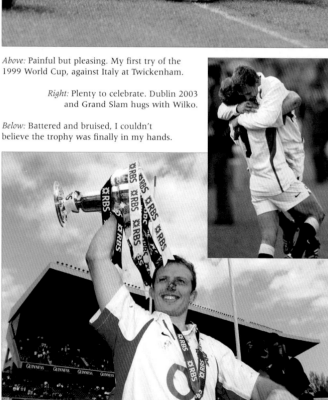

The ideal preparation for World Cup 2003 was beating the Aussies on their home patch in the summer. Martin Johnson, as always, was inspirational, both on and off the pitch.

Our back three of Josh Lewsey, Ben Cohen and Jason Robinson were instrumental to our success down under.

Post-match, June 2003. An even more important celebration against Australia would take place five months later.

What a World Cup! After the wet but wonderful win against France in the semi-final, the fans went crazy, home and abroad. Meanwhile we endured the ice baths in preparation for the biggest game of our lives. Cheers Jason et al.

One man, one team;
Johnno spurs us on (*below*).
That Final kick. How Jonny
nailed it! (*right*).

Left: World Champions, and don't we love it! It seems the fans back home did too.

Below: Six Nations 2004, England v Ireland, Twickenham. We managed just one score, my first-half try, in a defeat that we never really recovered from.

Below: House of Pain, on the summer tour Down Under. The All Blacks ran out 36–3 winners in the first Test at Dunedin. We weren't physically ready for that battle.

Right: Looking forward to a new beginning at Wasps after thirteen years at Northampton.

increasingly head for the courts if the game fails to show it can police itself properly.

We have all been shoed out of the back of a ruck and cheap-shotted at times. There is an unwritten law that you suck it in and get on with it. But unfortunately there are nutters out there who go into certain games with the sole intention to maim. I just pray that someone doesn't get seriously injured by a player purposely out to hurt him because the game will get severely tarnished as a result and all the hard work of the last decade will be totally blown away.

2003 England tour to New Zealand

Sunday, 1 June
Assembled at Pennyhill Park. Felt good to see boys again and catch up on gossip. Physio on thigh followed by 90-minute team meeting. Looks like Clive wants to play same side against New Zealand as against Ireland. Organized kit and food in room with Grays. Doesn't matter how many tours I go on I still get a buzz from packing and organizing break. Will miss that for sure when I stop.

Monday to Tuesday, 2–3 June
Anaerobic session at 7.45 a.m. with Dave Reddin [Otis] and a few of the lads. Feel quite fit but hope we don't overdo it as we did in 1999. Off to golf course for start-of-tour grudge match: Dawson and Dallaglio versus midfield marvels (Greenwood and Tindall). Our putting wins day and they are our bitches for a day. Flight is top draw. Business class whole way. Squad for Maori game were on earlier flight and had six-hour

stopover in Los Angeles. Nip to Venice Beach for some sun, sand and surf. Pity it is overcast. Boys on second flight, of course, devastated at that news. Second leg nothing but sleep so arrive in Auckland feeling fresh.

Wednesday, 4 June
Where did Tuesday go? It failed to register in any of our lives. Shame for Stuart Abbott as 3 June is his birthday! Luges and I spend much of day chilling in a bar with an espresso to keep us awake.

Thursday, 5 June
Gym session in morning. Run for first time at pace and feel sound. Weights just about kill me off. However, leave enough left in tank for rematch at Miramour Links Golf Club. Lol and I go three-up before wobbling and being pegged back to level. Lol plays dream four-iron to save day. Restless night but manage to get to 6.30 a.m. before being wide-eyed.

Friday, 6 June
Early to wake so potter about until Joanne calls. Absolutely chucking it down outside. Train at 10.30 a.m. and feel sharp and fit. Finish with anaerobic session with Barney Kenny and leg feels strong. Everyone mega paranoid of people watching sessions. Management constantly patrol perimeter. Lunch and a chinwag about old tours and classic evenings from past. Sleep before dinner out with Clive, Robbo [Andy Robinson], Will [Greenwood] and Jonny [Wilkinson]. Lovely food and not bad chat. Discuss move selection and patterns. Legs start to stiffen up so head to bed.

Saturday, 7 June
Another early rise. Jet lag still getting better of me. Walk to Bodyworks Gym with Barney to do some pulley work on thigh. Feel a little tired but exercises go well. Quick lunch. Food so far has been spectacular. Pennyhill Park chef David Brain is obviously pulling out all stops to guarantee his World Cup selection. Off to training where disaster strikes. Try to sprint but pull up with a little strain so miss rest of run. Not amused. Spend rest of day in physio answering questions about my fitness. Missing Joanne like crazy, but manage to talk to her on phone. That's better. First smile of the day. Australia dick Ireland 45–16 and look tidy at times.

Sunday, 8 June
Beautiful day, but unfortunately spend it with Backy, who also has a niggle, watching the lads do team run. There's not a lot of variety at moment other than sleeping, eating and training. On top of that I'm injured, so everything seems shit. Session at Wellington Oval, which I'm sure has plenty of viewing facilities for All Black spies. Most unlike our management to be so open, especially as we go through all our backs moves and lineouts. If there are any prying eyes they will have a field day. More physio and a pool session for me, followed by massage and acupuncture. Go downstairs to see midweek team off. Big game for Luges and Grays, who are both in side to play Maori so wish them best of luck. Rest of us head for Shed 5, nice restaurant on seafront. Not a soul around but food (Bluff Oysters) and wine (Cloudy Bay) goes down well. Back to hotel for more physio on leg. Not optimistic, but will keep trying everything.

Monday, 9 June
Matchday. Beat NZ Maori 23–9. Boys shoot off to gym early as All Blacks have it booked for 9 a.m. There is a bit of an overlap and apparently atmosphere is a bit sparky. Plenty of testosterone flying about. I miss it because I am in pool with Barney, where my hip is beginning to loosen up. Lads head out go-karting but I take raincheck as it would be unlikely to do me any good. After a nap I do some video analysis for weekend. Boy racers return having only written off one car. Settle down to watch match. Never seen or heard such one-eyed commentary in all my life. England are superb and play awful conditions brilliantly. Maori try to spin it but don't have the skills. Who are the naive ones then?

Tuesday, 10 June
Midweek boys return to Wellington with green faces after particularly dodgy flight. A few knocks, but all in one piece. It is decision day on the seven players to go to join Churchill Cup squad in Canada, so it's eyes down. Everybody is trying to avoid Clive and the 'Can I have a word?' line. Test team to play New Zealand is picked and I am in, even though I have not been fitness tested. I am given until tomorrow to prove my fitness and am hopeful after starting to run in afternoon session. Quick stretch in pool afterwards and then it's off to ambassador's reception with All Blacks and New Zealand and England netball teams. Hundreds of school kids are also there to hear the Prime Minister speak. It is a bit Old School but it is nice to see youngsters meet their heroes.

Wednesday, 11 June
Just when I think Wellington can't get any worse I have the day I have been dreading and have to pull out of Test match. Mixed emotions, initially one of frustration and anger at missing out on such a big game. I think this will be one of my biggest international disappointments. It's such a huge game to miss. But Luges, still reeling from the death of Nicky Duncombe, makes me realize it could be a lot worse. I turn away from my rugby disappointment and think of my family, friends and Joanne. The squad, to a man, come up and say how gutted they are for me, except Andy Gomarsall, who gets bench call-up as a result. Quite revealing, that. After lunch I go for second opinion and am recommended an MRI. Meet Luges for some bench weights then shoot off to Wakefield Hospital for scan. Results are very conclusive: a considerable tear high on thigh. Happy to finally know problem, but little peeved it has taken five weeks to get a scan. Unlikely to be fit for Australia game but will crack on. Clive pulls me to one side and mentions that all he wants me for is the second of two August internationals against France and the World Cup, and that I should just get myself fit for those. He is very relaxed about it and he makes me feel a bit better. Head next door for a Mexican and watch the England netball girls get thumped by 20 points. Hope that's not an omen.

Thursday, 12 June
Day starts well with a chat to Joanne. She seems down and has loads of school reports to write. We have a good giggle and manage to cheer each other up. Undergo rehab session with Otis and leg feels good and strong during run. Rest of lads

off to Middle Earth to visit *Lord of the Rings* cast and set. That sort of thing doesn't really flick my switch, so Otis and I go and play golf, only to find we are playing with Clive and Robbo. I partner Clive and can only hope the lads don't find out, or it's Brown Nose Central for me. Robbo has a dream day and takes the money but it is a good crack. No tour talk, just plenty of banter. Funny how refreshing it is to see the management getting stuck into each other. It makes them seem almost human.

Friday, 13 June
Start a busy day of training doing an 'agility with resistance' session. Can't knock Otis for the variation in his methods. It still amounts to a flogging but at least it's not monotonous. Bite to eat, then off to Westpac Stadium with team for run-through. It is supposed to be a closed session but all the hospitality boxes are full. There would be uproar if that happened at Twickenham. Another case for the defence of English arrogance. I don't think I have ever met such an arrogant bunch of rugby followers. They are so sure they will win tomorrow night. Off to gym for another workout with Otis and then back to pool for last session of day with Barney. Leg is feeling a lot stronger and I am now quietly confident about Australia selection. Dinner and a few cheeky ones in town with guys not involved in Test, then leave a garbled message for Joanne telling her how much I love her. Probably a mistake, but you know what it's like when you're away from the one you love and have alcohol in your system.

Saturday, 14 June
Matchday. England beat New Zealand 15–13. Nice start to day
when the phone rings and it's Joanne. She tells me that some
pisshead left a message on her phone last night and do I know
who it might be! Day really drags so goodness knows how the
team are feeling. Decide to fill time with physio and another
feed before Grays and I head to the team room to chill out.
We play snooker, and then he takes me back to the time we
shared a house by playing tunes on the piano. Must do that
more often as it sends a relaxing vibe right through me. Pack
bags ready for flight to Australia tomorrow, then off to match.
Win 15–13. How did we manage that? Backy and Lol are sin-
binned in second half and the All Blacks still can't get over our
line. Mixed emotions in changing room afterwards. Joy at
winning but disbelief that we could have played so badly and
got away with it. Needless to say the Kiwis find something to
blame other than themselves. Gutted to miss out. Memories of
'98 needed to be erased. The lads showed tremendous heart
and passion in defence, however the All Blacks coughed up
four or five golden opportunities and maybe should have won
comfortably. We need to have more of an edge in attack if we
are to compete in the World Cup. What could have been a
short and sweet reception at Tapa Museum is ruined by Derek
Morgan (our Welsh president) waffling on for about 15
minutes about his past and his rugby achievements. No
wonder other rugby nations think we are, in the words of New
Zealand's Andrew Mehrtens, a 'bunch of pricks' to lose to.

ENGLAND first played a Test match in Australia against the Wallabies in 1963. The game was played in Sydney and the home side won 18–9. Forty years on and the Poms were still not off the mark. But in Melbourne, under the roof of the Telstra Dome, lay the field of our dreams. It was firm underfoot, just perfect for what we had in mind.

And I would be involved this time. Thanks to some awesome work by our physio Barney Kenny and our fitness guru Dave Reddin, and to two, sometimes three physio sessions a day, I was able to pass a fitness test and make myself available for selection. Clive named me on the bench. While I was obviously disappointed not to get the number 9 shirt back, I hadn't expected it. It would have been a very, very harsh call on Kyran. It might not have been a particularly pretty performance in Wellington's Westpac Stadium, but it was a winning one. Moreover, I had not played for six weeks, and to be thrown straight back into that environment is, physically as well as mentally, very tough. In our position you've got to be sharp and up to speed, and I wouldn't have been match-sharp or in the right frame of mind to have started such an intense Test match. It was totally the right call by Clive.

He clearly loved being back in Oz, where he had spent some of his playing career, with an England team that demanded to be taken seriously. But while he had total belief that we could make history and beat the Wallabies, Clive never lost sight of the fact that the World Cup later that year was the bigger picture. So he devised a strategy whereby we treated the tour as if it were the business end of the World Cup. He heaped the pressure on us by recreating that tournament's knockout stages. That cranking up of pressure, week by week, from quarters through semis to the final itself, would happen again, hopefully, come November. The Maori game, he said, was the quarter-final, New Zealand the semi and Australia the final. By doing that the tour had a real knockout feel to it, and every game was a must-win. The nerves started to tingle. This, we told one another, was the feeling we would hope to have to deal with come the autumn, when there would be a pot of gold on the line.

Experience drawn from his six years in charge had convinced Clive that, far from being undone by pressure, we actually thrive on the stuff. Maybe that had been the missing link in previous years. We've always tended to be humble and non-critical of other sides, but sensing that everyone was piling into us Clive turned the thumb screws inside the camp. I once heard an interview with Tim Montgomery, the world's fastest man, who said that in order to be the best you have to believe you're the best. If you don't believe it in your head, he reasoned, you can't turn that into performance. Perhaps England had spent too long talking up the opposition. Whatever the case, Clive decided it was time we changed tack. Hence Backy sitting down to breakfast in Dublin earlier that year and declaring that we were going to put 40 points on Ireland, a side unbeaten in 10 games. And then us doing precisely that.

When it comes to putting pressure on me personally, Clive used to give me all the chat about what all the other English scrum-halves were doing, and that used to wind me up in a negative way. My view is this. If you're going to pick me in your team then believe that I am the man for your team and back me, and I'll be there 100 per cent; don't pick me and then say, 'By the way, Kyran is really close to you,' because that just does nothing for me. I have played my best rugby for England when I have been told I am the clear choice at number 9. When I was first appointed captain in 1998 and I therefore knew I would be in the team, my game was on fire. I wasn't worried about selection. It wasn't an issue. It was just a case of 'off you go'. There then followed a period during which I was told what I could and couldn't do, and I found I wasn't mentally strong enough just to focus on what I was doing. I was looking over my shoulder all the time and that was distracting me from my performance. I don't know whether Clive appreciates that now or not, but certainly the management's attitude these days is very different towards me. They've got a bit more confidence and belief in the fact that I know what I'm talking about.

Having been England captain on the Tour from Hell had only added to my disappointment at not being on the pitch in Wellington, but Melbourne on 21 June offered me another chance of vengeance, though for this I'd have to wear my Lions hat. The Telstra Dome, known in 2001 as the Colonial Stadium, had been the venue for the pivotal match in the three-Test series. We were one-up with the chance to kill off the Wallabies, but we'd blown it after leading at half-time. When we walked into the same changing room two years later, I felt a shiver through my body. I turned to Martin Johnson and said, 'Here lies the scene of possibly the worst half-time chat I've ever heard.'

All of us who went through that experience were still smarting, especially Ben Cohen, who was moody as hell all week.

'What's wrong with you?' I asked one day. 'You're really crabby.'

'I hate Australia, that's what. I've got nothing but shit memories of this place and I want to put them right.'

And if the Lions memory motivated certain individuals, the 'Dad's Army' jibe aimed at our forward pack by Toutai Kefu, Australia's vice-captain, succeeded in winding up the entire tour party. 'Look at their pack,' Kefu had chirped in a *Rugby World* interview. 'They've got guys like Martin Johnson, Neil Back and Jason Leonard who are almost in their mid-30s. England certainly has the players and the depth, but they have stuck with "Dad's Army". They have kept all the older players because they have been winning and they have failed to inject any younger blood.' It was the one slur that really hit home because it was so insulting. It was a really cheap shot. There was a lot of disrespect there, and it wound everyone up. Backy, aged 34 and about to become England's most-capped flanker, was livid. 'By all means slag me off for not being good at A, B or C,' he commented, 'but don't do it because of my age.'

As we got a sweat on in the changing room shortly before kick-off there was a lot of chat about 'Dad's Army'. What Kefu said was brought up numerous times, including the stuff about us not being able 'to handle the pressure away from home when it's applied', whereas 'as Wallabies we love and thrive on the pressure. The bigger the occasion, the more we love it.' It was time for England to have their say. Andy Robinson, who had been assistant to Lions coach Graham Henry in 2001, got stuck into us about physicality and taking no prisoners and the fact that they didn't rate us. Phil Larder then took his turn and was very calm, presumably because it was late in the day and his dentures might have come unstuck had he yelled. A knock on the changing-room door, one last squeeze in the huddle, and then it was time to face our critics.

England, we had been told, didn't know what a try was nor where the try line was. Just five minutes had elapsed when we strung together a move involving 14 phases and 31 pairs of hands, culminating in Will Greenwood touching down. We had spent a long time that week working on ball retention. It was always our intention to play and to constantly recycle ball. We wanted to batter them, but to do it in a certain way. To take them on physically and then to recycle ball. Keep the ball for 14 phases and you are going to have a sniff of the line against any team in the world. But to do that we needed high workrate and, above all else, we needed the pill. Early on we monopolized it. The Aussies couldn't get it off us. The bench boys were on deckchairs pitchside, and with every phase we sat a little straighter until we were perched on the edge. When Will touched down we all thought the same thing: 'Put that in your pipe and smoke it, boys! That, Campo, is what a try looks like!' There was a pocket of England supporters behind the bench, and as Jonny lined up the conversion they yelled, 'Boring, boring England!' It was classic stuff – very, very satisfying.

Tinds claimed the second try to add to his splendid score in Dublin. What was it Will Carling had said about him being the wrong choice if England wanted to do well in the World Cup? The trouble with Mike is that everyone is expecting the next Jerry Guscott. But Jerry is Jerry, Mike is Mike. Everyone is different. That is probably why we're successful, because we've got a lot of individuals who aren't trying to be what they're not. They're being themselves. Tinds has got attributes many centres across the world cannot get near.

His try came from set-piece ball, as did number three from Ben Cohen. Ben's try was different class. I had read a piece beforehand in which Wallabies full-back Chris Latham gave it the big one about how he was going to be the best full-back in the world and how his only rivals to the mantle were Doug Howlett (who is not even a full-back) and Joe Roff (who is a winger). Then I saw Wallabies forward Owain Finegan on a rugby show saying, 'The English are the best at bigging themselves up.' I thought, 'You want to look at your own players, chief.' Ben just made a complete fool of Latham. The England players loved it. Watching the video, we all agreed it couldn't have happened to a nicer person. As Ben tore through the Aussie defence it was as if he'd thought, 'I could mess about with you but I'm going to run round you instead.'

My tour had effectively begun 11 minutes earlier, when I came on for Kyran. It was fabulous to share in such a momentous occasion – one in which Johnno, whom presumably Kefu had seen as Captain Mainwaring, gave a simply awesome performance – and the sing-song which followed back in the changing room. 'Who do you think you are kidding, Mr Hitler?' we boomed out, our voices doubtless carrying along the corridor to where the Australians sat, presumably wondering how they had lost to a battalion of old soldiers. The maul that the forwards drove half the length of the field towards the Aussie line will live long in my memory. How the referee didn't penalize the Wallabies for pulling it down is just beyond me. England drive it 50 yards and then it collapses two yards from the line. Oh, c'mon.

Our achievement was hailed back home, the reaction Brian Moore gave to Sky News a particular favourite of mine. He, too, had clearly been wound up by Campo's carping. 'I was very, very pleased with the performance,' he said. 'You couldn't really fault much of it – and, of course, it shut David Campese up, which is a remarkable thing. Campese is entitled to his opinion, but what he shouldn't do is fit his opinion around a pre-conceived notion. To make some of the comments he has been making about England is simply wrong, there's no other word to describe it.' Moore was equally critical of the southern-hemisphere media's reaction to England: 'It showed a combination of utter insecurity and breathtaking arrogance to me. To not give England credit for the way they've played in the last 18 months just flies in the face of everything that even a partial observer has seen about the way they play.'

We had journeyed to the other side of the world in search of confirmation that we were on the right track going into the World Cup. We got that. But the respect of the southern hemisphere remained elusive. In neither New Zealand nor Australia did they respect what we achieved. Test matches don't come bigger than playing the All Blacks and Wallabies away, except for the semi-finals or final of a World Cup. Yet there was little or no credit given to us down there. There was always another obstacle they were able to put up between them and such an admission. England won, but they can't score tries; they can't play in wet weather; they can't play on hard grounds. There is always something we can't do. And every time we go out and knock down one of those arguments, another is put up.

People find it very, very difficult to give England unreserved praise. New Zealand said we were boring and played unadventurous rugby. But we played two games, in a monsoon and a tempest, and we won them both. Yes, the conditions did guard against us chucking the pill around, but we won. Then we went to Australia, where we were reminded that we hadn't played much rugby in New Zealand and were warned that indoors in Melbourne on a firm ground we would get found out. It didn't happen. In fact, we outscored the Wallabies three tries to one. If any other nation in the world had achieved what we did that June they would have had plaudits coming out of their ears. But because it's England, we've got to be knocked in some way.

All the rugby world had left to throw at us a few months before the World Cup was the presumption that we'd peaked too soon. That we couldn't get any better, even though everyone else would. When we came away there was, of course, no way of knowing how we would fare in the World Cup. All we knew was that in the summer of 2003 we'd achieved what no other English side had ever managed. And we were pretty proud of that.

2003 England tour to Australia

Sunday, 15 June
8 a.m. session with Otis. Progress to about 85 per cent so maybe I will make Aussie match. Fly to Melbourne and check in at Sheraton Towers on the south bank of Yarra River. Great gaff with view to die for from restaurant on twenty-fifth floor. Food is nothing short of sensational. One hell of a standard to

keep up for whole week. Rooming with Grays so maybe they will put me on bench. It would be harsh to drop Kyran after the way he played in Wellington.

Monday, 16 June

Day off to chill and maybe have a game of golf. Think again, Dawson! Physio with Barney at 10 a.m. followed by massage and, after a quick bite to eat, a trip to the gym for isolation exercises on leg. Lunch on run as Otis and Barney want to put me through same fitness test I failed last week to see if there is sufficient improvement. Feel strong and confident. Psychologically a good move by the medics because I am on a high after passing fit. Take myself up to hotel gym to lift some weights. Watch Derek Morgan row and power-walk in his Dunlop Green Flash pumps. Leave it, Del boy, you've had your day. Eat spendidly at Botanical restaurant in South Yarra.

Tuesday, 17 June

Wake feeling nervous as I have to train fully today. Stretch with Barney before post-New Zealand match debrief and then 20-minute ride to Scotch College for session. Scotch must be one of the most impressive inner-city public schools I've seen, with facilities second to none. Is it any wonder Aussie athletes are so high up in world sport when all the kids play all sports at all times? During break-time tennis courts, astroturf and playing fields are all packed. Session goes well and Clive tells me I will be on bench. No complaints from me. But I do get frustrated with certain aspects of our ruck clearing. In evening I present to squad our rules on contact so that we can progress, not just this week but into the World Cup. A lot of it comes from Wayne Smith at Northampton, but done well it is unstoppable. Clive gets a bit excited about it, which is good, until he singles out Luges as being crap. Needless to say he gets heaps from rest of lads. After meeting, head to Crown Casino with midfield marvels to play craps and we all leave considerably wealthier than when we arrived.

Wednesday, 18 June
Given a run-out in team to reacquaint myself. Am a little chirpy and have plenty to say. Some things don't change. After training pick up some golf spikes and buy some sexy, slinky jeans for Joanne. Hope they fit as she will look a million dollars in them. Luges and I go for haircut then more shopping. Now feel pooped. God that sounds so feminine. Pull yourself together, Dawson. Team night out at Red Emperor Chinese restaurant. Not the best night out, but there are good tales of previous tours and we discuss how best to spend last few days in Perth after Test. The banter reminds me how long I have been around as I seem to know all the stories.

Thursday, 19 June
Moonah Links, venue for the Australian Open, is chosen for big golf re-match between Dallaglio/Dawson and Greenwood/Tindall. At stake is pride and bragging rights. New shoes, balls, hat and buggy, and we're off. We win first after Will rockets an 80-foot putt past the hole and off the green. Three-up after six, Lol and I are on fire. But we three-putt twice and our lead is back to one. Tinds then finds his swing and the midfield marvels pull away. Our reign is over and abuse is on the way.

Friday, 20 June

Train at midday and have a couple of meetings to finalize defensive patterns. Clive pulls me aside and says I will be coming off bench at some stage. That gives me a little boost as I was hoping for a few minutes. Mind you, the way we intend playing this game Kyran will need back-up as he is going to have to run himself into the ground. Mixed emotions when we visit stadium. It is now the Telstra Dome, but the 2001 Lions remember it as Colonial Stadium, scene of our second Test defeat and Graham Henry's worst ever speech. How I would love to put right wrongs that cloud that part of my rugby life. Go to cinema later with Lol and Jason Leonard. Starting to zone in, which is an awesome feeling. It has been a while.

Saturday, 21 June

Matchday. England beat Australia 25–14. Chill in room until lunch then go for spotters. Arrive ready to prove critics wrong. Know we can. Not like '91 World Cup final where overnight change in playing style was drastic and suicidal. Back then I'd thought, 'Oh my God, what are you doing? This is just not England.' But now everyone knows we can play 15-man rugby (except the Kiwis and Aussies) and that's what we aspire to. Prove it in game. Forwards fairly immense, and when given opportunities backs click really well. They should have respected us. They should have watched us over last couple of years. Then they'd have known that get us on a good day and we'll play some outstanding rugby. In first 40 minutes we barely put a foot wrong. Ben's try gives me extra pleasure. He'd been really quiet all week to the point that a couple of times I pulled him aside and asked if he was all right. He wanted to erase bad memories. He certainly does that. His try, our third, is awesome as we run out comfortable winners. Aussies good afterwards. Knew it was a hard game and that they'd not been good enough on the day. They respect us in a way the NZ players did not.

Sunday, 22 June to Wednesday, 25 June

Time to wind down. Really want to go home. Management recognize this but want to show us training facilities and pitch and hotel in Perth, our base for the first few weeks of the World Cup. Could probably have done it in a day, but we spend three. Boys get to unwind, but there are so few days away from rugby and they are precious. If you get that emotional recovery right you turn up refreshed and recharged to go. Still, we are at the end of a long season and at last the beer is flowing. It would be rude not to.

9(ii)
Shooting For The Pot

THE GREATEST DAY OF ALL

It was slipped underneath my door, a note sealed in an envelope marked with the logo of the hotel where we were staying in Manly. It was 22 November 2003, a date I will not easily forget. Outside, the weather was grey and wet, not the best for those on holiday. But we were not. We were in Sydney to play in the final of the Rugby World Cup.

I picked up the envelope, opened the door and scanned the corridor in both directions. There was no-one there, but I recognised the handwriting. It belonged to Paul Grayson, my best friend, my half-back partner at Northampton and the guy with whom I'd made my England debut eight years and 56 caps ago.

He started off being funny, making reference to lines from *Blackadder* that only he and I laugh about. Then he got emotional about his family and his eldest son James, my Godson, and how much he loved me and how much I had changed in my humility since meeting Joanne. And then he got onto the reason both of us were in Australia.

'Today is your day,' he wrote. 'All your growing has been done, don't do it on the field. You're in control of the World

Cup final. This is where you belong. Enjoy it. The rest of the world can rejoice in Matthew Dawson the finished article . . . Win the World Cup. It will happen . . . They'll be looking at you and you'll go . . . You'll make the difference.'

I stood in the hallway and blinked back the tears. I couldn't read it a second time. It would have sent me over the edge. But once was perfect. Before the semi-final against France I had been frightened by the size of the occasion. I started asking myself whether I was good enough. A week on, the occasion was twice the size but I was ready.

It began in a church, the mission to perform a life-changing conversion from World Cup also-rans to champions. The 'church' in question was an unorthodox one, white and plastic in its construction and built beside our training pitch in the grounds of Pennyhill Park Hotel at Bagshot. You could not find a less forgiving place in all of England.

This was the 'Church of Pain', so called because it was the temporary facility housing yard after yard of state-of-the-art gym equipment. The units we worshipped were kilogrammes, calories and miles per hour. It was the place we came every day to get in serious shape for the challenge ahead. As candidates for World Cup selection we wanted for nothing. The pitch outside was a beautiful surface, the gym inside as comprehensive as I'd ever seen. There were three lanes of equipment and never any wait to get on the machine of your choice. With no contact work scheduled, it was a great chance to get in really good shape. And this time we did not overdo it.

Four years earlier, when the World Cup was held at home, we had overdone it. It had been sheer volume to the point where everyone was training for training's sake. We were away working for two or three months. We trained three or four times a day, setting alarms to wake ourselves up at 3 or 4 o'clock in the morning in order to take supplements.

Everybody involved with this England squad learned from the experience of 1999 and it is a million miles away from how we train and how we do all the stuff now. Back then, fitness was an area of English rugby which was patently not good enough and Clive Woodward decided to do something about it. Nowadays, England pride themselves on being a mega fit squad and playing to the death and being in the game right at the end. But the foundation stones were laid during the summer of '99.

That was when we worked ourselves to the bone at Couran Cove in Australia, with the Royal Marines at Lympstone in Devon, and on training pitches at Imber Court, Richmond Park, Twickenham and in Leeds. You name it, we sweated in it. And while it certainly opened my eyes to how far I could push myself and how fit I could be – since then my fitness levels have just shot up, and that goes for the whole England squad – I believe it ultimately played a part in our downfall. There is a fine line between getting your tank full for games and overloading. And I don't think we spent enough time on our basic technical skills and our plan of how we were going to play the game. When we lost the quarter-final to South Africa, I, for one, was absolutely knackered.

One day at Richmond Park remains indelibly etched in my memory. We trained all morning and then, at lunchtime, had a full team-contact session. Still that wasn't the end of it. Dave Reddin, our conditioning coach, decided we would finish with a group fitness session. To this day it is the hardest thing I've ever done. We were flogged. There were people being sick, unable to stand up in between recoveries. We were being told to take our hands off our heads and not bend over.

'Just breathe it in. Don't show weakness,' they said.

After doing two sets I was absolutely hanging, but there was still one set to go. Clive walked over and said, 'Fellas, what are you worrying about? It's only pain.' Each and every one of us looked up at him with the same thought. 'If you were within striking distance . . .'

Our time with the Marines at Lympstone was designed to bond us together as a unit. They are an incredibly impressive group of men and the activities we took part in were pretty awesome. But I came away questioning the value of the trip. Yes, we spent time together and got to know each other and did a bit of standard team bonding. But by the end of it, it was just that, a little 'standard'. I can't say something like that really influenced us as a unit any more than a night out at the pub together would have done.

At Northampton we sometimes go down to Sandhurst or Portsmouth. It's almost passé. What is the point of what we're doing? I feel if you're going to have a camp, go away where either it's going to be nice and warm or where there are good indoor facilities, and do some quality training and ball skills and then have activities that the boys enjoy. Because, at the end of the day, it's a bloody hard slog of a season.

People read so much into these types of activities; thinking that at 16-all against the All Blacks, as we were in our pivotal pool match at Twickenham in '99, the experience of having carried your mate through a submerged tunnel in total darkness is going to make the difference. I just disagree. I don't think it does. At 16-all, the next decision and execution to get us the next three points is the most important thing. So let's practise it and make sure we are the best in the world at doing it, rather than be the best in the world at crawling through holes under the ground (By 2003 I believe we had learned that. Think of the Final: 60 seconds left in extra time, scores tied. Time for one more move. One tilt at glory. 'Zig zag' was the call: upfield, drop goal, thank you very much.)

The preparations that would put us in that position were born out of the lessons learned from '99 and the professional coaching structure Clive had put in place. You couldn't turn a corner at Pennyhill Park without bumping into an expert: kicking, throwing, defence, scrummaging, nutrition, space-awareness, the list goes on. It was fantastic. And it reflected in the quality of our build-up.

Even though we trained as a squad, each player had an individually tailored programme. There was a lot more notice taken of the players' vibes than in the previous World Cup campaign. As a result the players were more honest with themselves and the management over injuries. If I said 'my legs are fucked' nobody doubted that.

A typical day at Pennyhill Park, between 21 July (when the squad reassembled following our post-tour break) and 8 September (when the World Cup squad was selected), went something like this:

7.00am: Alarm call
7.30: Weights
9.00: Breakfast

10.00: Training

1.00pm: Lunch

2.00: Sleep (we had to be in our beds at this time for two hours' rest)

5.00: Training

6.30: Dinner

For all the camaraderie that came from living the training experience together and working towards a common goal, it was also a really strange time. We were 43 players chasing 30 seats on the plane to Australia. As Mark Regan put it after the cut was made: 'For weeks it has been us against us. Only now is it us against them.'

Before then, there were three warm-up matches to be played. Again we had learned from 1999 when I have no doubt our fixtures contributed to us falling short as we played the United States and Canada and had two games against domestic selections dubbed Premiership All Stars which didn't challenge us at all. What good did dicking teams by 60 and 100 points do as a preparation for that pool game against New Zealand? We needed to be playing against one of the home nations or France, just to get us back into the real thick of international rugby.

Teams get stronger the longer a tournament goes and so the quicker you can get into your routine the better. We needed to hit the ground running very quickly because we had a game against the All Blacks second up. But after those four warm-up games, plus a 60-point opener against Italy, we simply weren't up to playing against the All Blacks for 80 minutes.

Contrast that with 2003 and a warm-up fixture list of Wales

and France away from home, followed by France at Twicken-ham. Three genuine Test matches on successive Saturdays, even if an England team comprising mainly fringe players made light work of Wales in the opening match, winning 43–9 in the Millennium Stadium. I was not involved, as Clive had told me in Australia in June that I would not be required until the home game against France.

That meant a week of warm-weather training under the baking Mediterranean sun without a match to look forward to at the end of it. We stayed outside Marseilles in a three-star hotel with short beds and mosquitoes for room mates. During the day we slogged it out on the playing fields before returning to our rooms to do battle with the insects. But it was essential preparation and despite the fact a mix-and-match England XV narrowly lost 17–16 in the magnificent Stade Velodrome on the weekend, we returned home with two massive shots of confidence: the first from knowing that whatever heat Australia might throw at us during the World Cup we could cope; the second being the knowledge that the best of France (our prospective semi-final opponents) had come within a whisker of being turned over by an under-strength England team.

We barely noticed the difference in climate being back at Pennyhill Park the following week, as the uncommonly hot English summer continued to push the mercury skywards. Mind you, we did have other things on our mind. This was the final week before World Cup selection and nerves were begin-ning to fray. I felt fine until I was told that Kyran Bracken had been preferred to me for the starting role at scrum-half against France in the Twickenham return match. I hadn't done anything wrong since the Grand Slam game in Dublin yet had not started a game in four due to injury, Kyran's impressive form in New Zealand and Australia, and Clive wanting to give opportunities to Andy Gomarsall (against Wales) and Austin Healey (against France). Now, twenty-four hours before the squad was due to be named, I was kicking my heels on the bench.

I still thought the game I was playing was the one England wanted and I could only think that when Clive said he wanted me for this game against France he hadn't expected Kyran to play as well as he did on tour. Clive did at least tell me I was going to get a half so I channelled my energies into preparing for that. I didn't spit my dummy at any stage and I like to think my reaction to not being picked was as important to the management as my performance on the pitch.

As it turned out I played just over a half because Kyran's back went into spasm in the pre-match warm-up and, despite him initially refusing Dr Simon Kemp's command for him to leave the field shortly before half-time – which reminded me of my set-to with the doc in Dublin six months earlier – he was hauled off with six minutes of the half left. 'I didn't want to come off and give my opponent a chance to come on,' Kyran later explained. 'Matt is a colleague and a team-mate but he's vying for the same shirt so in that sense he's an opponent. I had been told I was only playing half the game and I still had six minutes left.' Typical of the man. Total respect to him for that.

England ran out 45–14 winners, and by five tries to one. It was the perfect send-off to the World Cup, certainly better than the Gala dinner the RFU sold on the back of the England team being in attendance. Problem was, they didn't tell us they were going to do that. We thought we were being taken for granted, totally used and that it was not good enough. If you put on a Bob Geldof dinner you would have to pay for Bob to be there. What is the difference?

There we were, days before we left our loved ones for seven weeks and Joanne and I had to share a precious evening with 2,000 people I didn't know in a giant marquee erected in Twickenham's North car park. I signed shirts, photos and whatever else and didn't get to spend any time with Joanne. One guy came up and said, 'C'mon Matt, earn your corn'. 'If only you knew, mate,' I thought to myself, before putting on a pathetic false smile and signing his shirt.

Whatever my emotions they were nothing to those of my pal Austin on Judgement Day, when the England squad was named and missing was the name of Healey, along with Simon Shaw, Graham Rowntree and others who had worked their butts off all summer long in the hope of getting a dream trip to the World Cup.

The first I heard of Austin's fate was when he sent me a text saying 'you're going to need a new cribbage partner'. I replied: 'I don't believe you.' As I did, one arrived from Clive with a list of the 29 players who would accompany me Down Under. I was shocked Austin had been omitted and couldn't understand it. I thought he offered so much more than Andy Gomarsall. Only later did I see the wisdom of Clive's call. Gomars is an out-and-out scrum-half who had been playing at the top of his game, whereas Austin had been out the game for most of the year.

It was the right decision but, at the time, I didn't see it like that. My mate was being left at home and I'd never really got on with Gomars, because he'd never been bothered to listen to me. To be fair to him, though, all that changed when we arrived in Australia. We started talking and really responding to each other. Bridges were built and we got on really well. Maybe the management had had a word with him. Whatever, he was brilliant. Totally unselfish. When I was picked to start in the opener against Georgia he responded by selflessly working with me on my kicking, my passing and my defence.

Rugby World Cup 2003

Match 1: England 84 Georgia 6
(Subiaco Oval, Perth, 12 October 2003)

My joy at being selected to start the opening game lasted just over half an hour. I had beaten the jetlag and trained every single day since arriving (a team strategy to allow us to taper down in the build-up to play South Africa the following week). I had opened my try account with a close range, sniping effort, and I was really enjoying the feeling that comes with knowing you're playing well. Then, ouch. The walls caved in on me. I thought I was out of the World Cup.

England stole a line-out, I went to tidy up and get the ball away and one of the Georgians came in to tackle me. I tried to stand up and my leg twisted. At the time it felt like my medial knee ligament had really stretched, like an elastic band being pulled and then released. Clive had told us not to take any risks with niggles in this game, not with South Africa just six days away. But when I came off I didn't have the Springboks on my mind. I thought I could be going home.

I tried to pick something positive out of the wreckage of this personal catastrophe. I told myself that at least I would get to see Joanne six weeks earlier than I had expected. Then the size of the potential disappointment dawned on me. England could win the World Cup and I'd not be a part of it. I would spew for the rest of my life.

This stomach-churning emotion stayed with me for 24 hours until the doctor told me there was no 'ligament issue'. I had undergone a scan that afternoon and it had come up clear. Not only was I not going home but there was a good chance I'd be fit for the weekend. I let out a massive sigh of relief. I had a brace on my knee but I was going to be okay. I asked physio Phil Pask how that was and he explained it was due to the amount of stability and core work we had done over the summer.

But I was not out of the woods. There was an added complication. Kyran's back had gone in the Georgia warm-up and, as a precaution, Clive had sent for Martyn Wood, the Bath scrum-half. Five days before England played the Boks we had a crisis in my position. Kyran and I knew that if either of us didn't pull through one of us was going home. Although I was named in the team to play South Africa my fitness was not assured. The management told me they would give me until the day before the game to prove myself. 'If you're fit for the team run on Friday, that's good enough for us,' they said.

It was a real peaks and troughs week. I was very, very down on the Sunday, on Monday it was a lot better but I was still limping about. By Tuesday I was jogging around in the pool and by Wednesday I was running around and feeling good.

But it was Thursday when I had to really blitz it if I wanted to be in with a shout for Friday. I tried to go flat out but I was just in too much pain. I couldn't do it. I felt pain on the inside of my left knee at the base of my hamstring.

It was a massive call for me. I so wanted to play in that game. But Kyran had come through his fitness test so I owned up. I was not going to go into the game anything less than 100% fit – especially when there was someone like Kyran fit – and jeopardise the rest of the trip in whatever capacity. So on Friday, twenty-four hours before the big game, a game I had anticipated since the Twickenham clash the previous November, I pulled out. I had a cortisone injection into the bursar on my knee which made me feel a million times better. But only physically. Mentally I was in a world of depression.

I had wanted South Africa badly. For all the crap I had been put through on the field 11 months earlier; for the anguish afterwards of thinking my career had been ended by their thuggish tactics. Because of the golden memories of the 1997 Lions and my try in Cape Town. Because of the day at Twickenham in 1998 when I had been pressed into service as an emergency goalkicker and kicked England to victory, at a time when English wins over southern hemisphere sides were as rare as snow showers in the Sahara.

The squad rallied round me. There were little pats on my back from all the guys when they found out I wasn't playing, but they had a match to win and the mood in the camp was edgy. We had a comical final training session, disrupted by a load of television camera crews and a helicopter spying on the workout from up above. Apparently they thought Prince Harry was pitchside watching the session. He wasn't, of course, but Clive wasn't about to take any chances. He had our bus drive backwards and forwards in front of the cameras in the driving rain.

You could see the coaching staff were as nervous as we were but nobody was overly tense. We didn't train particularly well. In our defensive session Gomars was seconded to play the part of Joost van der Westhuizen and was making breaks left, right and centre around the fringes of rucks and mauls. Kyran was shouting, 'This guy's going to rip us apart if we defend like that'. But come game time the training paid off as we shut them out of the game because we were so well practised.

Match 2: England 25 South Africa 6
(Subiaco Oval, Perth, 18 October 2003)

The Boks had won over much of the media by the time the match took place. Corne Krige had impressed the journos with his contrition and his open and honest thoughts on the darkest day of his career. But I could not be so forgiving, not when it had been his acts of brutality which had threatened my future in the sport. And not when I heard his explanation.

'When you are in a situation like we were, you've got one of two decisions,' he said. 'You can either say "we're getting a hiding, I might as well give up" or you can say "I'm going down but I'm taking a few guys with me". It wasn't the right attitude and I apologised to the people I needed to and since then I haven't played like that again. But certain people react to certain situations and I'm not the kind of guy who lies down and says "we're getting a hiding, I'll just be a good sport".'

It might have made good copy for the press but I was furious. We've all been on the back of big defeats. All of us. Defeats that hurt us deeply. But just because I'm getting beaten doesn't mean I'm going to maim somebody or end their career. Krige may well be a fantastic speaker when he's got some hand up his arse telling him what to say, but in the heat of the battle when he needed to make his own decisions he made the wrong ones. And I cannot excuse him for that.

For all my personal prejudices there was no motivation for the team in the memory of November 2002. England versus South Africa was just a huge World Cup tie in its own right. Everyone's eyes were on it. It was a massive Test match, the sort which make you brick yourself as a player beforehand but which when you're not involved you realise how much you miss it and how much you would love to be. That was what went through my mind when the teams ran out.

I didn't think back to the so-called 'Battle of the Bok' at Twickenham when I saw the green and gold shirts emerge from the tunnel alongside the white of England. I was disappointed with the way they had carried on, on the pitch, and then blanked it afterwards. That for me reflected on their character as a rugby playing team. But there weren't many survivors from that game and I had no issue with the rest of the team. South Africa have got some fantastic players. My issue was with Krige and coach Rudolf Straeuli because they were the ones involved in it.

The tone was once again set by Krige, this time having a gratuitous dig at Martin Johnson a fortnight before the game, branding him 'one of the dirtiest captains in world rugby'. A bit rich, we all thought. Nothing needed to be said. Then it had been pretty tense when the two teams came face to face at the eve-of-tournament capping ceremony. Well, what did they expect? The Boks were the last people we wanted to socialise with. I certainly wouldn't have been all smiley and jokey with Corne and offering to buy him a glass of coke. It reached the stage where Clive complained that the two teams had to walk out together, fearing an episode in the tunnel.

'There is no love lost between the English team and the South African team and I don't think that it is the smartest idea to have the two teams lined up in the tunnel, shoulder to shoulder,' he said. 'It is not a big tunnel here, it's not Wembley and yet they expect all the guys to walk out with smiles on their faces. It's just not going to happen. I have to make sure that the referee, who is the important official, is down there. This is a highly charged game and I think that they should change it so that England or South Africa come out first. Just keep the two teams apart until the whistle blows.'

My concerns were largely centred around Kyran's back. Martyn Wood had been packed off home and in my absence scrum-half cover was restricted to Gomars. If Kyran's back went into spasm in the warm-up for a third successive game, Gomars would be on his own – in England's biggest game for four years, since South Africa eliminated us from the last World Cup.

I could see Kyran was not moving properly in the warm-up. I could tell from the way he was walking, the way he was bending over to practise passing, that he was in all sorts of bother. But I also knew that we would know soon enough whether Kyran was going to break down as he is such a robust player. Sure enough, the first kick-off went straight down his throat and he ran and got absolutely boomed. Each of us held our breath. But when the dust settled Kyran picked himself up and trotted off. We knew then that he was going to be all right.

For which we are all eternally thankful as he played a massive role in England winning a game in which we were far from clinical. The scores were tied 6–6 at half-time but we would have been six points down had Louis Koen not kicked so poorly. The boys got a real bollocking at the break from Andy Robinson about possession and keeping it. He said we needed to play down in the South African half as they were always going to give penalties away. Kyran and Jonny Wilkinson were getting shit, static ball which needed just to be booted downfield. Instead it was turned over.

But Jonny kicked sensationally and against the run of play we opened up a 12–6 lead. The way we were defending I knew we could win the game from there with kicks so I tried to pass a message to Paul Grayson on the subs' bench to get Jonny to go for drop goals. The problem was that the noise in the stadium was such that Grays could not hear a word I was yelling from my seat in the bleachers. When we play together for Northampton we have a long-standing call for drop goal: 'piss flaps'. It means Grays is going to sit in the pocket with a view to taking a pop at goal. So when there was a lull in play I boomed out the words 'Piss Flaps'. The record books show that Jonny kicked two and England ran out 25–6 winners.

England's performance was not perfect by a long chalk. Defensively we were pretty awesome. The best ever according to Phil Larder and Clive. As far as pressure in the heat of battle and the physicality of the game went it really doesn't get a lot better than that. But attacking-wise we were poor and our play at the breakdown was poor. Hell, we still won – and we scored the only try. And when I think of who scored it and what he had on his mind going into the game, thoughts about our attacking frailties seem way off the mark.

The score came in the 63rd minute. Louis Koen, whom we had noted takes an age to clear the ball from right to left, shaped to do precisely that. Lewis Moody was onto him like a heat-seeking missile, the ball ricocheted off Lewis into open field and Will Greenwood dribbled it over the unguarded try line before flopping onto it. The same Will Greenwood who had learned the previous week that his pregnant wife Caro was experiencing problems with her second pregnancy, at the same stage that their first child, Freddie, was born prematurely and did not survive.

Will kept this awful secret from his team mates so as not to risk distracting any of us from the job of beating the Boks. 'I'd noticed from before that people did treat you slightly differently and I didn't want that,' he said later. 'I didn't want the boys treading on eggshells, losing the ability to tell me to shut up in training. Not before the biggest game we'd faced in four years. But I'll never forget the phone call from the missus saying things weren't quite right. Your mind goes off in every direction possible. You start thinking "Why this, why now, why us?" '

For Will to have scored the winning try I hope gave him some comfort as he flew home the following day with all of our best wishes. And when he rejoined the party a week later, with Caro by now out of danger, there was a genuine feeling of joy in the camp. First and foremost we were thrilled for the pair of them, but it was also a timely boost for us as a squad as, in Will's absence, we had made heavy weather of beating Samoa.

Match 3: England 35 Samoa 22
(Telstra Dome, Melbourne, 26 October 2003)

I had a shocker, my worst game for years in an England shirt. Back in the team and fit again I had expected a lot of myself. No, I had demanded a lot of myself. But it didn't happen and with an hour gone we were losing the game to a rugby nation which, due to a lack of cash and players, had been talking about this being their last World Cup. Had we not come through to win, with late tries by Neil Back, Iain Balshaw and Phil Vickery, it might have been the last World Cup for all of this team, too!

Our chief disappointment, under the roof in Melbourne, was that we had realised after the South Africa game that teams now knew that the most effective way to frustrate us was to commit loads of men into the breakdown to slow down our ball. We had known that we hadn't kept the ball well enough against the Boks and thus hadn't got into our patterns and therefore had resorted to locking the game down and squeezing points out of people. Against Samoa we knew we had to adapt our strategy. Problem was we didn't.

At first things seemed okay. We got off to a great start, going straight through the guts of Samoa. But then they got the ball and we didn't see it again for 20 minutes. Fair play to them, they scored a great try and their handling was superb, but it was our own ill-discipline, more than any other single factor, which hurt us. I was disappointed that we just kept trying to force little passages of play and made a lot of handling and communication errors. There wasn't any fluidity to our game and I put my hand up, a lot of that was due to me. But not only me. We were all feeling the pressure.

We had come into the tournament as the number one ranked team, having beaten every major rival at home and away over the course of the previous 12 months. The feeling was that either we win the World Cup or we have failed. A certain fear of failure is healthy but players appeared really worried about making mistakes. Nobody seemed more uptight than Jonny Wilkinson, who in three games had not looked half the player he is.

It was something of a goldfish bowl environment and Jonny gets more press coverage than anyone, but he seemed unable to relax. He was worried about the media and worried about people taking photos of him. In Perth I remember seeing him cover his face to prevent the snappers getting a shot of him leaving a gymnasium. When we went to a water park he seemed to go to inordinate lengths to avoid being pictured.

At times it must be hellishly hard for him but my concern was that he was going into his shell off the field and that was having an effect on the way he was playing. His goalkicking held up brilliantly against South Africa when the rest of his game struggled. Then against Samoa his kicking game creaked. Ultimately we won and it was his inch-perfect cross-kick which set up Balsh's crucial try, but the alarms bells were starting to ring.

The following day we left the cold and wet of Melbourne for the sub-tropical heat of Australia's Gold Coast. Our week in Surfer's Paradise had been schemed as a week of R & R prior to our final Pool C match against Uruguay which, with due respect to them, was not likely to be our toughest fixture. But after our performance against Samoa we had an unexpected amount of work to do. As Martin Johnson admitted: 'We need to have a look at ourselves personally as players and get ourselves sorted out. We have got to sort out our heads. If we get into the knockout stage we are not going to beat teams making that many mistakes.'

A meeting of the players and management was called to address concerns that we were becoming too robotic and predictable in our play. We were getting very narrow and opponents knew where we were coming from. Our great strength had always been our unpredictability, opponents not knowing where we are going to attack next. That had changed to the point that there were no holes for me to threaten and everyone was moving on to Jonny.

It was a 'home truth' session but one conducted in a calm and composed manner. We analysed our playing pattern and concluded that it was not good for England. It was not a case of the coaches saying 'you're doing that wrong, do it right'. It was more a general acceptance that 'this is not how we want to be'. In the 1999 World Cup we had not recognised the tell-tale signs in time. This time we had. Or so we hoped.

However, England's problems ran deeper than that. By the time we arrived in south-east Queensland there was a growing crisis off the pitch with our name written all over it. In the closing moments of the Samoa game a mix-up had resulted in England fielding 16 players for a matter of seconds. Mike Tindall was having treatment, our bench thought he was off the field and sent Dan Luger on to cover for him. Only Tinds was apparently still in play.

Worse still, there had apparently been a confrontation between our fitness coach Dave 'Otis' Reddin and one of the world's top referees, New Zealand's Steve Walsh, after the final whistle. I say apparently as I was not witness to it. The first I knew of it was in the shower afterwards when Steve Thompson asked me if I had heard about Otis and Walsh? The word was that Walsh, who was acting as fifth official, had called him a 'loser', tried to trip him up and squirted water down his trousers. I couldn't believe it. I know Steve quite well and while he's a bit of a Jack-the-lad, he's also both a top man and a very good referee.

The temptation was to laugh it off as a heat-of-the-moment flare-up, only it was clear from the management's furrowed brows that this was not something which could be lightly dismissed. Tournament officials wanted to know whether England had deliberately ignored a match official when sending Luges on, and whether Otis had 'assaulted' Walsh. They were two charges levelled against England and all of a sudden we were forced to confront the worst case scenario – expulsion from the tournament.

That would have been scandalous given that the truth of the matter, which came out at the disciplinary hearing in Sydney, was that Otis was guilty of nothing in relation to his contretemps with Steve Walsh. Indeed, Walsh was handed a three-day suspension for verbal abuse of Otis. Our man was exonerated and while he did pick up a two-match touchline ban that was for the entirely separate matter of the substitution, an error for which Clive himself accepted responsibility, 'because I instructed Dave to do that'. The Rugby Football Union, represented at the hearing by team solicitor Richard Smith, was handed a £10,000 fine.

Personally I thought it was a storm in a teacup, a good story for the media to run with in an otherwise low-key week.

What we did in over-ruling the fifth official was wrong but I think he needed to be a little sharper. We weren't trying to pull a fast one. We were involved in a fierce contest, there was a break in play and we needed to get a substitute on. My view is that the official could have been more sensitive to the situation. Instead he seemed to take it personally, if his post-match comments to Otis are any guide.

Anyway, the fine was paid and England moved on. We briefly let our hair down with a trip to the Wet'n'Wild water-park, there was a game of 5-a-side, we had a day's golf with the media and sponsors Zurich at Hope Island, won by the team featuring Grays and Richard Hill, and there were three reasons to raise a glass. Word reached Jason Leonard that his partner Sandra had presented him with their third child, Francesca Belle, Martin Corry became a father for the first time when Tara gave birth to Eve Alexandra, and Will rejoined the squad after Caro came out of intensive care. After a week of worry – a week in which I turned 31 – we were refreshed in body and spirit.

Match 4: England 111 Uruguay 13
(Suncorp Stadium, Brisbane, 2 November 2003)

It was a chance to restate our credentials, to prove that while we had not played well, England were still the team to beat in this tournament. It was about proving it, not to our critics but to ourselves. A week away from the start of the knock-out competition we wanted a lift. 'Show no mercy' was the instruction, and the boys observed it to the letter.

The England record book was shredded. Biggest ever World Cup score and most tries in a World Cup-tie, with Josh Lewsey scoring five of the 17 to join Rory Underwood and Dan Lambert as co-holder of the record for the most tries scored in a match by an Englishman. As encouraging was that England made a statement about the way we can play, albeit against opposition made to play after just five days' rest.

The performance was both clinical and creative and much of the praise deservedly went to Mike Catt, on his first international start in two years. Catty pulled the strings in midfield, scored two tries and provided ample evidence that his ability to run the show at the highest level had not diminished during his time away from the squad. I was absolutely thrilled for him.

I was less enamoured with Joe Worsley, who stole many of the post-match headlines with his reaction to being sin-binned for a high tackle on Uruguay wing Joaquin Pascore. Catty had asked me to video him on his HandyCam, so I saw the incident unfold through the viewfinder. I was concerned by Joe's demeanour as he started walking off the field. He sort of strutted off. I said to myself, 'Come on, Joe, just get off the pitch'.

We were sitting behind the bench and when he started to clap the England fans all of us, to a man, said 'Joe, no . . . no, don't . . . Oh my God'. And that was before he bowed to the crowd in mock worship. 'Oh no, no, no'. After the game that was all everybody was talking about in the changing rooms. I heard that up in the box all the coaches were going loopy. And I think Clive was right to publicly condemn what Joe did because so many people had been waiting for an excuse to brand us as arrogant. We had done so well. We could, hand on hearts, claim not to have done a single thing to warrant the tag. Then you see something like that and your heart sinks.

Joe is a really good lad but that reflected badly on his decision-making ability. Under that sort of pressure you can't afford to have that type of wrong thought going through your mind.

The match won, we sat on the team bus on the way back to our hotel listening to the game between Wales and New Zealand in a state of disbelief. Everyone, including us, expected an England–Wales quarter-final yet Steve Hansen's side led after an hour in Melbourne. Briefly, it seemed that having worked so hard to make sure we topped Pool C and thus avoid a quarter-final date with the All Blacks, we would face them after all. Even though New Zealand eventually trumped Wales' four tries with eight of their own, we knew it was game on for the following Sunday – and that it was time to get our acts together.

Final Pool C Table

	P	W	D	L	F	A	Pts
England	4	4	0	0	255	47	19
South Africa	4	3	0	1	184	60	15
Samoa	4	2	0	2	138	117	10
Uruguay	4	1	0	3	56	255	4
Georgia	4	0	0	4	46	178	0

Matt Dawson's 2003 World Cup Diary Part 1

Tuesday, 30 September
Not the best day as I have to say farewell to Joanne for six weeks. Feel awful and empty as she has become such a huge part of my life. Meet at HQ for a run-through. Back to

Pennyhill Park (PHP) for onerous task of sorting kit for trip.
More shorts than jumpers, I hope! Try to sleep as so much to
do tomorrow.

Wednesday 1 – Thursday, 2 October
Final PHP flogging from fitness coach Dave Reddin. Run, row,
soccer shuttle. Knackered but feel fit. Given a piece of flag from
above Twickenham stadium – truly special memento which
could make the next few weeks even more special. Photo on
steps of plane for British Airways who, unbeknown to rest of
passengers, are re-routing to Perth in order to take England
party. Check in and wander into Duty Free. Signature hunters
are getting obsessive, especially for Jonny Wilkinson. Flight
BA015 to Singapore is totally painless as we have 'flat bed'
seats. What's all the fuss about flying long haul?! A blink of the
eye and we arrive. Buy ipod during stop over and spend next
leg of journey downloading tunes from Mike Tindall (Tinds).

Friday, 3 October
Arrive in Perth at one o'clock in morning to be greeted by
50 of Barmy Army. Jonny mauled as usual. Crash out in
Sheraton until time for fitness flush-out. Told to stay up late
to combat jetlag so decide that popping out for a couple of
beers with Lawrence Dallaglio (Lol) and Iain Balshaw (Balsh)
shouldn't be a problem. By 5.30am we think jetlag is beaten.

Saturday, 4 October
Feel a little ropey but know it is just a light weights session. By
the look and sound of boys who'd had an early night we have
got it right. Nobody slept a wink. Catch up on 40 winks in

afternoon before heading to Funtastico restaurant in Subiaco where those who have not already beaten the jetlag try out our method. Bale out at 1 o'clock but front-row posse plough on. Possibly not start to tour I had envisaged, but a real good buzz in camp. A few good stories, loads of laughs, all good ingredients.

Sunday, 5 October
Squad assembles five minutes late as have to chase Paul Grayson (Grays) and Tinds from their rooms. Jason Leonard (Jase) proceeds to sweat for 24 hours and you could see weight falling off him. Short and sharp team run, 20 minutes defence, 20 minutes attack. Split into two teams. One looks very much like a preferred Test team and thankfully I'm in it.

Monday, 6 October
Day gets off to excellent start when I am named in starting line-up to play against Georgia. Appears to be England's strongest team, or is that just wishful thinking? Not too tough a session, except for on the skin. Lads are getting quietly burned as sea breeze masks heat of sun. Back for quick bite and snooze before weights. Watch video of Georgia vs Italy in order to memorise some patterns. Phone Joanne but make fatal mistake of taking sleeping pill first. She is apparently not too amused when I start snoring.

Tuesday, 7 October
As days go this is not a vintage one as I finish with a bruised calf and a tooth missing. Full-on contact drills where non-matchday 22 decide to go a little overboard. Mark Regan

(Ronnie) and Danny Grewcock (DG) hand out couple of cheap shots. Get stamped on calf which stops me training and leaves me highly unamused. Immediately start intensive rehab to make sure I don't miss tomorrow as I feel Clive Woodward (CW) is itching to play Kyran Bracken (KB).

Fall asleep on drive to dentist in afternoon. But wake up soon enough when I get there. Tooth became loose last week after accidental clash with Josh Lewsey. As it was a capped tooth there was no immediate pain, however an X-ray showed it is badly fractured and that infection is imminent so it has to come out. Dr Simon Kemp okays gas and drugs for injection, then out it comes, though it feels as though dentist has tug-of-war team behind him trying to dislodge it. No pain, just the sound and awareness of exactly what is going on. No supper for me, just plenty of protein shakes and more ice for my calf. Doctor mentions he might pull me out of tomorrow's session. Don't think Clive will be amused so I might have to risk it.

Wednesday, 8 October

The tooth fairy didn't come! Treatment and a quiet word with the Doc to make certain that he tells Clive I am keen as mustard to train and that he is the one pulling me. I had a feeling he would drop me from weekend if I didn't train but as it is he is cool with me having a day off. Watch training with Balsh who has a calf pull. Pool session with Barney and Balsh. Feels good. No reaction. Quick lunch (my God it's good to eat again other than through a straw) then off to weights, physio. Crash out on physio couch till 6pm. Sit around with KB and am late for backs meeting. Oops. It is okay though as we are both together. No energy to go out so chill with backgammon crew.

Open awesome going-away present from Joanne. A photo and amethyst stone.

Thursday, 9 October

Wake up with air of apprehension as know will have to participate fully in session to clear the calf niggle. I hobble as usual to loo but after those initial 10 steps everything feels pretty normal. Thorough warm-up and all goes fine and dandy. More ice and rest to make sure okay for Saturday. Shower then remember amethyst Joanne sent me has to be buried to regenerate powers. Find flower pot in foyer and cunningly hide stone without drawing attention to myself. Evening busy with official Western Australia for all teams takes place on Lookout Point in Perth. Caps donned, photos snapped and opposition, especially South Africa, avoided.

Friday, 10 October

Day off, or is it? Lie-in followed by haircut and blond highlights. Boys dish stick out as expected but I quite like it. More lolling about until 02 beach party which we are assured will be fun and relaxing. On arrival plenty of photos for press and TV but Barmy Army are also in need of mementoes galore. Not seen the relaxation yet. Up to surf HQ for drinks, nibbles and barbeque with about 100 'I don't know who's' thrilled to be in company of England team. Sit and watch opening ceremony and Australia–Argentina match while topless body-painted models prance about and entertainers make enormous soap bubbles. Everyone else is sinking the ale and of course the noise increases. By end of day our heads are pounding and I couldn't be further from being relaxed if I tried. Okay, the sea and beach is appealing but the whole attention thing has made it a goldfish bowl environment. Exactly who has the party been in aid of?

Saturday, 11 October
8.30 on bus for team run which is slick. KB tweaks his back again so Gomars on stand-by. Watch All Blacks vs Italy and wandered into town with Luges. Back for 6.30 meet with Woody/Robinson and video. Excellent motivation for me. I love that two–three minutes of passion and desire you can soak up when watching magic moments from playing and training backed by some funky tune you can't then get out of your mind. Mindset chat with Robbo. Coaches want to see me start moving my defence up a few notches. Could be perfect chance. Also mention that I've got 40 minutes so 'give it plenty'. Mum and Dad rock up at Sheraton. I miss Joanne so much so when Mum gives me a photo album from her with all our photos in I feel a warm glow. SA give Uruguay one good thumping so now it is up to us to put down a marker. The start of my dream is about to begin. Let's hope it's long and vivid.

Sunday, 12 October
Match day. England beat Georgia 84–6. A long day as 8pm kick-off. Lie-in then off to park at end of road for line-out and walk-throughs. After lunch check in with Dave Reddin for Omega testing, which is a sophisticated test of your well-being. It measures strength of heartbeat, brain wave patterns and works out your energy level and mental state. Thankfully results good and so are my vibes. Back for doze before police convoy to Subiaco Oval. Facilities there awesome. Space and

convenient inside and a top track outside. But weather not on board as it chucks down right up to kick-off. Kyran pulls out of warm-up with back spasms so Gomars jumps in. KB's back is obviously going to be a concern for duration of trip. Game starts well. We put them under pressure and convert some opportunities. I manage to sneak over off the base of a scrum. Pleasing performance by everyone but I am less happy than most after straining my knee and coming off before half-time. I have no idea how serious it is and fear worst. Come back early on minibus.

Monday, 13 October
Will the 13th be unlucky for me? Early physio then back to bed, then more physio. Also have MRI booked for 2.30, with Tinds, KB and Richard Hill. Whole squad show empathy which gives me a boost while limping about in brace. Don't feel that good so fear the worst. DR doesn't tell me results until evening so remain edgy all day. At 8pm after team debrief he speaks to Woody and myself and says there is no ligament damage and that if swelling subsides there is a realistic chance for South Africa. Huge sighs of relief. More ice and physio, then early night with my lucky amethyst.

Tuesday, 14 October
Told that if I am fit for team run on Friday I will play. Because of injuries to scrum-halves, Martyn Wood has been flown out. Therefore if neither KB or I get fit for weekend one of us is going home. KB ends up having epidural because his disc has bulged quite badly. I don't train but have pool session and intensive physio.

Wednesday, 15 October
Knee feels really good today. Physios happy too so all looks well for weekend. Still stay out of training, which does not go well by the way. Not always a bad thing. Stay on after session to start running rehab with Pasky. About 60 per cent is fine so we leave it at that for today. Rest, ice and more physio is about as exciting as it gets in the afternoon. Clive announces unchanged team to press, even though Hilly and I still have to confirm our fitness. All media seem to be interested in is the battle between Joost and me at nine. Everyone raving about him which winds me up but only to point that I'd love to prove myself better than people give me credit. Team dinner at Fantastico. Food splendid. Eat so much I can hardly walk back onto bus.

Thursday, 16 October
Wonder what I've done wrong to deserve such a rollercoaster rugby career. I often contemplate how I would have been remembered if my fitness had not failed me at key moments in my career. Losing the captaincy in the summer of 2000, hamstring in Ireland (2001), calf before France (2003), thigh when in possession before New Zealand (2003) and now, when England have their most definitive match for four years, I get selected on merit and have to pull out after an injury sustained against one of rugby's minnows.

In some ways – and those numbers of ways are increasing – I cannot wait to quit this game and get on with a normal job. Nothing can be as emotional. The highs are what make it emotional but the troughs are so draining. The media bullshit, the rehab, my loved ones stressed and the damage it's doing to my body is testing my patience. If someone came along and offered me a career in a field that appealed I would bite their hand off today. Tomorrow, of course, might be different.

Because I know the end is coming in the next couple of years there's an element of apprehension that I don't really know what I'm going to do. There are things I probably could do but nothing where I'm just going to slot straight into. Sometimes I wish that there was because that would make my decision easier. Yesterday my calf stiffened up and today it's fine. In between, I get so stressed. I can't keep doing this.

As you will gather my fitness test does not go well. Clive and DR sit on balcony at Hale School as I try to up the pace from yesterday. It is too sore and in fact I irritate the knee problem. KB passes his test so will start. I should be okay for Samoa next week but that is scant consolation. Will have to prepare for media turnaround as I'm sure they'll have some sarcastic remarks to make. Wish I was feeling sick and nervous like all those 53 other times I've played for England. Instead I'm teetering on depression. The enormity of the game is what I train and practise for and to be omitted is heart-breaking. Yes, I'm at least here and not at home but right now it doesn't wash. Do nothing all day other than walk about hotel and reflect on a shit week. To add insult to my injury I have to venture to hospital for a cortisone injection to quicken recovery.

Taking the wider view, I'm still a little apprehensive about our fringe defence. With someone like Joost sniffing about we are going to have to be watertight. KB is hiding his back pain and creeps through training session. With some luck the adrenalin will kick in and he won't feel a thing, play well and we'll win.

Saturday, 18 October
Match day. England beat South Africa 25–6. Sour nerves with me all day. Horrible feeling when you are desperate for team to do well but in same breath you want to be missed. Day filled with physio-type activities, icing every two hours as the cortisone is still working. Not allowed to train today so just laze about. Everyone very relaxed but visibly focused on how huge a match this is. Follow lads into awesome atmosphere at Subiaco. Both sets of fans enjoying banter. Flags waving, faces painted and chants equal to passion displayed on pitch. Changing room jittery to say the least. Lots of shouting and screaming, classic nervous chat. First half performance is very poor. Bok pressure makes us wobble. However defence is unbelievable. Physicality was a priority in the week and to be honest it wins us the game. Half-time bollocking kicks us into gear and after that we look in total control. KB, Ben Kay and Will Greenwood have great games so it's suck it and see for selection next week. Come on knee, hang in there!

Sunday, 19 October
Early rise for three-hour flight to Melbourne. Assessed by medical team and given programme for next three days: hydro tomorrow, run Tuesday and with any luck back into full training Wednesday. Pop out with Tinds to casino to chill, then hook up with Catty, Jase and Balsh in St Kilda. They have a few but I decide to take it easy as I want this to be a big week. Back to Crown Casino for bite to eat and a $50 throw-in. Goes well and finish $2,700 up. Could my luck be changing? I hope so. Will Greenwood has had to fly home to be with Caro. Let's hope they overcome their personal traumas and they both

come through this. He has known about it all week yet still had the mental ability to withstand the biggest test of his career. Fair play, mate. Our thoughts are with you both.

Monday, 20 October
Hoped for lie-in but summoned to weights session at 8.45 at probably the most dodgy gym I've ever trained in. Don't think Jason Robinson will be spending much time amongst their clientele. Good to finally raise a bead of sweat even if I am a little tired. Back to hotel for treatment and more rehab. Wander into town with a gang for a coffee. Buy a music book as it's about time I get back to playing piano again. There's one in the hotel so I shall start embarrassing myself this week. Have to catch up with sleep until 7.30pm then grab a bite and watch Scotland vs USA. Leg has not reacted to training so at this stage it looks a goer.

Tuesday, 21 October
Leg feels okay but a bit sore, though not enough to bother me. Know it will be fine once I'm warmed up. Lengthy meeting to debrief South Africa. Coaching staff not happy with attacking attempt. Looks like Woody is going to play a strong team against Samoa on Sunday. I do all but full contact so should be fine, if selected. Weather is miserable and wet so session isn't of highest standard. Quick lunch then pool session with Pasky to flush out morning run, then sleep to 6pm. Quite a long chat with backs and Woody regarding scrums and line-outs and the options taken, then some picture messaging with Joanne on new phone.

Wednesday, 22 October
Aim of day is to get through whole session. Take a while to warm up but by time team run comes along it feels good. Two and a half hour session but body is okay so huge sigh of relief. Back at hotel, jump in pool to rehab. Standard sleeping afternoon, dinner and resting up for tomorrow's training.

Thursday, 23 October
Knee a bit creaky but okay to train. Pasky works his magic and I get through a tough attacking session. Absolutely batters it down at end of team run but stay for passing practise as there were a few dodgy chucks in the run. Team dinner out at Chinese but I don't fancy greasy, dodgy food so go with Luges and Ben Cohen to Botanical restaurant. Have interesting evening listening to the *EastEnders* lifestyle of Ben over some fantastic food and funky vibes.

Friday, 24 October
Day off so sleep in until 1pm. Lunch and a wander into town with Balsh and Tins. They don't fancy the cultural tour so I think I'll take it tomorrow. Meet up in crepe shop with Lol and Catty where we chat about our thrilling day. Not a lot to do in Melbourne to be honest. Food in hotel is shocking so pop into casino for fish and chips and a sharp gamble. Mum and Dad in Tasmania but hope to link up tomorrow. Missing Joanne like crazy but enjoy seeing her smiling face on phone every day.

Saturday, 25 October

8.30 start for final run at Scotch College. Don't train very well. Passing sloppy and quite fatigued. Visit Telstra Dome for line-outs and goalkicking. If there is anyone from Aussie camp with camera in the stands they have a golden chance to make a note of our full repertoire. Kick okay for first session back. Didn't sleep well last night so want to stay awake in afternoon in order to crash out later. Needless to say when I arrive in massage room the karma gets the better of me and my eyes close for hour. Meet Mum and Dad. Seems rain has followed them about. No worries for Sunday night, though, as roof will be closed. Team meeting and videos plus some carbs for supper just about wile the hours away until I hit the sack.

Sunday, 26 October

Match day. Beat Samoa 35–22. Wake for team meet. Passing drills to pass time. Pack bags as it's going to be a late night. Have snooze to try to pass the aching hours of boredom. Feel quite drained as it is a long rugby thinking day, but feel good and well prepared for match. Packed house at Telstra Dome. Those not in white are definitely on the side of the underdogs. Game does not go to plan. Samoa start brilliantly and catch us napping. The vibe in the changing room beforehand had worried me. Too much shouting and hollering. 'Come on, come on!' Sure sign that people are fighting to build themselves up. Too late five minutes before kick-off. Anyway, after our kick up rear in first 10 minutes and being 10 points down in front of a baying crowd, we fight hard and barring a few silly mistakes in contact, feel in control. Still, a barrage from the press is inevitable, but what's new. Not impressed with my own performance. Technically average though feel I control the mini-crisis with some good strategic calls. Afterwards hear about incident between Dave Reddin and fifth official Steve Walsh in tunnel. That surely has repercussions.

Monday, 27 October

Travel day. Bags loaded and off to Gold Coast. Few days off to chill, ease off and have a few beers. Standard rooms but plenty to do: golf, plenty of water parks, beach and of course Surfers Paradise. Grab nine holes with Grays and Will Greenwood. Then out to dinner at Hard Rock Café with gang. Dodgy night out as it ends up a karaoke evening. Hmm.

Tuesday, 28 October

Weights before visit to Wet'n'Wild for team day out. Proves to be a top giggle. Lots of posing and even more laughing as we rock and rolled through tunnels and over bumps. My dinghy buddy is Ben Kay, therefore being thrown out is a common occurrence. Spend most of my day riding on my stomach and scraping my face in the dark with the ominous thunder of Benny battering into me at the end of the tube. Notice that Jonny and Grays are not participating at all until last half hour. Not until later that I find out Jonny didn't want photographers taking shots of him. Concerned he may be taking things a bit too seriously. Without the release of tension anyone would go stir crazy. They will surely keep hunting him down. If not today, tomorrow. If not tomorrow, the next day and so on. Team night out to Shooters. Good banter, plenty of beers and laughs.

Wednesday, 29 October

Lazy morning followed by nine holes of golf. Team named for our final Pool game against Uruguay. I'm not involved but Martin Corry is, even though he is not yet back from England where he returned to be with wife Tara at birth of their first child. It would seem rude of the rest of us not to raise a glass in celebration of the birth of Eve Alexandra, not to mention Jason Leonard's newest arrival Francesca Belle. So we head into Surfer's for evening. Good crack but not out late as we're back in training tomorrow.

Thursday, 30 October

Feeling a bit strange; lethargic, sore, unmotivated, don't ask why. Go to Carrera sports ground, home of the Gold Coast Eagles to have a speed and weights session. Calf tight so can't carry. Finish off with some weights but in all honesty it is a half-hearted effort. Pissed off with calf stopping me again. Back to catch bus to Hope Island for Zurich Golf Day. Slightly annoyed as we were given today off and originally golf was optional. All of a sudden whole squad is summoned. If don't play have to turn up for barbeque at 6pm, thus ruining day off. Feel a bit better tonight but frustrate myself enormously by watching Samoa tape. I was awful, probably my worst game for England.

———————

WE WERE exactly where we wanted to be. We had won our group, were still unbeaten and now faced Wales in the quarter-finals. Win three more games, we assured ourselves, and nobody will remember that we did not play to anything like our potential early in the tournament. Only, it was a worry. The safety net had been removed. It was now win-or-bust. Lose and there would be no tomorrow.

Wales were the talk of the tournament as we checked out of our Gold Coast base and made the short trip up to Brisbane. Their coach Steve Hansen urged them to 'saddle the euphoria' surrounding their performance and use it to their advantage. It did make me chuckle that there was so much praise for Wales after a defeat and so much criticism of a winning England side but it was a slightly nervous chuckle because I knew that, for all we had achieved as a team in the past year, one defeat would wipe out the lot.

As I walked into the first press conference of quarter-final week I was struck by the size of the gathering. The numbers had swelled from a couple of dozen into literally tens of dozens. You can prepare for so much in professional sport but nothing you can do fully prepares you for the enormity of the World Cup circus. I thought to myself, 'Jesus, we dare not lose'. One game, one defeat and the walls of our world could cave in on us.

I remembered back to the last World Cup when New Zealand, who were widely seen as the outstanding team, got it wrong just once and were bundled out by France, who had done nothing all tournament and no way deserved to be in the final. So it could happen to anyone. The thought made me nervous. We really had to win this game.

In order for us to do so we had to sort out our indiscipline. An unacceptably high penalty count had been a feature of our tournament so far – only Tonga had a worse count than our 49 in four games – and against a team boasting goalkickers of the quality of Stephen Jones and Iestyn Harris it was clear we simply could not afford to continue the trend. So we addressed the matter. We analysed tapes of our previous performances and, realising that our greatest crime was over-eagerness, we devised a system to keep that enthusiasm in check. It involved a simple call – 'Dead' – which was to be yelled whenever one of us identified a ball that must be left alone.

I felt it was especially important for us to be on our best behaviour against the Welsh in light of the Steve Walsh incident at the end of our game against Samoa. I thought there could be a bit of a backlash against England. At the very least I expected the 50–50 decisions to go against us.

Match 5: England 28 Wales 17 (quarter-final, Suncorp Stadium, Brisbane, 9 November 2003)

They played as we thought they would. Very expansive, very fast, counter-attacking and all the rest of it. Trouble is, we didn't play anything like we thought we would. We were particularly disappointing but, not to put too fine a point on it, we were knackered.

We had spent too much time on the training paddock in the Queensland heat – three days of nearly three hours apiece – and even though everyone was mad up for a quarter-final we had just nothing in our legs. You could see it beforehand when we came off after doing our warm-up drill dripping in sweat and once the match itself started we were heavy-legged and sluggish. Dave Reddin was pretty upset afterwards, I think because he felt people would point the finger at him, when it was not his fault at all. It was even worse for Jonny and I because we also had to practise our kicking and so we ended up being on our feet for nearer three and a half hours, three days in a row. You don't notice it at the time, it's when you need your tank in the game itself.

I felt it had reached the stage that if it was not there tactically by quarter-final time it was never going to be. I thought we could have done nothing all week apart from a team run on Saturday and still have been fine.

That said, it was in the execution of the game-plan that we let ourselves down and we can't blame anyone other than ourselves for that. We just didn't put into play what we said we would. Strategically we were really poor. I couldn't question what the management were trying to get us to do because I think it was right. It was a case of key personnel not delivering and it was not the same people every week. Against Samoa I didn't deliver; in the other games, it was different players.

We were all at sea in the first half against Wales. Some of our option-taking was horrible. It was a headless performance. Everyone was running around like lunatics. There was so much wasted energy – energy which we didn't have to spare. It was as though we felt we needed to win the game in 10 minutes. By half-time, at which point we trailed 10–3 and by two tries to nil, I was apoplectic.

I had gone into the game with the mindset that I had been in a World Cup quarter-final before and lost, and I had no intention of experiencing that again. So when we got into the changing room and people were talking tactics and excusing ourselves for not doing what we should have been doing, I lost it. 'Fellas, shut the fuck up! We have promised ourselves we are going to deliver and do all these things, and give all our locker away and fucking throw everything at them. And yet we're calling bullshit calls. We're going to lose this game and we're going to be left with ifs and buts. For God's sake, this is make or break time. We have got to deliver now.'

I felt I was understanding the game and reading it really well. In fact, I felt bloody good thanks to a conversation I had with Paul Grayson in the week which, with hindsight, was the turning point in my World Cup campaign. Until then I had been a bit moody, a bit up and down, and Grays got me out of the rut. I'd been edgy since the Samoa game, because I knew I hadn't played well. I had tried telling myself that no-one had, and it was just one of those games, but that didn't wash.

So I asked Grays for what I call a 'Look in the Mirror' meeting, on the bus on the way to training. He looked me in the eye and told me what he saw. He said he felt I was on a rollercoaster. He said, 'It feels like I am reading a bit of your book (weeks earlier I had asked him to read through this manuscript). You're emotional. You're getting high, you're getting low. You're doing a bit of shouting and screaming. You're saying the right things but you're getting annoyed by certain things which shouldn't bother you. Rise above it, have a smile on your face. It's not important. Whether it be training, calls or moves, not getting enough rest, whatever. Let it go.'

It did me the world of good and from there on I felt I trained really well and really enjoyed myself. Yet in the changing room midway through the Wales game I was back to being angry and emotional. What had our Gold Coast meeting been all about? Had we not taken anything on board? We had said we would do chip-overs and grubbers to get round Wales' red line and make them think. But we didn't. We just ran into them. Brick wall to brick wall. And in defence we were so narrow. Wales were running around us and making us look vulnerable. It was not for a lack of effort on our part, but we weren't using our heads.

'This is the quarter-final of the World Cup, boys,' I said. 'Let's get down in their half of the field, let's apply some pressure, some real proper pressure, because they're giving away penalties left, right and centre. They're not going to let us score tries because they're giving penalties away. Fine, so we kick bloody goals.'

I was hot under the collar. I thought to myself that if we go out of this tournament without having given of our best I'll bloody kill myself. I had made a commitment to myself at the start of the pre-season that I would hold nothing back, that I wouldn't leave anything in my locker. I'd done that in the '99 tournament. I realise that now. Looking back I know I had something left in reserve. What it was I don't know but I didn't give it absolutely everything. This time would be different.

Clive Woodward then made a big call, but a necessary one. He brought on Mike Catt at inside-centre to take some of the heat off Jonny. It was an inspired move. Catty, who had been called into the squad only days before Clive named his 30 for the tournament and who had been stretchered to hospital after hurting his neck in training four days earlier, felt no pressure. He came on and immediately took the game by the scruff of the neck with his intelligent use of the boot. Within moments he had Wales on the back foot. Jason Robinson brought us level with a sensational diagonal run from deep which put Will Greenwood in for a memorable try and all of a sudden Wales looked like the Wales we have played against over the last few years, rather than the team which had run New Zealand and England ragged in successive matches.

With Catty stealing the spotlight, Jonny came onto his game, especially his kicking game. He kicked everything in the second half as we eventually ran out winners by 11 points. I was pleased for him because I had become concerned at how wrapped up he was in the whole thing. I feared he was taking too much on his shoulders, taking things too personally. It's not good for anyone to do that when the whole world is watching. As a team you have to share the burden.

Back in the changing rooms afterwards relief was the principal emotion. Very quickly we decided that something had to change in our preparation if we were to beat France, who had won their quarter-final against a really disappointing Ireland by barely breaking sweat. It wasn't an ultimatum given to the management, as one newspaper suggested. But we did bring it up and we were open and honest. Clive, Andy Robinson and Phil Larder listened and took it on board.

All week there were home truths spoken. 'We are very unhappy with the way that we are playing,' Clive told the media. 'We are certainly not at our best at the moment, everyone is aware of that, all the team, every individual. Now is the time for us to be very, very strong. You cannot be a Rolls Royce every week and certainly we are not that at the moment. But it is important that we don't over-react.'

Certain players, myself included, took it upon ourselves to speak up because we felt that if certain things were not said we would definitely lose to France. It was worrying to reflect on the fact that only ten weeks earlier our second team had pushed France's first string all the way in Marseilles and should have won. Now we were at full strength yet unfancied. Lawrence's feeling was that the French had caught up and probably overtaken us in their emotion. Their rugby ability, he felt, was still no better, because they had not been tested by anyone, but their confidence was sky high and that made them highly dangerous.

We took comfort from the 25 minutes straight after half-time against Wales in which we looked ruthless, dogged, determined and pragmatic. Any team playing us then would have been right under the cosh. But that was offset by an insecurity as to why we were only occasionally able to find that form.

I think we probably tried to develop too far. We had reached a point in the summer where we were playing bloody well and we should probably have been satisfied and said 'let's not try to become better than the best. Let's consolidate on what we've achieved'. The way we had played in Melbourne against Australia in June was where we wanted to be. That was World Cup-winning form.

But all hope was not lost. How could it be? Not when we were able to welcome back from injury a player of the calibre of Richard Hill, not when we had a captain with the inspirational qualities of Martin Johnson to lead us into battle, and not when we had learned the lesson of the week before and trained only once all week. Sure enough, come semi-final day the spring was back in our step. Now if we could just keep the faith.

Match 6: England 24 France 7
(semi-final, Telstra Stadium, Sydney, 16 November 2003)

We felt fresh and we felt ready to play. And that was after we had beaten France to reach the World Cup final. When it mattered most, England delivered. Just as Australia the previous night had overcome expectation to beat a team (New Zealand) sexier on paper, so substance triumphed over style on a night of unremitting rain inside the Olympic Stadium.

There are times when it feels so good to be alive and this was one of those. It was the night the real England at last stood up, the night we proved unequivocally to ourselves that we had what it takes to rule the world, the night 50,000 England fans turned a piece of Australia into a sea of white. France blamed the rain for washing away their hopes. That was simplistic in the extreme. The way we played we would have beaten them whatever the weather.

Andy Robinson had said in the press the day before that we had the game-plan to test the French in a way they hadn't been tested before. First of all, they hadn't been tested before. But Robbo was right. I can't overstate how effective, from minute one, our gameplan was, to go in close, then have a dabble up the short side.

France play like a wall defence between the two 15-metre lines and our strategy was to play around it. Either to go wide and go around it and then attack the short side, or to drive it, attack the short sides then keep attacking. We suspected they would give away penalties because it was wet weather and they would be ill-disciplined (they had two players sin-binned for foul play) and so we knew we could play territory.

It went perfectly to plan. I could see France thinking 'you

should be attacking in the middle where all our players are'. Did they seriously think we were going to pitch up for a World Cup semi-final with nothing new up our sleeve?

It was a performance built on passion. Plenty of thought went into it, but the inspiration came from the heart. The question had been asked beforehand, how badly do we want this? How much do we want the shot at immortality that victory would bring us? The scoreboard was about Jonny, who kicked all our points, a dozen in each half, in a marvellous riposte to his critics, but the real story was our forward pack.

They knew they had to crank up the physicality of their game a notch from the way they played against Wales if they were to dominate the French eight, and by God did they manage it. With half an hour to go France were toast. The forwards were just all over them to the point that the French boys seemed to lose the will to continue. You could see that they no longer wanted to really graft, to get stuck in, to dive on shitty ball. They appeared to want to give away penalties.

So often our discipline comes into question but all that opponents ever do against us is give penalties away. So what are we supposed to do, especially when we have a goalkicker of the quality of Jonny? Say 'Oh we won't go for goal, we'll give you a chance'? No way.

Richard Hill was awesome, considering he hadn't played for a month. Lawrence Dallaglio was brutal, really nasty, as he stepped his game up to a gear we knew he could reach. The front row as a unit, set-piece wise, were just phenomenal. Jonny hogged the headlines for his goalkicking, but he would be the first to pay tribute to his forwards for putting him in position.

Subconsciously I think we took a lot from the way Australia had totally stopped New Zealand from playing the night before. These were two very similar semi-finals, billed as bash against flash. The popular money was on the flash, which meant a New Zealand–France final. But none of it came from English wallets. There wasn't an England player who didn't fancy Australia, because they've got such a great all-round game. They possessed bags of experience and the priceless under-standing of how to win big games. Sound familiar?

France and New Zealand might have dazzled spectators with their early tournament fireworks but they were show-boaters: teams made up of very talented individuals one-on-one, teams great in dry weather under no real pressure and with no real defence in their faces. But these games were the semi-finals of the World Cup. At this level of competition you can't show-boat, you can't be throwing it through your legs, you can't be doing one-handed passes. You just can't get away with all that. Because you're playing against a big defensive unit in either Australia or England.

Carlos Spencer, the man they call King Carlos, was nowhere. He wasn't even in the game against the Wallabies. Defensively he shied away and left big gaps for Stephen Larkham. Did he really think Larkham was just going to pass the ball? That is arrogance to think Larkham would fall for that. The guy is quality. What about Imanol Harinordoquy, the France number eight, who made a name for himself by slagging off England and branding us arrogant for no good reason? Who do you think you are, mate? Have a look in the mirror. You came to the biggest game of your life and you were ordinary. There *is* arrogance in rugby but it doesn't wear a white shirt.

When the whistle blew our magnificent fans went wild, all 50,000 of them. So far from home the scenes were nothing short of extraordinary and it made us wonder how big a deal our World Cup campaign was at home. We could only guess. But I got a rough idea when I went back into the changing room and switched my phone on. Normally it would blink up one message, then perhaps another. It didn't bother. It went straight to 21.

I had nicked a ball from one of the ball boys, which had SF03 stamped on it to denote the match and the year. It was obviously a unique ball so we presented it to Jason Leonard along with a shirt with the number 112 on it to mark his achievement in breaking the world record for most-capped player.

Then it was back to our hotel, not for a celebration but a 1 o'clock meeting in which the message was hammered home that we had achieved nothing yet, because 'we haven't come all the way here to finish second'. It did no harm to remind us, but we all knew it already. After all, the biggest match of our lives was just six days away.

Match 7: England 20 Australia 17
(aet, final, Telstra Stadium, Sydney, 22 November 2003)
'Did that note go under the right door?'

The question came from Paul Grayson, standing in front of me in the changing rooms a couple of hours before the World Cup final. He wanted to make sure I had received his letter – the one he would later admit made him cry when he wrote it, the one I readily confess made me cry when I read it.

'Yeah,' I said. 'It went under the right door.'

Grays had felt moved enough to write to me on a personal level about things that are very difficult to say. 'You can't look a mate in the eye and say certain things that you can write down,' he later explained. 'You just can't do it. You well up, you bite your lip and it's lost in pointless tears.'

At that moment in time I couldn't talk about it. I couldn't tell him what his words had meant to me. How bloody good about myself he had made me feel, how he had chased away all the self-doubt and made me feel invincible on the day when, more than any other, I needed to feel that way.

I planned to thank him at a later time, hopefully when the game had been won and we were both aboard an express train bound for immortality. But not now. If I'd spoken about it at that point I would have dissolved.

Up until I received Grays' note the size of the occasion had me asking myself whether I was good enough. That startled me somewhat given that whatever talent I have had earned me two Lions tours and more than 50 England caps. But that is what the business end of a World Cup does to you. The stakes are that high.

The Australian media had done their best to unsettle us and put us off our game with a relentless campaign of Pom bashing. Injured Wallaby forward Toutai Kefu chose to brand me a 'dust mite', whatever that is, in his latest ridiculous tirade against all things English. It was he, remember, who dubbed the England pack 'Dad's Army' before Johnno and Co took Australia to pieces in the summer.

But the episode that got me going more than all that, more than the constant claims that our 'boring' style of play is some-how 'killing rugby', more even than the attempt by a Sydney tabloid to get locals to disturb our sleep the night before the final, occurred on the way to the Olympic Stadium.

The England bus drew up alongside a wedding cortège, a couple of open-top limos, at a set of traffic lights. I looked down, ready to offer a cheery smile to the newly weds, and was greeted by a one-fingered salute by some blond-headed cretin. Totally unprovoked. I thought 'Do you realise how much that's going to fucking help me tonight?' Honestly, some Aussies must think all England players are insensitive androids.

Armed with that anger and the inspiration provided both by Grays and the pre-match words of Johnno, I took to the field for a game which will forever live in my memory, a game which we should have had won by half-time. We played some really good rugby, Jason Robinson equalised Lote Tuqiri's early try and Jonny kicked a hat-trick of penalty goals to put us 14–5 ahead. The lead would have been even greater had not Benny Kay dropped the scoring pass I fed him over the Australia try line. I probably could have gone over but I didn't want to take any risks. Not in a World Cup final. So I drew my man and gave it to Ben, just to be sure!

For the first 25 minutes of the second half Ben was shitting himself. Half-time had come to the Wallabies' rescue and checked our momentum, which we never rediscovered in a second-half during which referee Andre Watson was inexplicably unhappy with our scrum. He kept saying: 'One (Woodman) and three (Vickery), I don't feel you're scrummaging right.' We all thought Vicks was doing really well and that Bill Young was popping out all the time, but he kept pinging Vicks all the time. We just couldn't work out why, particularly as our scrum was all over theirs.

With 15 seconds to go we clung onto a 14–11 lead but then disaster struck. At what should have been the last scrum of the game the Wallabies went fractions of a second early. Dougie (Woodman) wasn't quite down and tried to bale out. When he realised he couldn't he instead tried to sneak in the side. A split second before the whistle went I knew Andre was going to penalise us. Elton Flatley's boot did the rest.

Extra time brought a simple message from Clive to 'stop coughing up the ball and keep defending as you are'. He assured us that if we did so they would crack. We came together in a huddle and Johnno spoke. 'Fellas, you have worked your whole career for the next 20 minutes. Don't waste it.' He then pointed across to the Wallabies. 'Look at them.' And we did. They were hanging, they were bent over, they were tired. We had kept them in the game.

The one player not in the huddle was Jonny who had gone off to practise his goalkicking. It was a wise move as within two minutes of the restart Andre awarded us a penalty on halfway. Jonny stepped up. The kick, slightly with the wind and right, would require a draw. I picked a clump of grass, tossed it in the air, and watched the direction in which the blades fell.

'Jonny, are you sure? You've got to be sure on this mate, you've got to be sure. We can't waste this field position.'

Cool as you like, Jonny picked up the ball and said, 'Don't worry, I've got it'. He had and it should have been good enough to settle the issue, only we couldn't hold onto the lead once again. With a minute remaining Andre did us again and Elton, fair play to the bloke, kicked the game level at 17–17.

I couldn't believe it but now wasn't the moment for inquests and recriminations. There was still time, if we kept our heads, to salvage victory before the lottery of sudden death. Jonny kicked the restart deep and Mat Rogers cleared for touch. Not one of his best. We called the move 'zig zag'. It was the signal for line-out ball to be won and moved upfield in between the two 15-metre lines until Jonny was in range for a pot at goal.

Lewis Moody, on for Richard Hill, took the throw cleanly, Catty drove hard at the defence and set up a ruck. Time ebbed away. At the base of the ruck with Jonny in the slot, I could sense that the Wallabies were in the blocks expecting the field goal. Georgie Gregan was yelling 'field goal, field goal, they're going for the field goal' and out of the corner of my eye I could see Matt Cockbain ready to go.

But we were still a long way out and a drop goal would be far from guaranteed, especially as Jonny had missed all three of his earlier attempts from less taxing positions. A thought crossed my mind. 'A show-and-go really could be quite pretty here'. In a matter of seconds I had to weigh up the potential gain versus the potential calamity of me getting smashed and the chance being lost. Then I was gone.

As I broke through and clear of their first line of defence I had visions of a repeat of my try against Wales in Cardiff two years earlier when I had done the full-back and gone under the posts. But then I was walloped and it was look-after-the-ball time. Seeing me at the bottom of the pile-up Johnno decided to take the ball in again to give me time to get back into position. It was an awesome piece of thinking and of course he executed it perfectly. I spun the ball out to Jonny and via his weaker right foot he sent the ball through the posts.

I looked at the clock and it appeared to say 9:47. I thought

'Oh my God, there's only 13 seconds left, we've won the World Cup!' In our excitement we almost failed to defend the restart, but Trev came up with the catch, we rucked back the ball and as I passed the ball out to Catty I yelled, 'Kick it to the shit-house!' He obliged, absolutely booming it off the pitch. The whistle went, I remember hugging Catty and then it felt like I passed out.

I lay down on the floor, began crying and Grays was straight over to me. He pulled me up and we stood there hugging each other while madness ensued all around us. 'Thanks mate, thanks for everything,' I said.

'It was you who did it mate, not me,' he replied. 'You blew them away.'

Matt Dawson's 2003 World Cup Diary Part 2

Friday, 31 October
Massive relief in camp after World Cup disciplinary hearing restricts England's punishment over '16-man' cock-up to a £10,000 fine. People had been talking about us having points deducted or even being chucked out of tournament. Celebrate with a slice of my 31st birthday cake, made especially for me by our chef.

Saturday, 1 November
Relaxing day spent playing a few holes of golf on resort course. Andy Gomarsall is scrum-half tomorrow so I have at least a week to wait for the chance to get out of my system my performance against Samoa. Thinking about it irritates me

but there's nothing I can do now, except to make sure that I'm mentally ready when opportunity knocks again.

Sunday, 2 November
Match day. England beat Uruguay 111–13. A case of the good, the bad and the ugly. Thrilled for Balsh and Catty who look a million dollars as they shred the Uruguayan defence. They have waited a long time for their opportunity. Bad news comes when Balsh's two-try display ends on a stretcher. Ugly episode is Joe Worsley's reaction to being sin-binned. Prefer to remember Josh Lewsey's five tries, an English World Cup record.

Monday, 3 November
Train really well as squad. Good rhythm and flow. Thankfully we all realise that the style of rugby we tried to play in the South Africa and Samoa games isn't effective enough. Our mindset is that now we are in knockout stages our experience will come to the fore. Even though Sunday is a huge game I feel very confident England will produce a big effort.

Tuesday, 4 November
Lot of bullshit flying about at the moment. All of a sudden, because Wales nearly beat the All Blacks, they are world beaters. In contrast we are on the slide. Really? Another three-hour training session but we are all up for it as a squad, so keen is everyone to make the team sheet on the weekend.

Wednesday, 5 November

Doc wants to rest me from training due to my calf but I politely tell him to forget it as I know it will be a close call at 9; and if I am not able to train my chances of selection will diminish. Morning team announcement brings me good news. I'm in, although media feel Andy Gomarsall is a little unlucky not to make team. I'm chomping at the bit to play. Time now to get my head down and do my talking with the oval ball. Catty has a scare while training. Runs head first into a tackle bag and strains his neck. For a moment it is a scary issue. However, medics deal with it brilliantly, phoning for ambulance and taking no chances with X-rays. Media are at hospital almost before them, so our security is obviously not as good as we think.

Thursday, 6 November

Early start with physio so rush bowl of porridge before training. Attack-minded today which goes well. We all feel and look that little bit sharper. Looks like we'll be playing a more natural and hard-edged game on Sunday. If we get the likes of Robinson, Cohen and Greenwood in the spaces there could be an upturn in form. Bring it on! Have a 'Look in Mirror' session with Grays on bus. He says I am riding a rollercoaster at moment and that I am much happier and more effective when I don't get bogged down with things which need not concern me. So good having him as a best mate. Feel a million dollars after our chat.

Friday, 7 November

Great lie-in. No alarm or rushed breakfast. Leisurely bowl of porridge then off to Suncorp Stadium for kicking practice.

Dave Alred has spent a lot of time with me this week as Catty's selection on bench means I am second-choice kicker. Not too long a session but I've done enough each day to get into the groove. Suncorp Stadium is impressive to say the least, quite similar to the Millennium so I'm sure the Welsh will use it to psyche themselves. Go to Nudgee GC for nine holes and plenty of banter with Leonard, Grays, Balsh, Greenwood, Tins and Dallaglio. Not much of a day off but feel quite refreshed nonetheless. Loads of people starting to arrive in Brisbane and with Australia playing Scotland here on Saturday night the mood in the town is electric.

Saturday, 8 November
Final run of week is a lot shorter at request of players. Saying that, I still don't get back to room until 12.30. Wander to Pier 9 for lunch. The seafood is tremendous. Mum and Dad are having a ball, which is exactly what I wanted them to do. So pleasing to see them smiling and wowing about the time they have had as over the years both of them have always been there for me. Later in day watch the first two quarter-finals. All Blacks impress in beating the choking Springboks but Aussies are less so against a gallant but fading Scots outfit.

Sunday, 9 November
Matchday: Quarter-final: England beat Wales 28–17. These 8pm kick-offs turn the day into a week. It's bad enough being tense and emotional for any run of the mill Test match but with such a lot at stake the pressure is draining. Spotters at 11.30 at Brisbane Grammar and that's it until 6pm. I try to force some food into me at one and five o'clock but half a

jacket potato and some eggs on toast is about the limit. Hundreds of supporters pave the walk from the team room to the bus. Don't know whether to laugh or bury head as I feel extremely focused. Smiles get the better of me. Electric atmosphere at stadium, an awesome arena which inspires me. However, after warm-up I am fucked. Little do I know that others are as well and that Dave Reddin, seated in stand as he is banned from touchline, thinks we look lethargic. Maybe three days of training in the Brisbane heat has taken its toll. I have enjoyed the week but now don't have a full tank. Give it my all in first half and play okay but tire quickly and miss a couple of rucks where I am slow to my feet. Wales score twice early on but I remain convinced we have weapons to beat them. Question is: do we have balls to use it? Our decision-making disappoints me. Try to pipe up with calls to vary the play but they aren't used. Thankfully Catty comes on and saves day by playing territory. Game ends on sour note for me when I twist knee towards end.

Monday, 10 November

Travel day to Manly Pacific Hotel. Players and management reach decision that we will severely cut back on our training schedule this week in order to guard against any repeat of last weekend's sluggishness. Against France only our best will do.

Tuesday, 11 November

Supposed day off so plan to spend it lying in. No such luck as Austin Healey arrives and calls for breakfast. Oz has been flown in by Clive as emergency cover for Balsh and Josh

Lewsey. He's not allowed in our hotel, as while he's been called in as emergency cover, nobody has left the squad so how can I ignore his plea? Chew the fat which is cool as I haven't seen his cheeky smile for a while. Then back to hotel for video analysis, followed by visit to Dr Phil Lucas on outskirts of Sydney for bursar jab in knee. Needle phobia not too much of an issue for once. Chill on beach with Balsh and Will Greenwood until it is my turn to give a press conference with Phil Vickery. We talk up the French and Welsh. Standard stuff.

Wednesday, 12 November
Feel a bit strange getting up and not training. So strange that I have my training kit on all day. Force of habit. Post-Wales clear-the-air meeting takes two hours. Fingers pointed but to be fair most people put their hands up and take criticism on the chin. Lunch then long bus trip to Telstra Stadium, formerly Stadium Australia. We have traded off Friday walk-through at the ground for a full session today. Only an hour but session is sharp and intense. Boys in wetproofs to sweat a bit more as Dave Reddin thinks it's going to be warm on Sunday. Knee feels good but physio still worried as it's only been a day since jab.

Thursday, 13 November
Team announced at 11am and I'm in. Doctor gives me a final check but all seems fine. Tinds being dropped is the big news. Impossible not to play Catty after what he did against Wales. Can't really get out and about as Manly is choc-a-bloc with supporters. I'm sure I'll miss it when I've finished playing but it can be intrusive when all you want to do is chill, go for

a coffee, or do some shopping. Watch videos and have a chat with Robbo regarding freshness and originality of training. He's responded well and has come up with some good strategies for Sunday. Clive presents probably his best analysis ever. All the theories and practice seem so relevant to us for surprising the French. Jonny and I now have to implement it. Leg okay in training but my service is a shambles which pisses me off. C'mon Daws, rise above it and smile.

Friday, 14 November
Day off and I'm determined to have a genuine rest day. Slob on sofa and watch films, saving every ounce for Sunday night. Great to catch up with pals Tony Stratton and Mike Friend on beach later in day. Hardly a grain of sand spare to lay a towel. Friday must be POETS (Piss Off Early Tomorrow's Saturday) day over here too. Dinner with Mum and Dad as well as Jasper, who has been in hospital with eye infection. Excellent seafood. Mum and Dad in particularly fine fettle. Old fella has put a few kilos on, mind you.

Saturday, 15 November
After a quick chat with Phil Larder regarding cover defence, we have nothing else until 6pm. Boring though it may seem, I keep off my legs and don't even venture out of the hotel so as to keep my powder dry. Meet Anthony Catterson and his family in foyer. His brother and sister live down the road. Lovely to see a face out of rugby. Bit of physio, some mental rehearsal then off to Brookvale Oval behind hotel for line-outs and walk-through. Back in time to watch Australia's semi-final versus New Zealand. What a match! Shows what a well

prepared team can achieve. New Zealand can't think outside the square, try to run everything and are stuffed. Reinforces point that cool, calm heads will be crucial for us.

Sunday, 16 November

Match day. Semi-final: England beat France 24–7. This is it, Daws. One shot, one opportunity to show how you want to be remembered. Wake with a lot less pain and anxiety than I expected. Porridge and view of Manly Beach is easy to swallow as we gather in team room for final okay. Weather forecast raises a few eyebrows though: 60% chance of rain with blustery winds could make France's wide, wide game a little interesting. Force down a sandwich then crash until 4.30 when go straight into pre-match routine. A long hour spent on coach to the game gives ample time for reflection and attention to what is in store. Passers-by react to us in different ways, from kids not being the slightest bit bothered to drunken Aussies holding their miniscule crutches in disgust. Don't they realise how much they are winding us up? Obviously not. I'd love to be playing next week against Australia – the ultimate satisfaction!

Come match time the rain is lashing down. Awesome atmosphere in ground. There must be 50,000 England fans. Epic display by forwards and by Jonny in goalkicking department. All 24 points, thank-you very much. I could have run all day and I am initially upset to come off in the 69th minute. But to be fair match is won by then and there is so much still in our locker. Conditions don't allow us to express ourselves with our handling but we give a physical display second to none. France scrum-half Fabien Galthie refuses to swap shirts which I find odd. We both have two so why not, even if it is his last game? Stay up with the lads afterwards to celebrate Leonard's 112th cap. Couldn't have slept anyway. We're only in the World Cup final.

Monday, 17 November

Lunch with Mum and Dad who are both hung-over from wild night of partying. In fact most people in Manly look as though they hit it hard last night. Bump into Tim Clarke, who was my form prefect at RGS High Wycombe when I was 13. Other than that, plan a chill-out day until Lawrence invites me to the 'Here and Now' concert at Sydney Entertainment Centre. Tindall, Leonard, Johnson, Kay, West have a whale of a time reliving the 1980s with Human League, Paul Young, Belinda Carlisle, Go West and the star of the show, Kim Wilde. Meet them all backstage before returning to hotel to get ready for biggest week of our rugby lives.

Tuesday, 18 November

Body has shut down today. Too tired to train so do recovery in jacuzzi where I have some banter with a couple of Aussie old farts. The first thing they say is that they're so glad the English sent them to Australia. Chip on shoulder, I think! Really struggle to stay awake all day, snoozing at every opportunity. Body working hard to get right for final.

Wednesday, 19 November

Only have a light team training run which is a little slack. Good flow, but few handling errors. I feel okay but there are some comments from the medical staff about my fatigue. Getting over-excited about Joanne turning up. Can't stop talking about it. All the boys are winding me up about over-exertion. It will be tough to ignore. Rib and Rumps for team supper. Another early night. Amazing how focused you become when so much is at stake. Sleep, food, water, rest, sun all issues for us.

Thursday, 20 November
Day off. 5.45am limo to Sydney Airport to collect Joanne. What a sight for sore eyes as she runs through customs for the most welcome of hugs. Sleep until lunchtime then wander into town. Not out long as I want to make sure I am getting enough rest. Another doze in afternoon before taking taxi to show Joanne Sydney sights. Have organised supper followed by tickets to ballet at Opera House, which finishes off dream of a day. While watching the last scene my mind can't help going through moves and sequences for the final. So inspirational to see the power and precision of the dancers, set to the soothing notes of Handel. Catch Manly Ferry home and sleep like a baby next to his comfort blanket.

Friday, 21 November
Wake with Joanne thinking it's a normal day until my phone tells me I have a million messages. Breakfast out and even the waitress is giving me banter. Sneak into hotel by back way to avoid cameras and spend a lazy afternoon watching videos and eating. Phone still refuses to shut up. Rain has come so Aussies whinging more than ever that we're so boring. Why can't they just get on with it? Light training session. Mark Regan gets excited and pushes me over but Johnno clips him into line. Knee not right for goalkicking so there might be a change to

the bench. Can't better *Gladiator* for a Friday night movie. A bit of dice and then bed. Fear a long night as *Sydney Daily Telegraph* has helpfully called on its readers to keep us awake. Happily nothing comes of it. So much has flashed through my head today. So many messages from old friends. I have to smile when I realise what I'm doing tomorrow. Surreal.

Saturday, 22 November
Match day. World Cup Final: England beat Australia 20–17 aet. From the moment I wake my mind is playing the Test match in my head. Scrum moves, lineout peels, cover defence, over and over again. I realise that I have to find something to do to halt this or mental meltdown is assured. The nerves and sick and pain of pre-match tension is evident as I try to scoff the porridge and honey that has served me so well all tour. The mood of the lads has risen a few notches so banter and smiles are seen from only the usual few. For the rest it's time to back off. Talk shop to Andy Robinson before 11am to cement the team strategy in both our minds. That relationship has been a strong success on this trip. We have both aided our own performances. Catch a couple of hours' kip after a tiny lunch of pasta and toast then try to shut down. Want to get to 4pm before any of the pre-match routines. Iron shirt, check rucksack: gumshield, pants, boots, gloves, phone.

Everything seems identical to last weekend. The bus, the changing room, the music, the vibes. Comforted by that. Not until I run out onto pitch to have a light warm-up that the size of the occasion smacks me straight in the face. There is an ocean of white and red in the stands, Englishmen and women partying and singing like I've never experienced. Flags, faces painted, costumes, wigs, hugs, kisses, tears – and we haven't even started. Wander back in to changing room and then come out again to warm-up properly, followed by a bit of kicking, passing and speed drills. Back in again for team chat. The tension is awesome. The coaches go through their points for the umpteenth time and we sit there chewing over the cues and plays that concern us individually. My mind is crystal clear. I have repeated and executed the attacking options 1,000 times in my mind.

The first half seems to take an eternity. Even so I didn't want it to end. England's rampaging forwards create so many gaps. I am dabbling and linking. Australia score early but that only stiffens our resolve. From then on they can't get near us. Lawrence's break to Jonny and Jason Robinson makes for a classic try for JR. Ten minutes later I have the chance to put Ben Cohen away on the left. Less said about that the better. Boys sprint in at half-time (14–5 ahead) hoping the 10 minutes will fly by. Simple, tight rugby is going to win it, we tell ourselves. If we cut down errors, points would come.

Wallabies not in game until referee Andre Watson comes to their rescue by pinging our scrummage even though it is destroying theirs. As penalties start to mount up, Johnno begins to lose plot with ref and I have to pull him away. Quite frankly he is within his rights to be angry, as Aussies get out of jail, Elton Flatley kicking them level at 17–17 with fantastic pressure strike in dying seconds.

Extra time, but still no panic by us, just annoyance that we played so poorly in second period. Everyone looks so focused and so positive that I can't wait to get started again, particularly as I glance over to opposition and they look knackered.

That makes me feel good, though not as good as Jonny's 50-metre penalty which puts us ahead again. That, for me, will always be the kick that won us the Cup. The swirling wind and rain and conditions under foot made it a 60–40 kick. He nails it (by comparison, his winning drop goal was a doddle).

Just when we think we've finally got it in the bag the Aussies level again, through their ice man Flatley. But there is a minute left. Time enough. There is 35 seconds to go when we regain possession 45 yards out. Too far out for drop at goal, I decide, but their defence has only that on its mind. 'What about me?' I think to myself a split-second before I dummy and am in open field. Now, should I take on the fullback for potential glory or not? Opt for safer option so tuck ball under jumper and set up ruck. Surely Jonny is on for the drop. But there is no cheer so I guess someone else had taken it up. 'Get to your feet, Daws. Get there'. It comes back to me and I hit Jonny. He is on his weaker right foot and I fear he has not got a clean strike. For a moment I think it can't possibly make it. Wrong. Thank God. We are world champions.

Holding the Webb Ellis Cup in my hands feels great. The single most precious moment in my rugby life. Eventually the laps of honour end and we return to the changing room. We are the Champions is blaring over the tannoy. I sing it all the way down the tunnel and then belt it out as I walk into our locker room, shouting and screaming and singing really badly. Walk round the room shaking everybody's hand. None of us still can believe it. Wander around aimlessly trying to make sense of it all. No chance. Take loads of photos with the trophy, then Prince Harry, who has followed us around

Australia, comes in to say hello. Sit down for 5 to 10 minutes with head in hands and get a bit emotional again: reflecting on what we have done, the sacrifices my family and friends, as well as me, have made to enable me to achieve my rugby dream.

Brought back down to earth when I am selected for drugs test. The tester follows me around as I take fluids on board in order to be able to give a sample. Seems to take an eternity so turn my phone on and it flashes up 70 . . . 80 . . . 90 messages. Still unable to muster a sample so walk around the stadium. By now it is after midnight and the only people around are cleaning up the place. Finally sort myself out, then join up with rest of lads at Opium Bar in Sydney for a night of carnage.

Sunday, 23 November
Manage three hours sleep before woken by my body's reaction to the gallon of Red Bull I drank overnight. I am shaking like a leaf. Begin to answer the 150 text messages now stacked up on my phone and order some breakfast in bed. My mind is still away with the fairies but manage to do media stint after lunch before team heads to IRB Awards Dinner in Darling Harbour. What a disgrace! Video continuously shown of Australia winning World Cup in 1999 and there is a pathetic clap when we enter the room. Generally you can smell the hatred towards England. Brilliant. Mission accomplished. Time to go home.

England's 2003 World Cup squad and results

Forwards: Jason Leonard, Phil Vickery, Steve Thompson, Mark Regan, Dorian West, Trevor Woodman, Julian White, Martin Johnson (capt.), Ben Kay, Danny Grewcock, Martin Corry, Richard Hill, Lawrence Dallaglio, Neil Back, Joe Worsley, Lewis Moody; replacement: Simon Shaw

Backs: Josh Lewsey, Iain Balshaw, Jason Robinson, Ben Cohen, Dan Luger, Mike Tindall, Will Greenwood, Stuart Abbott, Mike Catt, Jonny Wilkinson, Paul Grayson, Matt Dawson, Kyran Bracken, Andy Gomarshall

(P7, W7, D0, L0, F327, A88)

Pool C
England 84 Georgia 6 (Perth, 12 October)
South Africa 6 England 25 (Perth, 18 October)
England 35 Samoa 22 (Melbourne, 26 October)
England 111 Uruguay 13 (Brisbane, 2 November)

Quarter-final: England 28 Wales 17 (Brisbane, 9 November)
Semi-final: England 24 France 7 (Sydney, 16 November)
Final: England 20 Australia 17 (aet) (Sydney, 22 November)

10
Celebration Time

It was the day to end all days. Or so I thought. Then I was awoken from dreaming about the day England won the World Cup and told that there were anywhere up to 10,000 supporters waiting for us in the Arrivals Hall at Heathrow Airport. At half past four in the morning.

Life didn't get any more surreal than this, I thought. Then it did. Monday 8 December, central London, three quarters of a million people waiting for a bus. On board, 31 rugby players. No Springsteen, no Beckham, no Pope John Paul, just us.

So this is what they meant when they said winning the World Cup would be a life-changing experience. This may be real life, but not as I have ever known it. I have taken tea with the Queen, drunk champagne with the Prime Minister, eaten breakfast with Sir David Frost and Michael Howard, Leader of the Opposition.

I have been stopped in the street, every street, and congratulated on what England achieved in Australia. I have been photographed with my girlfriend Joanne in *Hello!* magazine, spoken on a microphone to 750,000 people shoehorned into

Trafalgar Square and seen grown men fight in a queue for my autograph.

I have felt like a pop star, conducting 40,000 England fans in a rendition of *Wonderwall* by Oasis, in Sydney's Olympic Stadium and I have felt like a film star, leaving a restaurant in central London illuminated by enough paparazzi flash guns to power the National Grid. I have even been awarded an MBE. And I could go on and on . . .

Perhaps my life has changed for ever. Only time will truly tell. But I'm not going to let it change me as a person and the way I've been over the last 18 months to two years. I've loved every day. It's just been awesome. It seems a long time ago now that I was in the depths of despair professionally and personally but in actual fact it was not that long at all. I've been very fortunate.

'Cabin staff, doors to manual. Two minutes to land.' The voice of the captain of the British Airways' Sweet Chariot flight from Sydney to London informed us that our odyssey was at an end. After eight weeks Down Under we were home and the most prized possession in all of rugby union was with us.

From what some of the media boys had told us before we left Australia of the reaction back in England, we expected maybe a few hundred real diehard supporters to be awaiting our arrival. Mind you, it was still the middle of the night. Perhaps that was being optimistic. Then we got off the plane and reality hit us between the eyes.

The police were questioning whether they could allow us to walk through the Arrivals Hall, whether they could guarantee our safety. Sorry? Then we heard the chants, the unmistakable tune of 'Swing Low' coming from somewhere beyond Baggage Reclaim. We followed the sound, turned a corner and emerged into what can only be described as mayhem.

There was a sea of painted faces, flags and banners. There were television cameras and spotlights, photographers and flash guns. People were hanging off the balconies in the car parks, swinging on lamp posts, standing on trolleys. Any conceivable vantage point was taken. It was completely crazy.

Outside cars had been dumped just anywhere: on the middle of major roundabouts, by the side of the by-pass, in the central reservation. It was like 'I don't care if I get a ticket or get towed, I want to see the boys come home'. It was totally mind-blowing, so far beyond our wildest expectations as to be silly. And I loved every second of it.

When we finally battled our way through the well-wishers and onto the bus we sat there, players and management alike, united by a single thought: *My God, what are we in for in the next few months?*

It soon became very obvious. Every step I took out of the house it seemed that someone wanted to shake my hand and tell me how proud he or she was of what the England team had achieved. My testimonial dinner, a 720-seat event at the Royal Lancaster Hotel in central London, was a complete sell-out and a riotous night. The shirt I wore in the final fetched £12,000 in an auction.

On another night, I did a dinner at the Inter-continental Hotel in London with Lawrence Dallaglio and Jason Leonard. The three of us sat on a table with no security staff around us and we just got bombarded. There were people jumping over the table to get my signature, then leaning right across me, pushing me out of the way to try and get to Jason and Lol. It was physically intimidating to the point that I had enough and left.

At another do a couple of days later a queue formed for signatures. I was impressed. Then someone tried to queue jump and a fight broke out. They weren't your typical hooligans either. More like chief executives and managing directors.

And then came the Victory Parade and everything that had gone before was diminished by the sheer scale of it. They say it was the biggest ever street party in London. Even the 1966 World Cup footballers didn't get a day like this. From Marble Arch and along Oxford Street we rode aboard an open-top double-decker, up Regent Street to Piccadilly Circus, along the Haymarket and into Trafalgar Square.

I couldn't have constructed such a scenario in my most extravagant dream. Close to a million people shouting and screaming, the capital city at a standstill, gloriously littered with balloons and confetti. Lawrence said beforehand that the parade was not about the players, but the fans. But my word didn't us players enjoy it.

When we turned into Oxford Street I don't think any of us could really believe what we were seeing. It felt like we shouldn't really be there in such an exalted position. Had we really done something to warrant such adulation? It wasn't just on the streets either. Three television networks, BBC1, ITV and Sky, all broadcast the parade live, as if it was a Royal procession. My dad was interviewed on BBC1, Joanne was interviewed in Trafalgar Square by Sky News. It was unreal.

The procession turned into Trafalgar Square which was bulging at the seams. It appeared that only Nelson, from his vantage point high above the crowds, had any sort of elbow room. The bus drew to a halt and the BBC's John Inverdale, in his role as master of ceremonies, stuck a microphone in my face and invited me to tell the watching world about an incident with a metal detector at Sydney Airport.

I duly recounted the episode in which I set the alarm off and was asked to go back and empty my pockets. That I did, placing my loose change in the box before passing through the scanner. Again the alarm sounded. By now the security guard was getting really hacked off with me. He turned round and said, 'Sir, I'm going to have to frisk you'. I replied, 'Don't worry about it'. I then lifted up my shirt and pulled out the medal.

From there we moved onto Buckingham Palace where we stood in a semi-circle in one of the major ante rooms until Her Majesty arrived with a fleet of corgis at her feet. It was quite bizarre. Fortunately there was no humping of legs! I did laugh, however, when the first person she went to see was Mike Tindall. That morning the front page of the *Sun* newspaper had run a story claiming that Tins was dating Zara Phillips, the Queen's grand-daughter. That amused me almost as much as Prince Harry informing us, in the changing room straight after the final, that he had just received a text from 'his nan' inviting us to a party at the Palace when we got home.

And here we were. Joanne and I had a nice chat with the Princess Royal, who took a keen interest in Joanne's love of horses. Then, after a brief word with Prince William, who is a top man, we headed off to Downing Street for a very relaxed evening at Number 10 with the Prime Minister. It was very much a case of 'Right, come on, have a glass of champagne, have a chat, chill out a little bit'.

Tony Blair spoke fantastically well to us all, saying how proud the nation was. Michael Howard, who I'd met previously on *Breakfast with Frost*, was also there and he told me that he'd met my Grandad the week before in a Conservative club in or around Manchester. Talk about a small world.

From there most of the lads moved on to the first of Lawrence's two testimonial dinners but because Joanne was leaving for Africa the next day on a school trip to climb Mount Kilimanjaro we went for dinner at The Ivy. It was leaving there, at around 11, that we relived that famous scene from the film *Notting Hill* when Hugh Grant's character opens the door and is blinded by all the paparazzi flash guns going off.

The concierge had to take our bags to the waiting taxi because we couldn't see where we were going for all the flashes going off. When we had closed the door behind us Joanne and I just wet ourselves laughing at the absurdity of it all. Then a thought struck me. The last time I had been blinded by the light of Fleet Street's finest in central London had been three years ago during the infamous strike by England's players.

We had turned up at a charity fund-raising dinner and been photographed, not as national heroes but as reviled figures, unsure whether we would ever play for our country again. It's a funny old world, isn't it?

11
A Step Into the Unknown

We were consumed by a sea of humanity. The walk to the departure gate was impassable without a security escort, likewise the route to our team bus at the other end. Everyone, it seemed, wanted to pat us on the back, to associate with the World Cup winners. But that was then.

Seven months on the scene was altogether different. Sydney Airport got on with its business as the England rugby team, the champions of the rugby world, checked in. Where before we could not move, this time we ambled through largely unnoticed, doing a bit of Duty Free and killing time in the coffee shop.

At Heathrow, there were not 10,000 people waiting for us in Arrivals. Cars had not been abandoned here, there and everywhere in the mad dash for the best vantage point. This time we were not assigned a side exit and a planned route to the team bus, where our bags were already stowed. This time we queued to pass through Immigration, then we were kept waiting in the baggage hall because our gear was delayed.

The contrast was stark and it deserved to be. England had just lost for the fifth time in eight matches since the World

Cup. There was nothing for us to shout about, let alone anybody else. Three of us took the bus back to Pennyhill Park, where we had left our cars, while the rest of the squad dispersed at the airport.

The route home from our 2004 summer tour had been the same but everything else was different. Of the team that started the World Cup final against Australia, only Lawrence Dallaglio, Mike Tindall, Ben Cohen, Josh Lewsey and Richard Hill were in the team for the end-of-season rematch against the Wallabies. Martin Johnson, Neil Back and Jason Leonard had retired; Jonny Wilkinson, Phil Vickery and Trevor Woodman were lost to injury; Will Greenwood, Ben Kay and Jason Robinson had been left at home; and Steve Thompson and I found ourselves relegated to the bench.

Almost overnight England lost the vast majority of its World Cup-winning team. Experience, influence and a massive amount of talent haemorrhaged from the set-up at the same time as the rest of the world took a collective pledge to hunt down the world champions as never before. The outcome, in terms of results, makes grim reading. A nation that had lost one Test match in 25, between March 2002 and March 2004, won only one of six during the next three months.

We were bound to suffer a reaction to winning the World Cup; at least that's my opinion. There was no way on earth we were going to be able to continue that momentum. England won the biggest prize in the sport and then lost many of its biggest names. It was a step into the unknown, one that was impossible to prepare for.

For one thing, nobody had devised a plan for going

forwards after winning the World Cup, partly because it had never before been done mid-season (all the previous winners having come from the southern hemisphere) and also because it would have been seen as extreme arrogance. For another, the loss of many key players in the glorious aftermath left a hole too big to fill, especially given that Clive did not know who was going and when, and thus did not have the benefit of time to put in place a contingency plan.

After the World Cup he had two choices. To make whole-sale changes, shred the team and blood the new breed. Or to let people go to their retirements and change things gradually. He chose the latter, which I believe was the right thing to do as you've got to know players deep down before you expose them to international rugby and I don't think enough was known about the new generation to risk making wholesale changes at the expense of some of the greatest players ever to wear an England shirt.

So Clive adapted to the changing circumstances. First, to Johnno's decision to go, by making Lawrence captain before the start of the Six Nations. Then, to the loss of Jonny, by turning to Paul Grayson, Olly Barkley and, latterly, Charlie Hodgson. Other changes he implemented himself: dropping Backy and Jason in the Championship and then leaving behind Will Greenwood and Ben Kay when England toured New Zealand and Australia in June.

Of course it is not just a question of personnel. Before the World Cup when we were playing so well, we did our basics so well. We have now developed into this technical circus of players and ideas and manoeuvres and drills which, absolutely no question, improves one's ability. But I do wonder whether we've just got away from the hard-nosed brutality of playing Test rugby.

Twice since the World Cup, against France in Paris and New Zealand in Dunedin, we were, if not beaten up, then certainly bullied and on each occasion we had to have that little slap on the arse to kick us into gear. That never happened before. As captain, Lawrence was one of the most passionate men you'll ever meet but across the squad I think we needed a little bit more of that. He couldn't do the passion on his own. He was bloody good at getting people 2% better but you've got to be 98% to be efficient. If you're down at 75–80% in your passion and emotion another 2% is unlikely to alter the outcome of a match.

What a shame our campaign had to end in such ignominy Down Under. How sad that we had this tour bolted onto the golden memory of our World Cup season. I have told myself that I won't allow anything to tarnish the magic of the last 18 months, that I won't let anything get in the way of that life-changing achievement. But right now, if I'm being totally honest, we are smarting a bit.

Everyone now agrees that a period of English decline was inevitable post-World Cup. But at the start of the Six Nations Championship, this was not being flagged up by too many people. England were hot favourites to retain their crown and widely fancied to complete back-to-back Grand Slams; which suggested that no-one was listening when Clive made the point that going unbeaten through the championship would be every bit as tough as winning the World Cup.

The odds did lengthen when Johnno announced his

decision to step down, prompting Fran Cotton to speak for all of us by remarking: 'Martin Johnson is the all-time great England player. You come across his class only once in a generation'. It then emerged that Jonny required surgery on his neck and shoulder and would miss the entire campaign. Yet such was the confidence within the squad that we believed we could accommodate those losses.

Even without Jonny, Johnno and Backy – whom Clive somewhat surprisingly omitted from the squad – we were always going to be a good side. We showed that by fairly easily disposing of Italy and Scotland away from Twickenham in the first two rounds of the championship. It was only when we stepped up in class, against the likes of Ireland and France, that we fully appreciated how important those missing players were and how much poorer the side was without them.

To beat Italy 50–9 in Rome was no mean achievement, with Jason Robinson scoring a great hat-trick. It showed that the attitude of the squad was spot-on, that we had taken on board the demand of the management that we cast ourselves in the mindset of challengers in order to train and play with the intensity required to remain champions. On the evidence of what he saw John Kirwan, the Italy coach, said that only a bazooka could stop England. He was only half-joking.

When England beat Scotland by four tries to one the following weekend all seemed rosy. But despite the scoreline there was a lack of creativity to our performance at Murrayfield, with our tries owing everything to our aggressive defence. We couldn't be too harsh on ourselves at the time. To beat Scotland 35–13 on their own turf is no easy task. But the truth was that they caused us nothing like the problems we encountered in the remainder of the championship by sides genuinely attacking us.

Having played only one full game since the World Cup final I had no complaints at missing out on selection against Italy and Scotland. I came off the bench on both occasions. Don't get me wrong: I'd love to be standing here, like George Gregan, with 90-odd caps as first-choice scrum-half, never having been dropped. But that's never been the case. I just count myself fortunate that I got myself in absolutely tip-top nick at the right time for the right moment.

I no longer waste my time getting frustrated at not being picked. Andy Gomarsall had been playing well and deserved his chance. There had been a couple of occasions in the past where I was picked ahead of him and I thought to myself, 'Jesus, if I was in his position I'd be furious about that', so I was content to play second fiddle on this occasion. However, when I came on against Scotland I felt fit, comfortable and ready to start again. Clive must have noticed that because I was back against Ireland.

This was the game that shaped the second half of our season. The build-up was unsettling. First we were shocked by the dropping of Jason Leonard from the squad and the selection of the uncapped Matt Stevens in his place; then we were told it was time to take the shackles off. We planned to go out and play total rugby and win in style. Against Ireland, a team who should have made the World Cup semi-finals, a team boasting a great pack and match-winners like Brian O'Driscoll in the backs, our plan proved to be a grave mis-calculation.

By the end of the game we had managed just one try, my

first-half score. Our lineout had gone to pot, with 11 lost on our own throw, and we had been slaughtered in the scrums. Jason announced his retirement soon after and Backy followed suit, frustrated at being left on the sidelines. One defeat and so much changed. To be honest, we never really recovered from it.

And yet in the immediate aftermath I was not too downhearted. In fact, I remember feeling almost relieved that the pressure had been lifted of defending a five-year unbeaten home record and of not having lost any game since the World Cup. It was as though a line had finally been drawn under all that and we could start again. Not before time, I thought.

I think a lot of the other boys felt a bit relieved too, because we were still living the dream. All anyone wanted to talk about was the World Cup and it was so hard to move on to new targets and new goals. I thought losing to Ireland would flush all that out and yet it still didn't happen (it wouldn't until the second half of the game against France three weeks later). The defeat was simply explained away by a lack of preparation time and various off-field distractions.

That was true up to a point. I don't accept that off-field issues had anything to do with the result. It was more the lack of training days pre-tournament. The lineout drills had not been practised enough, nor had we had sufficient time to become comfortable with a new defensive system. The out-to-in system had been massively successful for Wasps so there was absolutely no reason why it shouldn't have worked for England. Everyone wanted to do it because we knew it could take us up to the next level, but we just hadn't practised it enough.

Against Wales a fortnight later Clive reunited 12 of the starting World Cup XV for a game which was supposed to signal the dawn of the new era. But the World Cup was still fresh in the mind as we wanted to beat Wales for all the abuse we had taken for beating them in the quarter-final in Brisbane despite being outscored by three tries to one. For a time, however, it seemed we would not even get the victory this time.

Leading 16–9 at half-time, they struck twice at the start of the second half as our defence again sprung a leak. All of a sudden we were five points adrift and in danger of becoming the first England team for 20 years to lose back-to-back Twickenham internationals. I can honestly say I never thought we were going to lose, but it was nonetheless a relief to us all to score 15 unanswered points in the last quarter and run out 31–21 winners.

Things hadn't been quite bouncing for us, but as soon as we got some continuity going it all clicked into place. We started going through the guts, picking and going. The forwards started to dominate and we appeared a totally different side. Frankly, we battered them in the last 20 and, in doing so, gave ourselves a springboard into the title decider against France, who had maintained their unbeaten campaign by wiping out Scotland 31–0 at Murrayfield.

Sadly, it proved a false dawn, even though we started bloody well against the French. When you play an international you sense pretty quickly how it's going to go because of the nature of the physical confrontation. For the first five or 10 minutes we were booming. The scrummaging was going well and we had them under pressure. Then, all of a sudden, we turned the ball over, they scored and it took the wind right out of our sails. We started fannying about, became loose and I could see the French start to lift themselves.

We became ill-disciplined and we didn't allow our match-winners to get in the game. If the game gets broken up all of a sudden players like Jason Robinson, Olly Barkley and me can start finding holes and start linking with Richard Hill. When was the last time you saw Hilda running down the wing? You just don't see it any more.

By half-time we trailed 21–3. In the changing room I said, 'Fellas, we've got to get ourselves back into a hard-nosed, hard-edged confrontation. We've got to start taking it to them.' We all knew the game could go in one of two directions: we were either going to get pumped by 40 points or we could stop the bleeding by really fronting up. The response was fantastic. We came out with lots of running off the fringes, good targets. France were suddenly scrambling and there was space for Jason, Josh Lewsey and Ben Cohen on the outside.

By the end the deficit was three points. We had nilled them in the second half and been disappointed to lose 24–21. It was a tremendous show of character and I came away from the Stade de France with a renewed optimism for the future. We had finished third in the championship – England's worst placing for years – but we had finally seen the light. We had finally let the World Cup go. We had finally moved on.

Three months later it was me who was doing the moving. I felt that I had been forced out of Northampton, the club with whom I had spent my whole senior career. I am quite clear about this. I would not have left Northampton and signed for

London Wasps had Saints not started the ball rolling. Even now, months later, I have not received so much as a thank-you for my 13 years of service to the club.

Nobody has written to me, or made any sort of contact. Not a dicky bird. There has been nothing official from the club to express gratitude for the past or wish me luck for the future. All I received was my P45. It seems they have tried to make me out to be the instigator of the split, but I won't have that. They got rid of me. I was pretty much asked to leave by the Board.

I know that ripped certain people apart. The Barwell family were devastated and, fair play to Keith, he took the bull by the horns and spoke to me when no one else did. But when he advised me to make other plans the first thing I said to him was: 'If this is going to happen it has to happen right. I'm not going to have it look like I'm leaving the club, because I'm not. Northampton are asking me to leave.'

That, though, was not the way it was leaked by a third party to *The Times* newspaper. The story, given back page prominence, made it appear that I had initiated the move. It made me look awful and I spent a horrid couple of weeks asking myself what exactly I had done to deserve such treatment while the rest of the country had the impression I was taking the club to the cleaners.

The matter had surfaced in January when Saints asked me what I wanted to do. I had to remind John Steele, the club's director of operations, that I had another year on my contract. He didn't even seem to know that. Unperturbed, he told me to go away and think about my future because they wanted to plan ahead. So I did. I went away. I spent a lot of time talking to my family, to Joanne and to the Beals and the Graysons – the people whose opinions I most value.

I couldn't make up my mind. One day I thought I could play in London, the next I thought 'No way, I can't leave Northampton, I've got to finish my career at Saints'. So I went back to the club to tell them I was staying and that was when Keith told me the Board had decided they wanted me to go.

A number of things disappointed me. Firstly, that none of the other Board members spoke to me personally. People I've known for years and years, people I've socialised with, played golf with and trusted, all of a sudden made themselves scarce. Once the Board turned against me there was no way back, even though not one Saints supporter gave me a hard time and been anything less than supportive since – something I will never forget. I will miss the buzz at Franklins Gardens on match day; the fans are a unique and fiercely passionate bunch who know their rugby. Northampton ended their campaign, ironically, at Wasps in the Zurich Premiership play-off semi-final and, because I was injured, I spent the afternoon in the Saints dugout. It was very tough and very disappointing to finish like that. That was not the way I wanted it to end.

Generally speaking, I've been really fortunate in my career. I have enjoyed massive highs – I feel hugely honoured now to play for Wasps – and just the odd horrendous low, but that afternoon at High Wycombe was one of them. I would have loved to play one final game at Franklins Gardens in order to say goodbye properly, but it wasn't to be.

With my future resolved, I was excited about the prospect of touring with England. Sean Fitzpatrick, the former All Blacks captain, had come out and claimed that certain England players were running scared of playing two Tests against New Zealand followed by one against Australia, but that was never true of me.

It is true, however, that the tour took on a different guise post-World Cup, what with the retirements, the injuries and the mental fatigue factor at the tail end of such a long and emotionally sapping campaign. What had always promised to be a severe challenge grew considerably in size as the weeks and months passed.

In an ideal world we would have liked to be preparing ourselves physically and mentally at home; resting up, getting ready to put England back on track. But we say that every single year. The bottom line is that we knew the tour was coming and we made a commitment to it. It would have been easy to have made excuses to have stayed at home. But we fronted up, we accepted the challenge.

1st Test: New Zealand 36 England 3
(Carisbrook Park, Dunedin, 12 June 2004)

They call Carisbrook the House of Pain and I hadn't needed reminding of it, having captained England there six years earlier on the Tour from Hell when the All Blacks ran out 64–22 winners. The score this time was different, but nowhere near enough for our liking. A New Zealand side on its first outing since the World Cup, and with an all-new coaching team that included my former Northampton gaffer Wayne Smith, walloped us by three tries to nil.

For the second match in a row the damage was inflicted in the first half. But while France made do with 21 points, the

Blacks ran up 30. We fannied around for 25 minutes and we got pumped. Once again the lineout was a disaster area and once again we were our own worst enemies, missing numerous first-up tackles and turning the ball over on countless occasions.

New Zealand had obviously been smashing the shit out of each other all week. They were getting passionate while we were getting very technical. We weren't ready physically for that. It reminded me of the second Test of the 1997 Lions tour in Durban, when South Africa were coming at us from all angles. When Joe Rokocoko went through at the first kick-off in Dunedin, Catty said it reminded him of the 1995 World Cup semi-final when Jonah Lomu broke through from the start.

I sensed that I would be a casualty of the defeat, and so it proved, but while I admit I didn't have my greatest game, I did everything I could possibly do. It was frightening to witness some of the calls, and the things some players were not doing. But I was one of six who carried the can for the defeat, with Steve Thompson, Mike Catt, Danny Grewcock, Chris Jones and James Simpson-Daniel joining me on the sidelines.

As captain, Lawrence was entitled to have his say and he made it count, demanding that the team toughened up mentally and matched his commitment to the cause in a physical sense. Clive reiterated the need to get physical and suggested that we had kept our self-control 'probably a little bit too well' in Dunedin.

2nd Test: New Zealand 36 England 12
(Eden Park, Auckland, 19 June 2004)

Simon Shaw became only the third England player to be sent-off in an international and Danny Grewcock received a suspension for careless and reckless use of the boot after coming on as a replacement. But I would take issue with anyone who says we were pushed too close to the edge. I think our preparation was spot on. At the end of the day we fell foul to a dreadful decision. New Zealand got away with murder in the first Test, but we let them do that because we didn't respond in the right way. They tried to get away with murder again at Eden Park, and in our determination not to let them we lost a man. We have to live with that.

The enduring frustration from this game is that we will never know what might have happened had Shawsy not been sent off. I don't know if we would have won had we kept 15 men on the field, I wouldn't like to say either way but I suspect one person does not equate to 24 points. What I am sure of is that we had the All Blacks where we wanted them early on and it is under those circumstances that New Zealand lose games.

We led 6–0 and had a penalty shot at goal for a nine-point advantage when Aussie touch judge Stuart Dickinson advised referee Nigel Williams that Shawsy had committed a sending-off offence. I thought the decision was a howler. It certainly ruined the game. However well England played after that, we were not going to win. If you had 18 men on the pitch the All Blacks would be dangerous on the outside, let alone with 14.

Afterwards, All Blacks coach Graham Henry, who I fell out with on the 2001 Lions tour, went out of his way to seek me out in order to bury the hatchet. Fair play to him for doing that. He extended the hand of friendship and I was glad to take it. He also sympathised with England's situation.

It had not only been the loss of Shawsy. Losing both centres, Stuart Abbott and Mike Tindall, in the first half-hour was also crucial. To give up three players of such influence in the first half was simply too great a handicap to overcome. A particular sadness for me, at the end of a game in which the All Blacks claimed all five tries scored, was that I have still to win a Test match in New Zealand.

More generally, there was a regret felt throughout the party that we had not left New Zealand with respect, although to be honest we always suspected that the locals wouldn't give the English respect whatever the result. We turned up and before we had even played a Test match they were giving it the big 'un. We went out for a team dinner in Auckland before the first Test and some local nob came over to where we were sitting, slammed his hands on the table, looked us all up and down and chanted, '*U, U, Umaga! Yeahhhhhhh! Go ABs!*'

We said nothing but I thought to myself 'Who the hell do you think you are, man? When you're sitting down having your dinner I don't come over and hurl abuse at you.' And they call the English arrogant.

In fact, for the first time the Aussies did not refer to us in that way on this trip. On the morning of the World Cup rematch, as it was dubbed in Brisbane, Stephen Larkham was quoted in *The Australian* as saying: 'They [England] have had a certain arrogance about them. That was the case over the last couple of years. That was before the World Cup. I think they handled themselves exceptionally well in the World Cup and

I think most teams have a different opinion of them now. We thought they would react differently after they won it, but they were very humble and not in the least bit arrogant. They were quite the opposite. It changed our opinion of them.'

I didn't think I'd live to see the day . . . sadly, though, it was also the day we conceded 51 points to the Wallabies in what was a wholly forgettable ending to English rugby's most momentous season.

Test: Australia 51 England 15
(Suncorp Stadium, Brisbane, 26 June 2004)
When an unheralded player is thrown into the opposing team seconds before kick-off you rather hope that will spell good news for your own chances, but Clyde Rathbone's unexpected promotion to the Australia starting line-up, after Wendell Sailor had pulled a hamstring in the warm-up, did not have the desired effect. He scored three tries inside 45 minutes.

Richard Hill and Lawrence scored our first tries of the tour but it was little consolation as England lost to the Wallabies for the first time in five years. I have no desire to dwell on the result, nor the means by which it was achieved. Suffice to say that neither was acceptable.

On reflection this was a tour too far. But that was never my mindset beforehand. Nor will it be on future trips. Before each of the three Tests my mentality was that we were going to go out and win. I have played in games – be it for club or country – where I've thought 'This is going to be a hard day at the office; we've got a slim chance of winning'. But that was never the case on this tour.

We learned the hard way, just as we have done virtually

every step of the way since the World Cup. But that was how it had to be because they were steps into the unknown. Every one of us underestimated what it felt like to have the title of world champions and what effect the team being decimated by retirement and injury would have. Only now do we know.

The tour served to highlight just how good the players were that England had in the team that won the World Cup. Even though we did have a very good coaching and administrative set-up – the backroom staff were brilliant – really it was the players who were running the show to a great extent. That was highlighted when all of a sudden we didn't have as many very experienced players and we were over-reliant on the coaching.

It was very hard for the coaches too, to go from one extreme to the other; having a world champion side to all of a sudden having only five of that side playing a year later against Australia (who were able to summon 12 of their Final starting line-up). So hand on heart, I can't say I was too surprised when Clive decided to step down in September. I had expected some changes, either in personnel or message, as my view post-tour was that the way we train needed to be refreshed in order for us to get back to being one step ahead of the rest.

Ten months on from winning the Webb Ellis Cup, the rugby world has been turned on its head. England are having to build anew, the Woodward era has ended and my nemesis, Corne Krige, has joined Northampton as club captain. I'm glad I've moved on, as he is not the sort of person I'd want as my captain, but more so because joining Wasps, the Premiership and European champions, has given me a new lease of life.

Since the tour, a lot of people have questioned my commitment to the sport. They are wrong to do so. While it is true that at the age of 32 I have reached a stage in my playing career where I need to look beyond a life in rugby, don't believe that my desire and passion to play for England has lessened one little bit. It never will.

2004 England tour to New Zealand/Australia squad

Abbott, Stuart (Wasps); Barkley, Olly (Bath); Borthwick, Steve (Bath); Catt, Mike (London Irish); Christophers, Phil (Leeds); Cohen, Ben (Northampton); Corry, Martin (Leicester); Dallaglio, Lawrence (Wasps, captain); Dawson, Matt (Northampton); Ellis, Harry (Leicester); Flatman, David (Bath); Gomarsall, Andy (Gloucester); Grewcock, Danny (Bath); Hill, Richard (Saracens); Hodgson, Charlie (Sale); Jones, Chris (Sale); Lewsey, Josh (Wasps); Lipman, Michael (Bath); Payne, Tim (Wasps); Regan, Mark (Leeds); Shaw, Simon (Wasps); Simpson-Daniel, James (Gloucester); Stevens, Matt (Bath); Thompson, Steve (Northampton); Tindall, MIke (Bath); Titterrell, Andy (Sale); Voyce, Tom (Wasps); Waters, Fraser (Wasps); White, Julian (Leicester); Woodman, Trevor (Sale); Worsley, Joe (Wasps).

Career Statistics

Milestones

31 Oct 72   Matthew James Sutherland Dawson is born in Birkenhead.

14 Dec 91   19-year-old Matt makes his Northampton Saints debut as a centre in the 51–0 victory in a friendly at Harrogate.

21 Nov 92   Scores his only drop goal to date in the 12–7 victory over Harlequins at the Stoop in Courage League Division One.

16 Dec 95   Makes England debut and becomes only the 4th Northampton scrum-half to pull on the famous white shirt after Dickie Jeeps in 1956, Trevor Wintle in 1966 and Jacko Page in 1975.

Along with Paul Grayson he marks the first occasion that clubmates have been the starting half-backs in an England team since Wasps team mates Rob Andrew and Nigel Melville played against Ireland in 1988.

It was also the first time that numbers 9 and 10 were BOTH making their test debuts for England on the same day since Rob Andrew and Richard Harding did so against Romania in 1985.

23 Nov 96   Makes his 100th first team appearance for Northampton Saints in the friendly at Bedford.

2 Apr 97   Is selected in the 36 man British & Irish Lions party for the tour to South Africa the following summer.

21 June 97   Matt's debut international try comes after a devastating break in the 72nd minute of the vital 2nd test of the Lions tour in Durban, South Africa and proves to be the key score in ensuring an unassailable 2–0 lead in the three match series.

20 Sep 97   Grabs a European record five tries in one match as the Saints trample over French outfit Nice 66–7 in the European Conference pool 4 game at Franklin's Gardens.

20 June 98   Captains his country for the first time in a test match as England, shorn of many of their established names due to injury and unavailability, slip to a 22–64 loss to hosts New Zealand in Dunedin.

20 Dec 98   Makes 100th league appearance for Northampton in the 19–14 victory against West Hartlepool at Franklin's Gardens.

17 Dec 99   Grabs a hat-trick of tries for Northampton and a record personal haul of 27 points as the Saints beat Edinburgh at Myreside in the Heineken Cup.

21 Jan 00	Scores his 500th point for Northampton during the 44–20 win over London Irish at the Stoop Memorial Ground in the Zurich Premiership.
5 Feb 00	Wins his 30th cap and skippers England to victory over Ireland at Twickenham on the day he surpasses Richard Hill as England's most capped scrum-half.
17 May 00	Injury 37 minutes into the Zurich Premiership match against Saracens at Vicarage Road just five days before the Heineken Cup final ends Matt's season and prevents him being part of the Saints team that lifts the prestigious trophy after they beat Munster 9–8 in the final at Twickenham.
28 Sep 01	Clocks up 200 first XV appearances for Northampton in the 25–17 victory over Cardiff at the Arms Park in the Heineken Cup.
30 Mar 03	Matt's 50th England cap against Ireland at Lansdowne Road is marked with his country's first Grand Slam since 1995.
22 Nov 03	Helps England win the 5th Rugby World Cup in a nail biting extra time 20–17 victory over Australia in Sydney.
6 Mar 04	Wins 60th England cap against Ireland at Twickenham, and scores his 15th international try.
4 Sep 04	Makes Premiership debut for new club London Wasps against Saracens at Twickenham.

ENGLAND CAPS

Caps	Date	Opponents	Venue	Comp
GEOFF COOKE ERA				
–	Sat 27 Nov 93	New Zealand	Twickenham	
JACK ROWELL ERA				
–	Sat 18 Nov 95	South Africa	Twickenham	
1	Sat 16 Dec 95	Samoa	Twickenham	
2	Sat 20 Jan 96	France	Parc des Princes	5NC
3	Sat 3 Feb 96	Wales	Twickenham	5NC
4	Sat 2 Mar 96	Scotland	Murrayfield	5NC
5	Sat 16 Mar 96	Ireland	Twickenham	5NC
6	Sat 12 Jul 97	Australia	Sydney Football Stadium	CC
CLIVE WOODWARD ERA				
7	Sat 29 Nov 97	South Africa	Twickenham	
8	Sat 6 Dec 97	New Zealand	Twickenham	
9	Sat 21 Feb 98	Wales	Twickenham	5NC
10	Sun 22 Mar 98	Scotland	Murrayfield	5NC
11	Sat 4 Apr 98	Ireland	Twickenham	5NC
12	Sat 20 Jun 98	New Zealand(C)	Carisbrook, Dunedin	
13	Sat 27 Jun 98	New Zealand(C)	Eden Park, Auckland	
14	Sat 4 Jul 98	South Africa(C)	Newlands, Cape Town	
15	Sat 14 Nov 98	Netherlands	McAlpine St, Huddersfield	WCQ
16	Sun 22 Nov 98	Italy	McAlpine St, Huddersfield	WCQ
17	Sat 28 Nov 98	Australia	Twickenham	CC
18	Sat 5 Dec 98	South Africa	Twickenham	
19	Sat 20 Feb 99	Scotland	Twickenham	5NC
–	Sat 6 Mar 99	Ireland	Lansdowne Road	5NC
20	Sat 20 Mar 99	France	Twickenham	5NC
21	Sun 11 Apr 99	Wales	Wembley Stadium	5NC
22	Sat 26 Jun 99	Australia	Stadium Australia, Sydney	CC
23	Sat 21 Aug 99	United States	Twickenham	
24	Sat 28 Aug 99	Canada	Twickenham	
25	Sat 2 Oct 99	Italy	Twickenham	RWC
26	Sat 9 Oct 99	New Zealand	Twickenham	RWC
27	Fri 15 Oct 99	Tonga	Twickenham	RWC
28	Wed 20 Oct 99	Fiji	Twickenham	RWC/PO
29	Sun 24 Oct 99	South Africa	Stade de France	RWC/QF
30	Sat 5 Feb 00	Ireland(C)	Twickenham	6NC

Res	Shirt	Scoring	Subs	Mins
W 15–9	–		Bench rep	–
L 14–24	–		Bench rep	–
W 27–9	9			80
L 12–15	9			80
W 21–15	9			80
W 18–9	9			80
W 28–15	9			80
L 6–25	9		Rep by Healey (41)	41
L 11–29	9			80
D 26–26	18		Repl Bracken (59)	21
W 60–26	21	Try	Repl Bracken (70)	10
W 34–20	9	Try		80
W 35–17	9			80
L 22–64	9	Try		80
L 10–40	9	Try/Conv/PG		80
L 0–18	9			80
W 110–0	9	Try		80
W 23–15	9			80
L 11–12	9			80
W 13–7	9	Conv/2PG		80
W 24–21	9		Rep by Bracken (69)	69
W 27–15	–		Bench rep	–
W 21–10	16		Repl Bracken (34)	46
L 31–32	9			80
L 15–22	16		Repl Bracken (51)	29
W 106–8	9	Try		80
W 36–11	9	Try		80
W 67–7	9	Try		80
L 16–30	9			80
W 101–10	9	Try	Rep by Beal (31)	31
W 45–24	18	Conv	Repl Healey (40)	40
L 21–44	9		Rep by Corry (72)	72
W 50–18	9			80

ENGLAND CAPS – *cont.*

Caps	Date	Opponents	Venue	Comp
31	Sat 19 Feb 00	France(C)	Stade de France	6NC
32	Sat 4 Mar 00	Wales(C)	Twickenham	6NC
33	Sat 18 Mar 00	Italy(C)	Stadio Flaminio, Rome	6NC
34	Sun 2 Apr 00	Scotland(C)	Murrayfield	6NC
35	Sat 18 Nov 00	Australia	Twickenham	CC
36	Sat 25 Nov 00	Argentina	Twickenham	
37	Sat 2 Dec 00	South Africa	Twickenham	
38	Sat 3 Feb 01	Wales	Millennium Stadium	6NC
39	Sat 17 Feb 01	Italy	Twickenham	6NC
40	Sat 3 Mar 01	Scotland	Twickenham	6NC
41	Sat 7 Apr 01	France	Twickenham	6NC
42	Sat 20 Oct 01	Ireland(C)	Lansdowne Road	6NC
43	Sat 23 Mar 02	Wales	Twickenham	6NC
44	Sun 7 Apr 02	Italy	Stadio Flaminio, Rome	6NC
45	Sat 9 Nov 02	New Zealand	Twickenham	
46	Sat 16 Nov 02	Australia	Twickenham	CC
47	Sat 23 Nov 02	South Africa	Twickenham	
48	Sun 9 Mar 03	Italy	Twickenham	6NC
49	Sat 22 Mar 03	Scotland	Twickenham	6NC
50	Sun 30 Mar 03	Ireland	Lansdowne Road	6NC
51	Sat 21 Jun 03	Australia	Colonial Stadium, Melbourne	CC
52	Sat 6 Sep 03	France	Twickenham	
53	Sun 12 Oct 03	Georgia	Subiaco Oval, Perth	RWC
54	Sun 26 Oct 03	Samoa	Colonial Stadium, Melbourne	RWC
55	Sun 9 Nov 03	Wales	Suncorp Stadium, Brisbane	RWC/QF
56	Sun 16 Nov 03	France	Stadium Australia, Sydney	RWC/SF
57	Sat 22 Nov 03	Australia	Stadium Australia, Sydney	RWC/F
58	Sun 15 Feb 04	Italy	Stadio Flaminio, Rome	6NC
59	Sat 21 Feb 04	Scotland	Murrayfield	6NC
60	Sat 6 Mar 04	Ireland	Twickenham	6NC
61	Sat 20 Mar 04	Wales	Twickenham	6NC
62	Sat 27 Mar 04	France	Stade de France	6NC
63	Sat 12 Jun 04	New Zealand	Carisbrook, Dunedin	
64	Sat 19 Jun 04	New Zealand	Eden Park, Auckland	
65	Sat 26 Jun 04	Australia	Suncorp Stadium, Brisbane	

Res	Shirt	Scoring	Subs	Mins
W 15–9	9			80
W 46–12	9			80
W 59–12	9	2 Tries	Rep by Gomarsall (77)	77
L 13–19	9			80
W 22–19	20		Repl Bracken (61)	19
W 19–0	9			80
W 25–17	9			80
W 44–15	9	2 Tries		80
W 80–23	9		Rep by Bracken (58)	58
W 43–3	9		Rep by Bracken (73)	73
W 48–19	9		Rep by Bracken (80)	80
L 14–20	9		Rep by Bracken (37)	37
W 50–10	20		Repl Bracken (59)	21
W 45–9	20	Conv	Repl Bracken (56)	24
W 31–28	9			80
W 32–31	9			80
W 53–3	9	Conv	Rep by Gomarsall (57)	57
W 40–5	9	Conv		80
W 40–9	9			80
W 42–6	9		Rep by Bracken (26–34, 69–71)	70
W 25–14	20			27
W 45–14	20			46
W 84–6	9	Try	Rep by Gomarsall (35)	35
W 35–22	9			80
W 28–17	9		Rep by Bracken (67)	67
W 24–7	9		Rep by Bracken (39–40, 70)	70
W 20–17	9			100
W 50–9	20		Repl Gomarsall (62)	18
W 35–13	20		Repl Gomarsall (54)	26
L 13–19	9	Try		80
W 31–21	9			80
L 21–24	9			80
L 3–36	9		Rep by Gomarsall (64)	64
L 12–36	20		Repl Gomarsall (57)	23
L 15–51	20		Repl Gomarsall (46)	34

BRITISH ISLES TESTS

Caps	Date	Opponents	Venue
1	Sat 21 Jun 97	South Africa	Newlands, Cape Town
2	Sat 28 Jun 97	South Africa	Kings Park, Durban
3	Sat 5 Jul 97	South Africa	Ellis Park, Johannesburg
–	Sat 30 Jun 01	Australia	Wooloongabba, Brisbane
4	Sat 7 Jul 01	Australia	Colonial Stadium, Melbourne
5	Sat 14 Jul 01	Australia	Stadium Australia, Sydney

Understanding the stats:

Each "appearance" in the 22 for a test match is listed including those where Matt did not actually get onto the field of play.

Appearances as England captain are marked with a (C) following the opponents name.

The key to the competitions is as follows: 5NC – Five Nations Championship; 6NC – Six Nations Championship; CC – Cook Cup; RWC – Rugby World Cup; WCQ – World Cup Qualifier.

The figures in brackets following Matt's tries and replacements are the minute in the match concerned.

The 'Mins' column indicates the number of minutes on the pitch in the match.

Res	Shirt	Scoring	Subs	Mins
W 25–16	9	Try		80
W 18–15	9			80
L 16–35	9	Try	Rep by Healey (80)	80
W 29–13	–		Bench rep	–
L 14–35	20		Repl Howley(80)	1
L 23–29	9			80

ENGLAND CAP SUMMARY

Opponent	ST	REP	T	C	PG	DG	PTS	W	D	L
Argentina	1	0	0	0	0	0	0	1	0	0
Australia	4	4	0	0	0	0	0	4	0	4
Canada	1	0	1	0	0	0	5	1	0	0
Fiji	0	1	0	1	0	0	2	1	0	0
France	5	2	0	0	0	0	0	5	0	2
Georgia	1	0	1	0	0	0	5	1	0	0
Ireland	6	0	1	0	0	0	5	4	0	2
Italy	5	2	3	2	0	0	19	7	0	0
Netherlands	1	0	1	0	0	0	5	1	0	0
New Zealand	5	2	2	1	1	0	15	1	1	5
Samoa	2	0	0	0	0	0	0	2	0	0
Scotland	6	1	1	0	0	0	5	6	0	1
South Africa	6	0	0	2	2	0	10	3	0	3
Tonga	1	0	1	0	0	0	5	1	0	0
United States	1	0	1	0	0	0	5	1	0	0
Wales	6	2	3	0	0	0	15	7	0	1
TOTALS	**51**	**14**	**15**	**6**	**3**	**0**	**96**	**46**	**1**	**18**

Matt's 17 international tries as a starting scrum-half (15 for England plus 2 for the Lions) ranks him in 4th place in the all-time list for tries scored by number 9s in Test matches, behind Joost van der Westhuizen (36), Justin Marshall (23) and Gareth Edwards (20).

REPRESENTATIVE APPEARANCES

ON TOUR WITH THE BRITISH & IRISH LIONS

Date	Opponents	Venue	Res	Subs	Scoring
Wed 28 May 97	Border	East London	W 18–14	Rep	
Wed 4 Jun 97	Mpumalanga Pumas	Witbank	W 64–14	SH	Try
Sat 14 Jun 97	Natal	Kings Park, Durban	W 42–12	Rep	
Tue 12 Jun 01	Qld. President's XV	Townsville	W 83–6	SH	
Sat 16 Jun 01	Queensland	Ballymore, Brisbane	W 42–8	Rep	
Tue 19 Jun 01	Australia A	Gosford	L 25–28	Rep	2 Conv
Sat 23 Jun 01	NSW Waratahs	Sydney Football Stadium	W 41–24	SH	Conv
Tue 3 Jul 01	ACT Brumbies	Canberra	W 30–28	SH	3 Conv/3 PG

ON TOUR WITH ENGLAND

Date	Opponents	Venue	Res	Subs	Scoring
Sat 13 Jun 98	New Zealand A	Rugby Park, Hamilton	L 10–18	SH	Captain
Sat 19 Jun 99	Queensland	Ballymore, Brisbane	W 39–14	Rep	

GAMES FOR ENGLAND 'A'

Date	Opponents	Venue	Res	Subs	Scoring
Tue 5 Jan 93	France A	Welford Road, Leicester	W 29–17	SH	
Wed 3 Feb 93	Italy A	The Rec, Bath	W 59–0	SH	Try
Fri 5 Mar 93	Spain	Athletic Ground, Richmond	W 66–5	SH	
Fri 19 Mar 93	Ireland A	Donnybrook	W 22–18	SH	2 Tries
Sat 22 May 93	British Columbia	Victoria	W 26–10	SH	
Sat 5 Feb 94	Italy A	Piacenza	W 15–9	SH	
Fri 18 Feb 94	Ireland A	Athletic Ground, Richmond	W 29–14	SH	Try

Career Statistics

Date	Opponents	Venue	Res	Subs	Scoring
Sat 18 Mar 95	Natal	Kings Park, Durban	L 25–33	SH	
Wed 24 May 95	Victoria	Olympic Park, Melbourne	W 76–19	SH	3 Tries
Sun 28 May 95	Queensland	Ballymore, Brisbane	L 15–20	SH	
Tue 10 Dec 96	Argentina	Franklin's Gardens	W 22–17	SH	
Fri 1 Mar 02	France A	Limoges	L 13–19	SH	

GAMES FOR ENGLAND UNDER-21

Sat 2 May 92	French Military	Twickenham	D 21–21	C	Try
Sun 6 Sep 92	Italy U21	Welford Road, Leicester	W 37–12	C	
Wed 14 Oct 92	Ireland U21	Kingston Park, Newcastle	W 39–28	C	

GAMES FOR ENGLAND 18 GROUP

Wed 18 Apr 90	Ireland	Oxford	L 6–15	Rep	
Sat 21 Apr 90	France	Carmaux	L 9–20	C	
Wed 23 Jan 91	Australian Schools	Twickenham	L 3–8	SH	
Sat 30 Mar 91	Ireland	Limerick	W 15–0	SH	
Wed 3 Apr 91	France	Franklin's Gardens	W 28–13	SH	
Tue 9 Apr 91	Scotland	Aspatria	W 21–3	SH	
Sat 13 Apr 91	Wales	Colwyn Bay	L 10–13	SH	

GAMES FOR THE BARBARIANS

Thu 2 Jun 94	Matabeleland	Bulawayo	W 35–23	SH	Try

GAMES FOR THE MIDLANDS AGAINST TOURING TEAMS

Sat 2 Dec 95	Samoa	Welford Road, Leicester	W 40–19	SH	Try

Note: The positions denoted under the Representative Rugby section are:
SH – scrum-half; C – centre; Rep – replacement.

MATT'S NORTHAMPTON CAREER

Season	Div	App	T	C	PG	DG	Pts	App	T	C	PG	DG
				LEAGUE						**CUP**		
1991–92	CD1	7	1	1	2	–	12					
1992–93	CD1	10	1	–	–	1	8	4	–	–	–	–
1993–94	CD1	14+1	2	–	–	–	10	2	–	–	–	–
1994–95	CD1	9	3	–	–	–	15	2	–	–	–	–
1995–96	CD2	16	9	–	–	–	35	1	–	–	–	–
1996–97	CD1	16	2	–	–	–	10	1	–	–	–	–
1997–98	ADP	17	5	5	14	–	77	3	–	–	–	–
1998–99	ADP	22	6	17	8	–	88	2	–	–	–	–
1999–00	ADP	9	2	12	21	–	97	2	–	3	1	–
2000–01	ZP	10+1	1	7	10	–	49	3	3	–	–	–
2001–02	ZP	10+5	–	–	–	–	–	3	–	–	–	–
2002–03	ZP	15+1	3	3	2	–	27	3	–	–	–	–
2003–04	ZP	3+1	–	–	–	–	–					
TOTALS		158+9	35	45	57	1	428	26	3	3	1	0

Notes: Appearances as a replacement are marked after the (+) sign.

Key to the Division is as follows: CD1 – Courage League Division One; CD2 – Courage League Division 2; ADP – Allied Dunbar Premiership; ZP – Zurich Premiership.

Appearances in post season playoffs are NOT included in the League column.

Matches in the Knockout Cup have been played under various different title sponsors as follows: Until 1997–98 – Pilkington Cup; from 1997/98 to 2000/01 – Tetley's Bitter Cup; from 2001/02 to date – Powergen Cup.

Games in Europe include appearances in the European Conference in 1996/97 and 1997/98 and the main Heineken Cup thereafter.

All previous statistics compiled by Stuart Farmer Media Services Limited up to 13 September 2004.

Career Statistics

Pts	EUROPE						ALL GAMES					
	App	T	C	PG	DG	Pts	App	T	C	PG	DG	Pts
							15	5	3	5	–	41
–							19	2	–	–	1	13
–							21+1	5	–	–	–	25
–							14	4	–	–	–	20
–							18	10	–	–	–	50
–	3	1	–	–	–	5	23	7	–	–	–	35
–	5	5	–	–	–	25	25	10	5	14	–	102
							26	8	19	8	–	102
9	4+1	3	8	14	–	73	16	5	23	36	–	179
15	2	–	–	1	–	3	17+1	6	7	11	–	77
–	3	–	2	2	–	10	17+5	–	2	2	–	10
–	5	1	1	1	–	10	23+1	4	5	3	–	39
							3+1	–	–	–	–	–
24	22+1	10	11	18	0	126	237+9	66	64	79	1	693

Career Injuries

26 May 93	Right hamstring
7 Sep 93	Left elbow joint
17Jan 94	Neck injury
23 Feb 94	Left elbow joint
10 Mar 94	Right hamstring
7 Apr 94	Left knee hyper extension injury
5 Sep 94	Left hamstring strain
5 Nov 94	Left hamstring strain
5 Apr 95	Right hamstring strain
2 Oct 95	Right posterior knee pain
12 Aug 96	Low back pain
25 Nov 96	Right hamstring strain
28 Aug 97	Left elbow joint strain
11 Nov 97	Left shoulder injury
29 Dec 97	Left shoulder injury
31 Jan 98	Left shoulder injury
1 Sep 98	Left knee pain
14 Sep 98	Right hamstring strain
4 Jan 99	Left quadriceps strain
26 Oct 99	Right hamstring strain
30 Dec 99	Left shoulder joint strain
6 Mar 00	Left knee hyper extension
21 Mar 00	Left shoulder joint strain
5 Apr 00	Right costal cartilage
2 May 00	Left shoulder subluxation
19 May 00	Left shoulder dislocation
3 Jun 00	Left bankcart and T plasty left shoulder joint
6 Jan 01	Right AC joint (grade 1)
20 Mar 01	Left hamstring strain

Career Statistics

10 Aug 01	Left knee hyper extension
10 Sep 01	Right calf strain (grade 2)
23 Oct 01	Left hamstring strain (grade 1)
12 Nov 01	Concussion
7 Jan 02	Right ankle joint subluxation
28 May 02	Left calf strain (grade 1)
6 Aug 02	Left thigh haematoma
26 Sep 02	Deep peroneal nerve neurothapy (calf numbness)
7 Oct 02	Neck injury
14 Oct 02	Left wrist subluxation/crepitis
23 Oct 02	Low back pain
23 Oct 02	Right calf strain (grade 1)
25 Nov 02	Right neck pain with neuropraxia to hand
2 Dec 02	Right knee medial ligament strain (grade 2)
3 Feb 03	Head injury (right visual disturbance)
14 Feb 03	Left calf cramps
2 Apr 03	Right calf strain
22 Apr 03	Right calf strain
5 May 03	Left elbow strain
9 May 03	Left elbow pain
12 May 03	Right rectus femorris (quads strain, grade 2 strain)
12 Oct 03	Left knee bursar swelling (steroid injection)
26 Oct 03	Dead calf right
9 Nov 03	Right knee bursar swelling (steroid injection)
20 Dec 03	Calf strain
18 Apr 04	Jarred shoulder

Index

Abbott, Stuart 260
Ackford, Paul 185, 191–192
Addison, Jeff 95–96
Adebayo, Ade 19, 21
Alatini, Pieta 81
Alred, Dave 146, 149, 173, 335
Andrew, Rob 27, 106, 200
Anne, Princess Royal 95–96, 351
Archer, Garath
  Australia, New Zealand and South
    Africa tour 1998 91
  international experience 76
  Six Nations 2000 115
Ashton, Brian 106

Back, Neil
  Australia and New Zealand tour 2003
    261, 265, 269
  Barbarians Zimbabwe tour 1994
    28
  Lions Australia tour 2001 155, 177,
    180
  Lions South Africa tour 1997 71
  Six Nations 2003 219–220, 230, 236,
    245, 267
  South Africa match 2000 211
  South Africa match 2002 212
  video tape 235
  World Cup 2003 296

Balshaw, Iain
  Australia match 2000 124
  Dawson's needle phobia 58
  development as young international
    103
  Lions Australia tour 2001 148, 153,
    156–157, 180
  playing style 19
  Six Nations 2001 189
  World Cup 2003 296–297, 303, 305,
    311, 313
Bannister, Roger 228
Barbarians Zimbabwe tour 1994
  27–31
Barnes, Stuart 106
Baron, Francis 122, 126
Barwell, Keith
  ambitions for Northampton 50
  appointment of Smith 197
  attempting to sign Johnson 45–46
  England players' strike 127
  pulling players from overseas tours
    73–74
  rugby turning professional 44–45, 48
  support for Dawson 12–13, 49–50,
    221, 362–3
Bateman, Allan 71
Bates, Steve 31
Baxendell, Jos 92

Index

Bayfield, Martin 45, 198
Beal, Jo 198
Beal, Joshua 198
Beal, Nick
  Australia, New Zealand and South
    Africa tour 1998 92
  cactus leaf incident 29–30
  Dawson's neck injury 209
  friendship with Dawson 198
  Lions South Africa tour 1997 71
  support for Dawson xiii–xiv,
    197–198
  World Cup Sevens 1993 19–21
Beal, Thomas 198
Beaumont, Bill 127–128
Beim, Tom 92
Bell, Duncan 88, 91
Bentley, John 69, 71
Benton, Scott 92
Best, Dick 27
Black, Steve 149, 152
Blair, Ben 210
Blair, Tony 351–352
Blyth, Andy 216–218
Boyce, Max 111
Bracken, Kyran
  Australia and New Zealand tour 2003
    252–253, 266, 271, 274, 275
  Australia tour 1993 24
  Canada tour 1993 23–24
  Dawson's shoulder injury 117
  Dawson's views on 227–228
  dropped by England 41, 52
  England caps 2001 196
  England under-21s 15
  Five Nations 1995 35
  international debut 24–27
  Lions South Africa tour 1997 72
  Packer circus 47
  rivalry with Dawson 23–28, 34
  Six Nations 2002 199
  Six Nations 2003 227, 230, 245
  World Cup 1995 35
  World Cup 1999 98

  World Cup 2003 289–291, 293–294,
    305, 307, 308–309, 310–311
  World Cup selection process
    285–286
Brain, David 261
British Lions
  1997 tour statistics 71–72
  2001 tour statistics 180–181
  Australia tour 1969 63, 65
  Australia tour 2001 133–181
  motivational factors 136–137
  New Zealand tour 1993 64–65
  selecting Dawson 63–65
  South Africa tour 1997 61–63,
    65–72
  spies at training sessions 168–169
  team-building exercises 145–147
Broun, Alex 145, 178
Brown, Spencer 92
Brown, Stewart 15–16
Bulloch, Gordon 180
Burke, Paul 9
Burnham, Jasper 208–209
Burrell, Paul 162

Calder, Finlay 189
Campese, David 248
  criticisms of England 255–257, 272
  World Cup Sevens 1993 20, 21
Carling, Will
  criticism of Tindall 231–232, 270
  Lions New Zealand tour 1993 64–65
  Packer circus 47
  stripped of England captaincy 47
  support for Dawson 42
Cassell, Justyn 19, 20
Catt, Mike
  advising younger players 103
  Dawson's views on 105–106
  Lions Australia tour 2001 142, 148,
    180
  Lions South Africa tour 1997 72
  Six Nations 2000 103, 105–107
  Six Nations 2001 188

Catt, Mike – *cont.*
  World Cup 2003 301, 311, 313,
    321–322
  World Cup final 2003 xi, 331, 332
Catterson, Andy 338
Chamberlain, Phil 63
Chapman, Dominic 92
Charvis, Colin 180
Christophers, Phil
  Six Nations 2003 227, 246
  South Africa match 2002 212
Chuter, George 91
Clarke, Ben
  Australia, New Zealand and South
    Africa tour 1998 87, 92
  England initiation ceremonies 38
  international experience 76
Clarke, Tim 340
Cleary, Mick 83, 158, 176
Cockbain, Matt 331
Cockerill, Richard
  Australia, New Zealand and South
    Africa tour 1998 84–86, 91
  Barbarians Zimbabwe tour 1994 29
  criticisms of Woodward 130
Cohen, Ben
  Australia and New Zealand tour 2003
    268–269, 271, 276
  Australia match 2002 211
  Dawson's unhappiness at
    Northampton 196
  death threats 186–187
  development as young international
    103
  Lions Australia tour 2001 138, 145,
    176, 180
  New Zealand match 2002 210
  Six Nations 2000 101, 103, 105
  Six Nations 2003 230, 238, 243, 246
  video tape 236
  World Cup 2003 313
Cohen, George 105
Cohen, Peter 105
Cohen, Simon 166

Cordingley, Sam 124
Corry, Martin
  birth of child 300
  holiday with Dawson 224
  Lions Australia tour 2001 171, 180
Cotton, Fran 70, 136, 170, 179, 357
Crompton, Darren 91
Crystal, Dr Terry 188
Cullen, Christian 87, 249
Cusworth, Les 56, 67

Dallaglio, Lawrence
  absence from England 1998 tour
    squad 77, 82
  Australia and New Zealand tour 2003
    265, 275
  autograph hunters 349–350
  captain of England 355
  Dawson's newspaper diary 161
  Five Nations 1999 111
  golf playing 259, 260, 275
  Lions Australia tour 2001 149–150,
    180
  Lions South Africa tour 1997 62, 71
  role in RFU dispute 122, 125, 128
  Six Nations 2000 114
  Six Nations 2003 219–220, 241, 245
  South Africa match 2002 210
  talking to referees 200
  testimonial dinner 352
  video tape 235
  Western Samoa match 1995 43
  World Cup 1999 99
  World Cup 2003 303, 313, 323, 325
  World Cup Sevens 1993 18, 20–21
  World Cup victory parade 350
Davidson, Jeremy
  Lions Australia tour 2001 148, 180
  Lions South Africa tour 1997 66, 71
Davies, Mark 149
Davison, Bill 214–215
Dawson, Emma (sister) 1, 3, 11
Dawson, Lois (mother)
  birth of Matt 2

Index

Davison punch incident 214–215
fear of Matt being injured 10–11
Five Nations 1999 112
Lions Australia tour 2001 156, 158, 160, 177
Matt arrested for theft 6
Matt getting lost 3
Matt leaving home 12
Matt's bad behaviour 192
Matt's childhood bike accident 1–2
Matt's fiftieth cap 241
Matt's neck injury 209, 214
Matt's newspaper diary 172
Matt's relationship with Joanne 221–222
Matt's sledging accident 4
Matt's unapproachable attitude 165
move to Hampshire 1
National Anthem 44
Six Nations 2000 105
Six Nations 2003 235
support for Matt xiii, 10–11
World Cup 2003 xi, 307, 313–314
Dawson, Matt
  2001 Lions tour diary 145–159, 171–179
  2003 Australia tour diary 273–276
  2003 New Zealand tour diary 259–265
  2003 World Cup diary 302–316
  admiration for Shelford 16–17
  airport metal detector incident 351
  apologies for newspaper diary 161–162, 171
  appointed England captain 73–74
  appointment of Northampton captain 182–183
  Argentina match 2000 130–131
  'arguing' with Pountney 203–205, 244
  arrested for theft 6
  arrogant attitude 39–40
  Australia and New Zealand tour 2003 247–276
Australia match 2000 124–125
Australia, New Zealand and South Africa tour 1998 74–92
Australia and New Zealand tour 2004 364–70
autograph hunters 349–350
bad conduct 190–191. 201–205
Barbarians Zimbabwe tour 1994 27–31
birth of 2
bleeding nose incident 244–245
Buckingham Palace reception 351
cactus leaf incident 29–30
Canada tour 1993 23–24, 64
career milestones 353–355
career statistics 353–367
childhood 1–6
childhood bike accident 1–2
coached by Ron 5–6
commitment to England 369
Daily Telegraph diary xii, 134–135, 142–144, 161–162, 171–179, 183
Davison punch incident 214–215
death of Duncombe 224–226
debut at Northampton 14
difficult relationship with Emma 11
dispute between clubs and RFU 48–50
diving board injury 78
dropped from England squad 55–56, 184–185, 191, 194–195
England initiation ceremonies 37–38
England under-18s 9–10
England under-21s 10, 14–15
fiftieth cap 241
fine for newspaper diary 133–134, 163, 166–167, 173
first England cap 37–38, 42–43
first rugby game 4
fitness training 280–282
Five Nations 1996 54–55
Five Nations 1999 111–113
friendship with Grayson 234

Dawson, Matt – *cont.*
  game tactics 238
  godson James 89, 234, 279
  golf playing 58, 148, 150, 259, 260,
    264, 275, 315
  hamstring injury 23
  hate mail 93–94, 115
  head-shaving incident 65
  Heathrow reception for World Cup
    squad 348–349
  Hello! magazine 347
  injury history 309, 352–353
  Ireland red carpet incident 239–241
  joining Northampton 11–12
  joining Wasps 363
  knee injury 288–290, 308–312
  Larkin's reports 33–34, 52–54
  leaving Saints 361–363
  Lions Australia tour 2001 133–180
  Lions South Africa tour 1997 61–63,
    65–72, 136, 138–139
  living in New Zealand 15–17
  living with Joanne 220–221
  low point in career xiii
  MBE award 348
  media commitments 184–185
  meeting Joanne 207, 223
  move to Hampshire 1
  neck injury 207–208, 210–217
  nerves 43–44
  Northampton's relegation 32–33
  Omega testing 307–308
  over-emotional 182–185, 191–192
  Packer circus 47
  paparazzi 352
  players' strike 119–120, 125–130
  playing football 4–5
  playing style 54–55
  poor academic record 7, 9
  Powergen Cup 2002 198–203, 238
  Powergen Cup 2003 228–230, 238
  'pretty boys' 13–14
  prima donna attitude 26, 31–32
  Prime Minister's reception 351–352

pulling out of Argentina tour 75–76
reaction to needles 56–59
rebellious teenager 6–7
recalled to England squad 199
relationship with Natalie 163–164,
  171, 181
rivalry with Bracken 23–28, 34
role in RFU dispute 122, 125–128,
  130
royal snub incident xii, 94–96,
  115–116
rugby turning professional 44–48
school rugby 5–9
security guard job 12
selected for Lions 63–65
sharing house with Luger 224
shoulder injury 111, 116–117
Six Nations 2000 94–98, 100–101,
  103–111, 114–116
Six Nations 2001 181–182, 184,
  185–194
Six Nations 2002 199
Six Nations 2003 219–220, 224–227,
  230–245
South Africa match 2002 211–215
South Africa tour 1995 35
sports psychology 228–230, 267–268
support from Barwell 49–50
support from Ron 7–8, 10–11
talking to referees 200
teaching job 13
team-building exercises 145–147
testimonial dinner 349
unapproachable attitude 165
unhappiness at Northampton
  196–198, 205–206
views on Bracken 227–228
views on Catt 105–106
views on England captaincy 101–103
views on fair play 82–84
views on future career 309–310
views on Greening 109
views on Henry 135–144, 148, 151,
  158

views on Johnson 162–163
views on Lenihan 135–137, 140, 144
views on Lions 134, 170
views on media 90–91
views on rough play 201–202, 211,
 257–259
views on rugby finances 121–123
views on team accommodation 89–90
views on team bonding 282–283
views on Venter 199–202
views on Wilkinson 243
views on Woodward 195–196
Western Samoa match 1995 37–38,
 42–43
Wonderwall song xii
World Cup 1995 35–36
World Cup 1999 98–100
World Cup 2003 279–332
World Cup final 2003 xi–xii, xiv,
 329–332
World Cup gala dinner 286–287
World Cup opening ceremony
 306–307
World Cup Sevens 1993 18–21
World Cup victory parade 347–348,
 350–351
Dawson, Ron (father)
 birth of Matt 2
 coaching Matt 5–6
 Davison punch incident 214–215
 Five Nations 1999 112
 Lions Australia tour 2001 156, 158,
  160, 171, 177
 Matt leaving home 12
 Matt playing for England under-21s
  10
 Matt starting rugby 4–5
 Matt's bad behaviour 192
 Matt's childhood bike accident 1–2
 Matt's fiftieth cap 241
 Matt's neck injury 209, 214
 Matt's rebellious behaviour 6–7
 Matt's relationship with Joanne
  221–222

Matt's unapproachable attitude 165
Matt's unhappiness at Northampton
 205–206
move to Hampshire 1
National Anthem 44
royal snub incident 115–116
Six Nations 2000 104
Six Nations 2003 235
support for Matt 7–8, 10–11
work at Mobil Oil 3
World Cup 2003 xi, 307, 313–314
World Cup victory parade 350
de Beer, Jannie 100
de Glanville, Phil
 England initiation ceremonies 38
 Packer circus 47
 Six Nations 2000 101
Diprose, Tony
 Australia, New Zealand and South
  Africa tour 1998 78, 92
 Lions South Africa tour 1997 71
Dooley, Wade 23, 65
Duncombe, Nick 224–226, 253, 263

Edwards, Gareth 28
Eminem 235
England
 16 men on pitch incident 298–299
 1998 tour statistics 91–92
 2003 Six Nations statistics 245–246
 Argentina match 2000 130–131
 arrogant image 96–97, 248–249
 Australia and New Zealand tour 2003
  247–276
 Australia match 2000 124–125
 Australia match 2002 210–211
 Australia World Cup final 2003
  327–332
 Australia, New Zealand and South
  Africa tour 1998 74–92
 Buckingham Palace reception 351
 Canada tour 1993 23–24
 coaching team 283
 'Dad's Army' nickname 269, 271

England – *cont.*
  Dawson's first cap 37–38, 42–43
  dropping Dawson 55–56
  fitness training 280–282
  Five Nations 1995 35
  Five Nations 1996 54–55
  Five Nations 1998 107
  Five Nations 1999 111–113
  France World Cup semi-final 2003
    324–327
  Georgia World Cup match 2003 288,
    307–308
  Heathrow reception for World Cup
    squad 347, 348–349
  inexperience of 1998 tour squad 76
  initiation ceremonies 37–38
  Ireland red carpet incident 239–241
  New Zealand match 1993 25–27
  New Zealand match 2002 210
  New Zealand Test 2003 265
  players' strike 119–120, 125–130
  pressure of media in World Cup
    316
  Prime Minister's reception 351–352
  Robocops reputation 110
  Samoa World Cup match 2003
    296–297, 314–315
  Six Nations 2000 94–98, 100–101,
    103–111, 114–116
  Six Nations 2001 181–182, 184,
    185–194
  Six Nations 2003 219–220, 224–227,
    230–246
  Six Nations championship statistics
    186
  South Africa match 2002 211–215
  South Africa tour 1994 31
  South Africa tour 2000 120–121,
    211
  South Africa World Cup match 2003
    291–295, 311
  spies at training sessions 237, 261
  training boycott 48–49
  typical training programme 283–284

  under-18s 9–10
  under-21s 10, 14–15
  Uruguay World Cup match 2003
    300–301
  Wales World Cup quarter-final 2003
    318–322
  Western Samoa match 1995 37–38,
    43
  World Cup 1995 35
  World Cup 1999 98–100
  World Cup 2003 279–332
  World Cup 2003 Pool C results
    302
  World Cup Sevens 1993 18–21
  World Cup victory parade 347–348,
    350–351
  World Cup warm-up matches
    284–286
Erickson, Wayne 83, 84
Evans, Ieuan 62, 71
Evans, Mark 226

Feek, Greg 81
Fidler, Rob 87, 91
Finegan, Owain 271
Fitzpatrick, Sean 363
Five Nations
  1995 35
  1996 54–55
  1998 107
  1999 111–113
Flatley, Elton 330
Freeman, Cathy 177
Friend, Mike 338
Frost, Sir David 347

Galthie, Fabien 339
Garforth, Darren 29
Geldof, Bob 287
Gibbs, Scott
  Five Nations 1999 112–113
  Lions Australia tour 2001 171, 180
  Lions South Africa tour 1997 70,
    71

Index

Gibson, Daryl 81

Gifford, Phil 250

Gomarsall, Andy
  Argentina tour 2002 76
  Australia and New Zealand tour 2003
    250, 252, 263
  England under-18s 10
  Italy match 1996 56
  Six Nations 2003 227, 245
  World Cup 1995 35–36
  World Cup 2003 291, 293, 307, 308,
    332–333
  World Cup selection process 286,
    287–288

Grant, Hugh 352

Grayson, Emma 38, 234

Grayson, James 89, 234, 279

Grayson, Paul
  Australia and New Zealand tour 2003
    250–251, 259, 261, 265, 274
  birth of son 89
  Dawson's concussion 35–36
  Dawson's neck injury 208, 209
  dropped by England 100
  England debut 37, 42–43
  England initiation ceremonies 38
  European Cup 2000 117
  Five Nations 1999 112
  friendship with Dawson 64, 198, 234
  golf playing 300, 315
  Lions South Africa tour 1997 65–66,
    71
  recalled to England team 233–234
  rugby turning professional 44
  Six Nations 2003 219–220, 233–234,
    238, 243, 245
  support for Dawson xiii, 104, 197,
    279–280, 320, 327–329
  World Cup 1999 99–100
  World Cup 2003 294, 304, 320,
    327–328
  World Cup final 2003 332

Greef, Werner 212, 215, 258

Green, Will 91

Greening, Phil
  Australia, New Zealand and South
    Africa tour 1998 91
  Dawson's views on 109
  Lions Australia tour 2001 150, 180
  Six Nations 2000 109

Greenwood, Caro 295, 300, 312

Greenwood, Dick 11

Greenwood, Freddie 295

Greenwood, Will
  Australia and New Zealand tour 2003
    260, 270
  golf playing 259, 275–275, 315
  Lions Australia tour 2001 180
  Lions South Africa tour 1997 70–71
  Six Nations 2001 188
  Six Nations 2003 219–220, 227, 238,
    243, 245, 246
  video tape 236
  World Cup 2003 295, 300, 311, 312,
    322

Gregan, George 331

Grewcock, Danny
  Australia, New Zealand and South
    Africa tour 1998 77, 82–83, 91
  Lions Australia tour 2001 171, 180
  Six Nations 2003 245
  World Cup 2003 305

Grey, Nathan 258

Guscott, Jeremy 42, 101
  comparison with Tindall 270
  Lions South Africa tour 1997 69–71
  Packer circus 47
  World Cup 1999 99

Hanley, Steve 112

Hansen, Steve 316

Hardwick, Rob 49

Hardy, Simon 247

Harinordoquy, Imanol 224, 326

Harriman, Andy 18–21

Harris, Iestyn 318

Harrison, Justin 169

Hart, John 82, 84

Hawke, Colin 62
Healey, Austin
  advising younger players 103
  Australia, New Zealand and South
    Africa tour 1998 82, 89, 92
  complaints about 2001 Lions tour
    155–156
  criticism of Dawson 63
  Dawson's newspaper diary 144, 161
  disciplinary hearing 166
  diving skills 78
  golf playing 58
  international experience 76
  Lions Australia tour 2001 140,
    147–150, 153, 155–156,
    160–161, 166, 167, 172, 175,
    177–180
  Lions South Africa tour 1997 67,
    71, 137
  newspaper articles 140, 178
  Six Nations 2000 108, 110–111
  support for Dawson 162, 164
  World Cup 1999 99
  World Cup 2003 336–337
  World Cup selection process 286,
    287–288
Healey, Louise 160
Henderson, Rob
  Lions Australia tour 2001 142,
    147–148, 153, 171, 177, 180
Henry, Graham
  analytical attitude 148
  Dawson's criticisms of 135–144, 158
  Dawson's newspaper diary 134,
    139–140, 163, 171
  England tour match 1998 80
  Healey's disciplinary hearing 167
  Lions Australia tour 2001 134–179
  Lions Melbourne Test half-time
    speech 167, 174, 275
  mistakes in selecting Lions team 66
  pep talks 152, 154–155, 167,
    173–174, 176
  relationship with media 170

selection policy 137–138, 148
training sessions 146, 149, 151
uninspiring coach 161
Hepher, Ali 214
Hewitt, Norm 84–85
Hignell, Alistair 129
Hill, Richard 31, 106
  absence from England 1998 tour
    squad 77
  Australia and New Zealand tour 2003
    258
  Five Nations 1999 112
  golf playing 300
  Lions Australia tour 2001 171, 180
  Lions South Africa tour 1997 66, 71
  Six Nations 2003 241, 242, 245
  South Africa match 2000 211
  video tape 235
  World Cup 2003 308, 309, 323, 325
  World Cup final 2003 331
Hills, Murray 251
HM Queen Elizabeth II 351
Hodge, Duncan 115
Hodgson, Charlie
  Six Nations 2003 230, 233, 243, 245
Hopley, Damian 19, 20
Howard, Michael 347, 352
Howarth, Shane 186
Howe, Tyrone 180
Howlett, Doug 81, 254, 271
Howley, Rob 63
  golf playing 150
  Lions Australia tour 2001 137, 144,
    147, 149, 150–151, 153, 155, 159,
    171, 174, 180
  Lions South Africa tour 1997 66–67,
    72, 137–138, 139
Hule, Rob 15–16
Humphreys, David 241
Hunter, Ian
  Dawson's Northampton debut 14
  friendship with Dawson 200
  Lions New Zealand tour 1993 64
  rugby turning professional 44, 46

Index

Inverdale, John 351

James, Dafydd 142, 171, 180
Jenkins, Neil
  Five Nations 1999 112
  Lions Australia tour 2001 145, 149,
    180
  Lions South Africa tour 1997 61, 66,
    69, 71, 136, 139
John, Chris 10
Johnson, Martin
  absence from England 1998 tour
    squad 77, 82
  approached by Northampton 45–46
  Australia and New Zealand tour 2003
    268, 269, 271
  Australia match 2000 124
  broken hand 182
  Dawson's newspaper diary 159, 160,
    161, 173
  Dawson's views on 162–163
  England retirement 355
  Lions Australia tour 2001 145, 153,
    158, 171, 173, 180
  Lions call-up 23
  Lions South Africa tour 1997 71
  Packer circus 47
  pep talks 173, 178
  qualities as England captain 101, 232,
    239–241, 323
  role in RFU dispute 122–123,
    125–126, 128–129
  Six Nations 2003 230, 239–241, 245
  South Africa tour 2000 121
  support for Dawson 162–163
  talking to referees 200
  video tape 235
  World Cup 1999 100
  World Cup 2003 290, 297–298, 323,
    329
  World Cup final 2003 329–331
Johnstone, Brad 110
Jones, Derwyn 29–30
Jones, Ian 82–83, 257

Jones, Stephen 87, 110, 318
Jones, Tom 111
Joseph, Jamie 25, 27
Joubert, Andre 62

Kaplan, Jonathan 244–245
Kay, Ben
  Australia and New Zealand tour 2003
    254
  Six Nations 2003 245
  video tape 235
  World Cup 2003 311, 315
  World Cup final 2003 329
Kefu, Toutai 269, 271, 328
Kelleher, Byron 81
Kemp, Dr Simon 59, 244–245, 286,
  305
Kenny, Barney 260–262, 264, 266, 274
  World Cup 2003 305
King, Alex 92
Kirwan, John 357
Koen, Louis 294, 295
Krige, Corne 201, 210–215, 369
  World Cup 2003 291–293
Kruger, Ruben 62

Labuschagne, Jannes 212–213
Lam, Pat 102, 182
Lambert, Dan 301
Lander, Steve 202, 203
Laporte, Bernard 193
Larder, Phil
  Australia and New Zealand tour 2003
    269–270
  criticisms of Lions squad 156–157
  Dawson's newspaper diary 171
  egotism 151
  restricted by Henry's views 158
  support for Dawson 172
  team tactics 176
  training sessions 81, 146, 147, 149
  World Cup 2003 294, 322
Larkham, Stephen 326
Larkin, Paul 33–34, 52–54

Latham, Chris 271
Lenihan, Donal
  criticisms of England team 96
  Dawson's criticisms of 135–137, 140, 144
  Dawson's fine for newspaper diary 133–134, 145, 163, 166, 172
  Dawson's newspaper diary 159, 171
  Healey's disciplinary hearing 167
  Ireland red carpet incident 240
  Lions Australia tour 2001 154–155
  pep talks 174, 179
  relationship with media 170
  spies at Lions training sessions 168
  training sessions 158
Leonard, Jason
  absence from England 1998 tour squad 77
  Australia and New Zealand tour 2003 269, 275
  autograph hunters 349–350
  birth of child 300
  Dawson's newspaper diary 161
  golf playing 150
  Lions Australia tour 2001 148, 180
  Lions South Africa tour 1997 71
  record number of caps 327
  Six Nations 2000 107
  Six Nations 2003 224, 226–227, 245
  video tape 235
  World Cup 2003 304, 311, 327
Lewis, Denise 177
Lewsey, Josh
  Australia and New Zealand tour 2003 255, 257–258
  Australia, New Zealand and South Africa tour 1998 77, 88, 92
  physical fitness 88
  Six Nations 2003 231, 246
  stamping incident 255, 257–258
  try-scoring record 300–301
  video tape 236
  World Cup 2003 300–301, 305, 333

Lomu, Jonah
  England match 2002 210
  England tour match 1998 80
  rough play 211
  World Cup 1999 98–99
Lucas, Dr Phil 337
Luger, Dan
  16 men on pitch incident 298–299
  Australia and New Zealand tour 2003 253, 260–261, 263, 275
  Australia match 2000 124
  Dawson's neck injury 209
  death of Duncombe 226, 253, 263
  Lions Australia tour 2001 155, 180
  sharing house with Dawson 224
  Six Nations 2003 220, 245, 246
  World Cup 1999 99
  World Cup 2003 307, 313
Lynagh, Michael 21

Mallett, Nick 125
Mauriac, Paul 215
McAleese, Mary 239
McBride, Willie John 159
McBryde, Robin 180
McGeechan, Ian
  Barwell pulling players from overseas tours 74
  coaching Lions 61, 63, 65
  coaching skills 143
  criticism of Northampton players 33
  Dawson's arrogant attitude 40
  Lions South Africa tour 1997 66, 68, 136–138
  rugby turning professional 46
  support for Dawson 32, 40–42, 55
  training Northampton squad 39–40
McGruther, Dick 74–76
McRae, Duncan 139
Meeuws, Kees 81
Mehrtens, Andrew 189, 265
Melville, Nigel 40
Merceron, Gérard 226
Miller, Eric 66, 71

Mitchell, John 153
  Australia, New Zealand and South
    Africa tour 1998 78–81, 85–86, 88
  support for Dawson 88
Montgomery, Tim 267
Moody, Lewis
  Australia, New Zealand and South
    Africa tour 1998 77, 91
  Six Nations 2003 245
  South Africa match 2002 212
  World Cup 2003 295
  World Cup final 2003 331
Moore, Brian 272
Moore, Matt 92
Morgan, Derek 240–241, 265, 274
Morris, Darren 180
Morris, Dewi
  competition to supersede 24, 31, 34
  Lions New Zealand tour 1993 23
  retirement from international game
    41, 52
  TV commentator 224
  World Cup 1995 35
Morris, Robbie 47, 245
Morrison, Ed 137, 147
Mulder, Japie 211
Murdoch, Rupert 46
Murphy, Geordan 190–191, 200, 241
Murray, Scott 180

Nicol, Andy 178, 189
Noon, Jamie 251
Northampton, 1994–1995 season
    32–33
  1995–1996 season 39–41, 44, 51–52
  1995–1996 statistics 52
  1999–2000 season 116–118
  appointment of Pountney as captain
    182
  attempting to sign Johnson 45–46
  Dawson joining 11–12
  dispute between clubs and RFU 48
  European Cup 2000 117–118
  Heineken Cup 2000 116
  Powergen Cup 2002 200–203, 238
  Powergen Cup 2003 228–230, 238
  rugby turning professional 44–45,
    48
  Tetley's Bitter Cup 2000 116

O'Brien, Paddy 212, 215
O'Driscoll, Brian
  golf playing 148, 150
  Lions Australia tour 2001 142, 143,
    171, 177, 180
  Six Nations 2004 358
O'Gara, Ronan
  assault incident 139
  golf playing 148
  Lions Australia tour 2001 165, 176,
    180
O'Kelly, Malcolm 180
O'Shea, Conor 200
Ofahengaue, Willie 21
Ojomoh, Steve
  Australia, New Zealand and South
    Africa tour 1998 92
  England initiation ceremonies 38
  international experience 76
Oliver, Anton 82
Owen, Mick 84

Packer, Kerry 47
Pask, Janice 17
Pask, Phil 17, 53, 289, 309, 312–313
Pearce, Gary 200
Pearce, Stuart 113
Perry, Matt
  advising younger players 103
  Australia, New Zealand and South
    Africa tour 1998 92
  Lions Australia tour 2001 171, 174,
    180
  World Cup 1999 99
Phillips, Zara 351
Picton, Keith 12
Pool-Jones, Richard 92
Potter, Stuart 92

Pountney, Budge
  appointment as Northampton captain
    182–183
  'arguing' with Dawson 203–206,
    244
Prescott, Richard 94–95
Pretorius, Andre 210
Prince Harry 344, 351
Prince William 351

Quinnell, Scott
  cardboard cut-out 187
  Five Nations 1999 112
  Heineken Cup 2000 116
  Lions Australia tour 2001 167, 171,
    174, 177, 180
  Lions South Africa tour 1997 71

Randell, Taine 87, 250
Raphael, Dr John 57–58
Ravenscroft, Steve 92
Reason, Mark 41
Reddin, Dave 274, 281, 303
  Australia and New Zealand tour 2003
    259, 263–264, 266, 273
  Dawson's knee injury 308, 310
  Omega testing 307
  overtraining England squad 319
  Walsh incident 298–300, 315
Redman, Nigel 71
Regan, Mark
  Lions South Africa tour 1997 71
  professionalism 109
  Six Nations 2003 245
  World Cup 2003 305
  World Cup selection process 284
Reihana, Bruce 81
Richards, Dean 47, 191
Richards, Peter 92
Robinson, Andy
  Australia and New Zealand tour 2003
    260, 269
  Dawson's complaints about 2001
    Lions tour 154

Dawson's newspaper diary 171
  egotism 151
  golf playing 264
  pep talks 173, 177
  restricted by Henry's views 154, 158
  team tactics 106
  training sessions 146, 149
  World Cup 2003 294, 307, 322, 324,
    342
Robinson, Jason
  Lions Australia tour 2001 142–143,
    149–150, 156, 169, 171, 180
  playing style 19
  Six Nations 2001 188–189
  Six Nations 2003 230–231, 246
  Six Nations 2004 357
  South Africa match 2002 212–214
  video tape 236
  World Cup 2003 312, 321–322
  World Cup final 2003 329
Robson, Dr James 67, 70
Rodber, Tim 73, 101
  absence from England 1998 tour
    squad 77
  Canada tour 1993 64
  criticism of Northampton players 33
  dropped by England 100
  Five Nations 1999 112
  friendship with Dawson 200
  hamstring injury 24
  Lions South Africa tour 1997 61–62,
    71
  Packer circus 47
  rugby turning professional 44–45
  World Cup Sevens 1993 18–20
Roff, Joe 167, 271
Rogers, Mat 331
Rokocoko, Joe 254
Ross, Glen 14, 15, 32
Rowell, Jack
  Dawson's criticisms of 102, 106
  Dawson's playing style 54–55
  disregard for younger players 102
  dropping Dawson 55–56, 67

Index

retiring as England coach 74
selection policy 31, 35
Rowntree, Graham
  Australia, New Zealand and South
    Africa tour 1998 83, 85, 87, 91
  international experience 76
  Lions South Africa tour 1997 71
  Six Nations 2003 242, 245
  stamping incident 257
  video tape 235
  World Cup selection process 287

Salley, Joanne
  Australia and New Zealand tour 2003
    260, 261, 263–265, 275
  Buckingham Palace reception 351
  Dawson's neck injury 209
  Hello! magazine 347
  living with Dawson 220–221
  meeting Dawson 207, 223
  paparazzi 352
  Six Nations 2003 226, 239
  support for Dawson xiv, 222–223,
    279
  World Cup 2003 289, 302, 304, 306,
    307, 313, 341
  World Cup final xi
  World Cup gala dinner 287
  World Cup victory parade 350
Sanderson, Alex 246
Sanderson, Pat 92
Scully, Dave 19–21
Shaw, Simon
  Australia and New Zealand tour 2003
    250
  Lions South Africa tour 1997 66, 71
  Six Nations 2000 108
  Six Nations 2003 245
  World Cup selection process 287
Sheasby, Chris 19
Shelford, Buck 16–17, 248
Sicilly, John 15–16
Simpson-Daniel, James 38–39, 246
Sims, Dave 87, 91

Six Nations
  2000 94–98, 100–101, 103–111,
    114–116
  2001 181–182, 184–194
  2002 199
  2003 219–220, 224–227, 230–246
  2004 356–61
Smith, Greg 99
Smith, Ollie 246
Smith, Richard 299
Smith, Tom 71, 170, 180
Smith, Wayne
  appointed by Northampton 196,
    204
  coaching skills 135, 142–143
  Dawson pulling out of Argentina
    tour 75
  Dawson's move to London 223
  Dawson's neck injury 208, 209, 217
  Dawson's unhappiness at
    Northampton 206
  New Zealander 248
  rules on contact 275
  sports psychology 229–230
  support for Dawson xiii, 88, 196–197,
    199, 233–234
Spencer, Carlos 254, 326
Stanger, Tony 72
Steele, John 127
  appointment of Northampton captain
    182–183
  Dawson's disciplinary hearing 204
Stevens, Matt 358
Stimpson, Tim
  Australia, New Zealand and South
    Africa tour 1998 92
  Lions South Africa tour 1997 71
  South Africa tour 2000 121
Stirling, Brian 124
Straeuli, Rudolf 210, 290
Stratton, Di 222
Stratton, Tony 222, 338
Stringer, Peter 241
Sturnham, Ben 91

Tait, Alan 66, 69, 71
Tattersall, Colin 8
Taylor, Brett 57–58, 64
  Dawson's Northampton debut 14
  'pretty boys' 13–14
  teaching job 13
Taylor, Mark 180
Taylor, Simon 150–151, 180
Teichmann, Gary 62
Telfer, Jim 68
Thompson, Sam 3–4, 6
Thompson, Steve 47, 109, 196, 200
  Australia and New Zealand tour 2003
    254
  Six Nations 2003 245
  video tape 235
  World Cup 2003 299
Thorne, Reuben 81
Thorneycroft, Harvey 39–40
Tindall, Mike
  16 men on pitch incident 298
  Australia and New Zealand tour 2003
    270–271
  Buckingham Palace reception 351
  comparison with Guscott 270–271
  development as young international
    103
  golf playing 259, 275–275
  Six Nations 2000 103
  Six Nations 2003 231, 238, 243,
    246
  South Africa match 2002 210
  video tape 236
  World Cup 2003 303–304, 308, 311,
    313
Toia, Anton 157
Townsend, Gregor
  Lions South Africa tour 1997 69, 71,
    137–138
  rugby turning professional 45
Tuckerman, Alec 5
Tuckerman, Spencer 4, 5
Tuqiri, Lote 329
Turnbull, Ross 47

Underwood, Rory 42, 43, 301
Underwood, Tony 71
Uttley, Roger 89

Van Nistelrooy, Ruud 83
van der Westhuizen, Joost 62
  World Cup 1999 99
  World Cup 2003 291, 309, 310
Venter, Brendan 199–202
Vickery, Phil
  Australia, New Zealand and South
    Africa tour 1998 77, 91
  Lions Australia tour 2001 171, 180
  Six Nations 2000 108
  South Africa match 2002 210
  World Cup 2003 296
  World Cup final 2003 329

Wainwright, Rob 71
Wallace, David 180
Wallace, Paul 66, 71
Walsh, Steve 298–300, 315, 318
Watson, Andre 329, 330, 343
Webb Ellis, William 119
Weir, Doddie 71
West, Dorian 109
  Australia and New Zealand tour 2003
    247
  Lions Australia tour 2001 175,
    180
Wheeler, Peter 129
White, Julian 245
Whiteside, Norman 113
Wilkinson, Jonny
  Australia and New Zealand tour 2003
    260, 270
  Australia match 2002 211
  Australia, New Zealand and South
    Africa tour 1998 77, 88, 92
  autograph hunters 303
  Dawson's views on 243
  dislike of media coverage 297, 315
  England captaincy 104, 230,
    232–233

excessive training 319
Five Nations 1999 112
Lions Australia tour 2001 142–143,
    153, 159, 167, 169, 171, 173, 177,
    180
rough play 211
Six Nations 2000 107, 108, 115
Six Nations 2001 188
Six Nations 2003 219–220, 226–227,
    230, 232, 234, 238, 242–243, 245
South Africa match 2002 212–210
training sessions 153, 159, 173
video tape 236
World Cup 1999 99
World Cup 2003 294, 297–298, 319,
    321–322, 325
World Cup final 2003 329, 330, 331,
    344
Williams, Ali 251–252
  stamping incident 255, 257
Williams, Barry 71
Williams, Chester, 20
Williams, Dave 159, 160, 184
Williams, Martyn 180
Williams, Shane 186
Windo, Tony 91
Wood, Keith 65
  Lions Australia tour 2001 147,
    168–169, 171, 180
  Lions South Africa tour 1997 71
Wood, Martyn 289, 293, 308
Woodman, Dougie 329, 330
Woodman, Trevor 245
Woods, Tiger 185
Woodward, Clive
  16 men on pitch incident 299
  ambitions for England 89–90
  appointing Wilkinson England
    captain 232
  Australia and New Zealand tour 2003
    247–248, 250, 254–255, 259–260,
    262–263, 266–267, 274–275
  Australia, New Zealand and South
    Africa tour 1998 77–79, 84, 87–90

changing England's playing style
    103
  coaching team 283
  Dawson appointed England captain
    73–74
  Dawson pulling out of Argentina
    tour 75
  Dawson's neck injury 209–210
  Dawson's views on 195–196
  dislike of criticism 130
  dropping Dawson from England
    squad 184–185, 191, 194–195
  European Cup 2000 117
  fitness training 281–282
  Five Nations 1999 113
  golf playing 264
  players' dispute with RFU 49, 123,
    126, 126–127, 130
  playing Catt in midfield 106
  quitting England job 369
  selection policy 86
  Six Nations 2000 97, 100–101, 103,
    106, 108
  Six Nations 2001 184
  Six Nations 2003 233, 236, 237,
    239
  Six Nations 2004 356–61
  South Africa match 2002 210
  South Africa tour 2000 121
  sports psychology 266–268
  support for Dawson 195–196
  support for Tindall 231
  views on Dawson's newspaper diary
    183
  views on media 254–255
  views on Williams stamping incident
    257
  World Cup 1999 100
  World Cup 2003 288–289, 291,
    293–294, 299, 301, 305, 307–310,
    312–313, 321–322
  World Cup final 2003 330
  World Cup selection process 285,
    286, 287

Woodward, Clive – *cont.*
  Worsley incident 301
World Cup
  1995 35–36
  1999 98–100
  2003 279–332
World Cup Sevens 1993 18–21
Worsley, Joe
  Six Nations 2003 227, 245

World Cup 2003 301–302, 333
Worsley, Mike 245

Young, Bill 329
Young, Dai
  Lions Australia tour 2001 161,
    171, 180
  Lions South Africa tour 1997
    71